THE WAITE GROUP'S
NC GUIDE

Piroz Mohseni

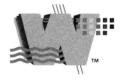

Waite Group Press™
A Division of
Sams Publishing
Corte Madera, CA

Publisher: *Mitchell Waite*
Associate Publisher: *Charles Drucker*

Acquisitions Manager: *Susan Walton*
Acquisitions Editor: *Joanne Miller*

Editorial Director: *John Crudo*
Project Editor: *Laura E. Brown*
Developmental/Technical Editors: *Frank Pittelli, Scott Rhoades*
Copy Editor: *Deirdre Greene/Creative Solutions*

Production Manager: *Cecile Kaufman*
Cover Designer: *Karen Johnston*
Book Designer: *LeeAnn Nelson*
Production Editor: *Mary Barbosa*
Production: *Jeanne Clark, Jenny Dierdorff, Brad Lenser, Andrew Stone*
Indexer: *Tim Tate*
Cover Illustration: *PhotoDisc, Inc.*

Printed in the United States of America
97 98 99 • 10 9 8 7 6 5 4 3 2 1

Mohseni, Piroz, 1972–
    The Waite Group's NC guide / Piroz Mohseni.
       p.   cm.
    Includes index.
    ISBN 1-57169-106-5
    1. Network computers. 2. Client/server computing. 3. Computer networks I. Waite Group. II. Title.
    QA76.527.M64 1997
004.6'186--dc21

97-19460
CIP

Dedication

To my parents

About the Author

Piroz Mohseni is a software consultant specializing in Java, Web, and database technologies. He is involved in a variety of Web projects. Prior to this, he was an assistant scientist at Ames Laboratory in Iowa. He received a B.S. degree in computer engineering from Iowa State University in 1995. He is the author of *Web Database Primer Plus* from Waite Group Press.

Table of Contents

Contents

Chapter 1   The NC Paradigm

Chapter 2   NC Specifications

Chapter 5   The NC and Java

Chapter 6   The NC and Databases

Chapter 7 Distributed Applications on the NC

Chapter 8   The Distributed Object Model

Chapter 9 Electronic Commerce

Chapter 10 Computer Telephony Integration

Chapter 13   Java Development Tools

Chapter 14 What's Next?

Appendix A A Guide to ActiveX

Appendix B **Push Technologies**

Appendix C **Online Resources**

Acknowledgments

Completion of this project would not have been possible without the support of many individuals. I'd like to thank my family for their continued support and encouragement. Special thanks go to Dr. Reza Ehtessabian, his wife Arlene, and their children Roxana, Jon, Jason, and Jared for their kind support throughout the past years. I'm grateful to my uncle, Ali Mohseni, for his support and for writing Appendix A. I'd like to thank Bhanu Morampudi for contributing Chapters 7, 12, and 13 and for all the thoughtful discussions.

The following people have in one way or another helped and supported this work, and I sincerely thank all of them: Steve Goldsmith, Vince Iuliano, Babak Fakoor, Jason Fox, Alireza Ardehali, Steve Young, Shaoqing Wang, Lisa Johnson, and all the folks at Waite Group Press. Special thanks go to Laura Brown for being a great project editor.

Introduction

Welcome to the world of network computing! A world in which the boundaries between computers are slashed away and the computer and network become one integrated device. Change is nothing new to the dynamic computer industry. With the incredibly rapid growth of the Internet, a major shift in networks and network computing has taken place. This book provides an overview of this exciting evolution in computing. *The Waite Group NC Guide* attempts to capture the essence of network computing and the open standards that it promotes. It covers a variety of issues facing IT managers and executives as they shift their strategies toward a network-centric model of computing. The Guide also satisfies the curious MIS professional who wants to learn more about the impact of network computing on software development. Specific products are mentioned where appropriate, but the overall focus of the book centers on the concepts needed to understand and evaluate new technologies suited to individual computing environments.

The book begins with a swift introduction to the network evolution by providing a historic perspective. This first chapter also presents arguments as to why network computing is needed and what problems it can address.

Chapter 2 offers a broad discussion of the two main network computer specifications to date: NC Reference Profile 1, a joint project by several vendors, and the Net PC standard, endorsed by Microsoft and based on that company's Windows operating system.

The Guide then shifts in Chapter 3 to the software world and how to develop and deploy software in a network-centric computing environment. Software includes operating system, user interface, applications, and back-end programs. All of these components are affected in one way or another by the network. Security also plays an important role in software design and implementation.

Chapter 4 discusses the specifics of software on the servers. The thin-client devices rely heavily on servers, whether a file server, an application server, or a database server. This dependence is evident in the way a browser depends on a Web server to receive information. This chapter discusses functions of a server in a network and what it must contain.

Java has risen as a popular programming language for network-centric environments due in part to its portability. Chapter 5 provides an overview of some of Java's attractive features as a programming language for network applications. Aside from the general features of the language, some of the components of the Java Development Kit that add to its network functionality are discussed.

A major beneficiary of network computing will be database applications. Distributed databases and distributed applications go hand in hand to provide a seamless and reliable interface to users. Chapter 6 discusses Java Database Connectivity, which is the link between Java (a network programming language) and databases (network-centric data storage and retrieval programs).

Chapters 7 and 8 expand on the distributed application design by discussing distributed objects and component models such as JavaBeans. Chapter 8 is devoted to a survey of CORBA and its architecture, and its competitor DCOM.

In Chapter 9, electronic commerce and the implications of network computing on this rapidly changing sector are discussed. Several specific standards such as CyberCash, SET, and Java Commerce framework are presented.

The world of networks is not limited to data networks. A large and established network already exists in the telephone network. Chapter 10 discusses how telephony can be implemented in a network-centric model and how data and telephone networks can complement each other. Telephony applications such as call centers and the Java Telephony API are presented.

Chapter 11 is devoted to a relatively new network-based operating system called Inferno. This OS is highly suited to the network device market, which includes a variety of network-aware electronic gadgets. This sector promises rapid growth in the near future as its infrastructure expands.

Managing devices and computers in a network environment is a complex task. Chapter 12 provides an overview of the Java Management API. Because the API is independent of the underlying management protocol, it can be used to develop generic management applications.

Chapter 13 provides an overview of some of the Java development tools available to the programming community. Web sites containing up-to-date information and evaluation copies are included.

Finally, Chapter 14 looks to the future of network computing and its implications on our daily lives. Aside from changing computing as we know it today, network computing will introduce computing to areas currently not associated with a network.

There are three appendixes in the Guide. Appendix A discusses ActiveX and the technology behind it. As long as Windows remains a dominant operating system, ActiveX is going to play an important role in bringing the benefits of the network to Windows applications. Another growing area is push technology, and Appendix B is devoted to a brief discussion of this topic. It introduces Castanet as a practical implementation of push technology in a network-centric environment. Appendix C is a listing of all the URLs in the Guide, along with a brief description of each one. It is a useful reference to the latest news about a variety of topics.

The NC Paradigm

Change is unavoidable and in many cases unpredictable. Change can be evolutionary or revolutionary. In the world of computers, it seems to be both. Massive directional changes can sweep the industry in a very short time. The concept of *network computers*, commonly referred to as *NCs*, is one such change. In less than a year after formalized announcements about network computing from industry leaders, consumers were faced with a number of products and solutions from which to choose. New products are announced almost daily and existing products are constantly enhanced. This book is an attempt to provide an overview of this new technology and its implications on the software, corporate information technology (IT), and personal computer industries.

An Overview of Computing Models

To put things in perspective, it is helpful to consider network computing as part of the computer evolution that began in the 1950s. The computer of 40 years ago was not the same as today's computer. There are very distinct differences in the technology and use of computers. Such differences are mainly the result of several paradigm shifts that have rattled the industry.

The computer began as an experimental device. It was developed and used in large research institutions. The earliest computers came in the form of large and expensive machines commonly referred to as *mainframes*.

Mainframe

The mainframe had its own personality. It was consistent with the industrial revolution that had arrived a century earlier. The mainframe was a big, centralized machine. It did everything from processing to printing to storage. Programs were typically submitted as batch jobs and executed according to a priority schedule. The mainframe resembled a factory. Instead of raw material, it used data; instead of finished products, it produced information. Users usually accessed the mainframe from a terminal. These terminals were connected directly to the mainframe. They were very localized. The terminal had no processing power of its own. It simply accepted input from the user and sent it out to the mainframe. Perhaps that is why it got the title of *dumb terminal*. Figure 1-1 shows a conceptual view of the mainframe model.

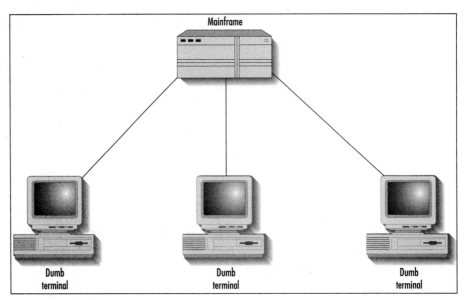

Figure 1-1 Mainframe model

Mainframes were good at what they did, but advancements in technology brought some of the mainframe's shortcomings to the surface. As more business functions were shifted to automation, centralized mainframes could not keep up with the processing demand. Mainframes were not very scaleable, and the cost of upgrading and maintaining them was very high. In addition, mainframes resembled a centralized control unit, a concept not well liked by many "free" thinkers. Furthermore, business functions were rapidly spreading among departments and functional units. This departmentalization approach was not suitable for the centralized model of the mainframe. There was a need to distribute computing, just as business tasks were distributed.

Advancements in chip technology and the microprocessor industry made it possible to begin a paradigm shift from the centralized mainframe to independent personal computers on the desktop.

Personal Computers

The personal computer (PC) also had its own personality. It was a relatively inexpensive machine that could operate independently. It had its own storage device and its own processor. It would receive input from users via a keyboard and produce output to a printer or a monitor. The software industry went into a frenzy and produced millions of applications and programs for the PC. These applications represent the heart and soul of the PC. Just like you buy food at a grocery store, you bought programs at a software store. Additionally, people had a choice in what software they could buy. They could purchase software that they thought would help them solve their problems. So the PC was more than a hardware revolution: It brought about a major shift on how software was perceived and deployed by the end user. Figure 1-2 shows the personal computer model.

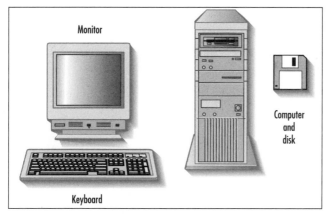

Figure 1-2 Personal computer model

At about this time, a popular device called a *modem* that enabled computers to communicate with each other through an ordinary phone line hit the market. That was important, because it planted the seeds for breaking geographical barriers. Simultaneously, other communication mechanisms and protocols were being developed and concepts such as local area networks were becoming commonplace. The PC was an independent machine, but it was becoming apparent that the PC could do a lot more if it worked with its peers via networks.

Client/Server

Once the PC earned the power of communicating with other machines, a new paradigm was formed. This paradigm also had its own personality. It was like a big brother/little brother (or big sister/little sister) relationship. The old mainframe companies saw an opportunity to enter the market once again and play the role of the big brother. The PC was a small machine compared to the big mainframe computers. Client/server was an effort to divide the tasks typically done by a computer application. Tasks requiring huge data storage and retrieval operations, large memory requirements, and fast processing would be done by a big machine called the *server*. Less intensive tasks such as application user interface, small processing jobs, and basic data entry and retrieval would be done by a small machine called the *client*. This model is shown in Figure 1-3.

Depending on where the performance bottleneck was, either the client or the server had to be modified. A client was not totally dependent on the server. It was an independent desktop, but for certain applications, it required the assistance of the server. The server, too, didn't depend on clients, although the purpose of its mere existence was to serve clients. When no client required its services, it would be busy doing some other routine task.

On a different front, another possibility was being examined: the UNIX operating system. UNIX was a lot more flexible than the PC, and that flexibility led to fragmentation in the industry. However, UNIX had one major advantage over the PC. It had an inherent bond with networking, with early activities such as email and UNIX-to-UNIX copy (UUCP). Furthermore, it was the platform of choice at research institutions involved in the development of a network of networks, commonly referred to as the *Internet*.

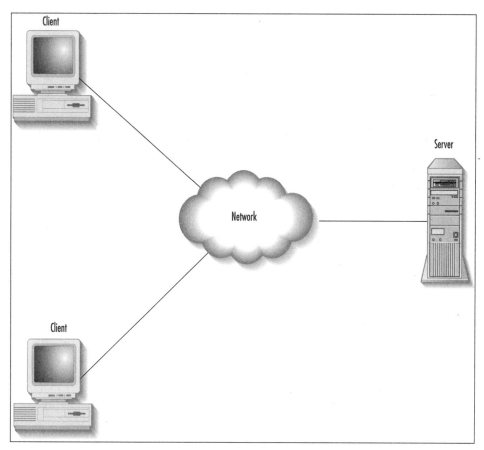

Figure 1-3 Client/server model

network Centric

Starting in late 1994, the computer industry began another journey that has led to the network-centric model, on which the NC is based. The culprit was the Internet, specifically a component of it referred to as the *World Wide Web*. The Web established a communication medium among all computers that included not only text but pictures and audio. Prior to the Web, the only thing that came anywhere close to the commonality of the Web was the VT100 terminal, which almost all computers either supported or were able to emulate. There were other standards, of course. The X11 standard, or the Windows standard on the PC side, provided a common view of applications and network resources. In that regard, the Web was more of an evolution than a revolution. The Web built on top of concepts portrayed by X11 and similar technologies. What set the Web apart was that it brought this technology to the masses and made network access as common as using local resources. The Web played a very important role in bringing the network to the forefront of computing and helping users realize its usefulness. The network-centric model of computing is represented in Figure 1-4.

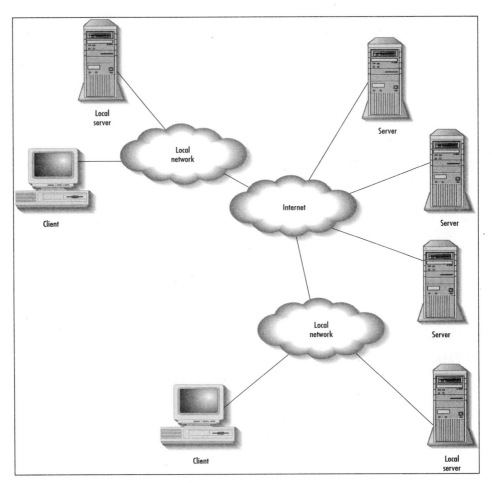

Figure 1-4 Network-centric model

Shortly after the Web's arrival, plans were introduced to integrate the Web with other types of servers (such as databases) and to use the Web as an application platform by giving it programming capabilities. Technologies such as CGI, Java, JavaScript, VBScript, and ActiveX emerged. The Web was no longer a static collection of pages, but a fully functional programming environment in which real applications could be executed. A browser depended on the network to download the pages and applications. It depended on the Web server to serve the pages and applications. Once the information and data were retrieved, the client used the processing power of the machine it was running on to execute any application that was downloaded. A new model had emerged that was different than anything the mass PC market had seen before. It started another paradigm shift. What was important about this shift was its economic effects. Network access, execution of remote programs, and downloadable codes had been technologies enjoyed only by high-end workstation users. Those same technologies were now becoming commonplace for millions of users with lower-end machines.

What Is the NC?

You now have a perspective of where network computing fits in the computing models. Still, the exact nature of network computing remains a question. For the purpose of this book, I will use a broad definition. The NC is a client device that functions by using the distributed network as a source for data, applications, and communication. Several aspects of the above definition must be emphasized.

First, the NC is a client device. Going back to the client/server model, the NC is not the big brother. It acts as a client to one or more servers. These servers may be Web servers, application servers, or database servers. The NC is a device: It does not have to be a computer or even resemble one. A product like WebTV could be considered an NC once certain modifications are done to it to support an application environment.

Second, the NC lives and dies by the network. If the network goes down, you cannot expect your NC to continue functioning as usual. This is the nature of the new network-centric paradigm. In the same way your phone won't do anything useful if it is not connected to the phone network, the NC won't do much computing if it is not connected to the distributed network.

Third, the NC is part of a distributed network such as the Internet or a corporate intranet. In the mainframe days, terminals were connected to the main machine via direct lines or a closed, proprietary network. In the client/server era, there were a number of closed and proprietary networks. The market for such networks is very small compared to distributed networks such as the Internet. Although it is possible to build an NC to work in a particular network, the definition here disallows that. A positive aspect of the NC is its open design and ability to connect to different networks as long as they comply with certain standards discussed in Chapter 2, "NC Specifications."

Notice that I have not mentioned any specific examples thus far. This is intentional, because the NC is more of a concept than a physical entity. The concept has been implemented in a variety of ways and is bound to be found in other implementations by different vendors. For an initial discussion, the definition is nonspecific and conceptual. Later chapters offer specific examples.

The NC Software Paradigm

One of the most common divisions of computer-related subjects is between hardware and software. The NC paradigm includes both. In other words, both NC hardware and software are different compared to existing or past paradigms. Keeping the concept of the NC in mind, the following is a discussion of what software is like in an NC environment.

Because the NC is network based, its application software is provided by the network. The NC may not have local storage capabilities (e.g., disks). In that case, the software must be downloaded from the network and executed locally. Any storage operations must go through the network back to the server where the data is physically stored. The NC usually has some basic software stored in ROM (read-only memory). Such software usually includes a control interface, a browser, an email program, and other basic programs. Application programs such as a word processor may also be included in the ROM, but they will probably be downloaded from the network. From now on, when I refer to NC software, I am talking about these application programs, not the small utilities stored on the NC itself.

One of the first problems that comes to mind is the practicality of downloading applications over the network. This concern is legitimate because the current paradigm has encouraged the creation of large, do-it-all, complex applications. Take a look at the memory and disk space requirements for some of the new applications and you can see a definite push toward "bigness" and completeness. There is an irony in that, however. On the average, users take advantage of a very small percentage of the functionalities offered by an application. Another fact is that many applications are task based. That is, each part is designed to complete a specific task. Because humans are not very good at performing multiple tasks simultaneously (at least not yet!), they take advantage of one task at a time. So a perfect paradigm for NC software is applications that are highly task oriented and modularized. Rather than downloading the entire application, only the part that is needed for completing the current task is taken from the network and executed locally.

The software industry has had a good solution to creating such applications for nearly 20 years, except it never flourished. The NC paradigm may be the right environment for object-oriented technology to take off and finally fulfill its promises. Object-oriented technology enables developers to divide their applications into smaller tasks performed by individual objects. Technologies such as JavaBeans and ActiveX, along with CORBA (common object request broker architecture) and DCOM (distributed component object model), allow objects to communicate with each other. Within such a framework, it is possible to download individual objects to perform specific tasks on the NC, as shown in Figure 1-5. Within such a paradigm, the execution of network-based application software becomes practical.

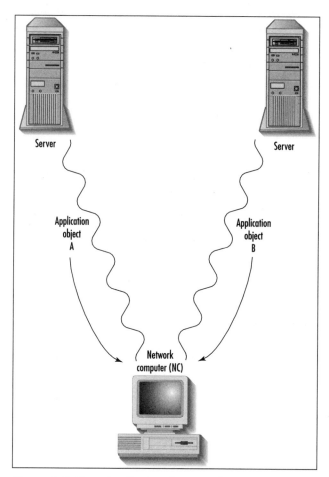

Figure 1-5 Downloading application objects

The concept described above is not totally new. When you load your favorite word processor, it normally provides you with a simple editor so you can type your document. Although the application includes a spell checker, the spell checker is not invoked until you specifically ask for it. At that time, the appropriate module is loaded from your hard drive and executed to check the spelling of your document. In the NC world, the spelling module is downloaded from the server and then executed. The result is the same: Your document is spell-checked. The difference is how the software behaves to accomplish that task. Cache technology is very useful here to reduce the number of times a program must be downloaded from the network. Just as your Web browser does not contact the server for a page it has in its own cache, the NC does not contact the server for an application module that is in its memory. Network access is more common, but it is not a cheap operation compared to local memory access.

Another helpful technology is the push model for distribution of content and applications. This model works similar to how a television works. Different channels show different things. As a viewer, you select the channel you want to watch. The push model "broadcasts" a particular content or application on a regular basis. That way, you always get the latest version. In the case of applications, rather than broadcasting the entire application each time a change is made, only the changes are sent out. This greatly reduces download time. Several products are already based on this technology; they are discussed later in this book.

In summary, object-oriented models are ideal for NCs. In particular, component-based models where an application can be composed of several independent objects fit the NC model very well. The current language of choice for the NC is Java from Sun Microsystems. Chapter 3, "Software for the NC," provides a detailed discussion of NC software requirements. Chapter 5, "The NC and Java," is devoted to the aspects of the Java language that qualify it for NC application development.

Why Network Computing?

Throughout this chapter, I have intentionally kept network computing as a concept. In this section, some of the benefits of using network computing are outlined at a conceptual level. The main reason for this approach is so you can apply the concepts to your own situation as appropriate. Also, it is imperative that you have a conceptual understanding of network computing before you evaluate the many implementations out there.

Cost

One of the biggest arguments behind network computing is its low cost. Cost, however, is a relative concept, so we must compare network computing to something. The fairest comparison is the client/server model.

Consider a typical desktop computer in an office. Aside from upgrade and maintenance costs, there are software support and management costs associated with the client/server model. The experts have thrown around numbers as to the average cost of maintaining a PC. Without getting into the specifics, let's consider what costs would be directly reduced by using an NC rather than a PC.

With the network-centric model, the majority of applications reside on the server. Therefore little, if any, application management costs are associated with the NC. Furthermore, the cost of upgrading applications is substantially reduced because the application is updated once and in one place. There is no need to distribute updates via disks or CDs.

Most NC specifications do not require a local storage unit such as a disk. This is one component that can malfunction on a PC, so there is a definite potential for saving here. Some specifications disallow any movable parts on the NC. This adds to the importance of centralized file systems and routine backups.

Finally, the NC is supposed to be a simpler machine than a typical desktop computer. This simplicity and robustness should help reduce costs. Some increased costs are associated with the server and the network itself, however, because these components are very important in a network-centric environment. The good news is most IT organizations are already incurring such costs in their existing client/server environments.

Maintenance

The NC is easier to maintain than a typical PC. It has fewer parts and its scope of operation is more limited than a typical PC. If you have ever tried installing, configuring, and using a board on your PC, you can appreciate the problems associated with PC maintenance. Replicate those problems to an organization level and you can see how system and network administrators suffer.

The NC doesn't have many components, so there are fewer things that can go wrong with it. Application maintenance is greatly simplified because the application resides on a server. The NC has the potential of becoming as easy to use as your telephone.

Portability

An NC is much more resourceful than the desktop computer or even the mainframe. A network is a collection of resources. The NC is designed to take advantage of the vast resources of the network. By moving to a network-based model, you can greatly enhance the resources available to a single computing unit (which in this case is the NC).

The NC is more portable than a desktop computer, but it encourages the sharing and use of resources on a global level. To get a glimpse of the possibilities, look at how the Internet has become a potential wealth of information.

Where the NC Is Used

The question of where the NC is used is a difficult one to answer conceptually. Network computing can and will have many implementations targeting different users. There may even be a division among NCs geared toward different applications. Potentially, the NC can be used in three different environments.

Corporate IT

The NC is ideal for environments in which large number of desktop computers are used to perform limited, specific, and routine tasks. A typical call center or technical support center may fall within this category. The NC reduces the cost of maintaining each station and brings a sense of uniformity to the operation by providing resources at the network level.

The NC is also appropriate for environments in which the same applications are used by a large proportion of the machines. By providing a network-centric application platform, the NC helps reduce costs and maintenance efforts.

There are many operations within corporate IT in which the potential of the NC can be exploited. To realize the potential, one must look at the explosion of intranets within large and small companies. If you examine the use of intranets closely, you will discover that the majority of use comes from network-centric applications such as interactive Web pages and applications. Many intranets already use the Web as the front-end of their legacy systems. The same reasons that prompted the success of intranet within these organizations will create the market for NCs.

Personal Use

Some variation of the NC, such as the WebTV, will undoubtedly target the consumer market. As more and more houses open their doors to the information age and the Internet, there will be more of a need to access this vast resource in a cost-effective and efficient manner. An analogy might be helpful here. Households don't use sophisticated switches to access the telephone network—they use a simple telephone. Similarly, an expensive desktop computer is not needed to access and use distributed networks such as the Internet. A simple device will do, and the NC is a prime candidate to be that simple device.

When surfing the Net, most people use only one application on their PC: the browser. Within the browser, they can not only access information but run interactive applications. Surely a simple device can run that one application. The NC will likely be integrated with some other common household devices such as the telephone or television. Again, there is a great potential here for growth.

The "Device" Market

One of the things the network will do is shift the burden from the client to the server. This shift clears the way for smaller and less expensive clients that perform very specific tasks. Because the server will do most of the work, these clients do not have to be very sophisticated. When the microprocessor hit the market two decades ago, a number of devices began using it and became more sophisticated as a result. Camcorders, stereos, and telephones are some examples. A similar wave is approaching the device market; this time, the network is behind it. With wireless technologies exploding, the network will become more and more accessible to very small and simple devices. These devices will be able to do more by using the network.

Summary

This chapter has provided a conceptual overview of the NC. A chronological overview of the different computing models such as the mainframe and client/server puts the NC in perspective. The NC is based on the network-centric model, in which the network plays an important role in connecting individual clients to the resources on the network such as database servers and application servers.

Software development for the network-centric model is somewhat different than software development for other computing models. The network-centric model has unique requirements because the applications are downloaded from the server and must maintain communication with network resources. Object-oriented technology promises to address many of the software needs of the NC. Similarly, push technologies, where the content or the application is distributed over the network, can help.

The NC has many advantages over the conventional desktop computer by reducing cost, easing maintenance, and increasing portability. The NC is a concept, and many implementations will hit the market geared toward different users and different applications. The information technology market is a definite candidate for shifting to the NC and the computing model behind it. The consumer market and the device market also will benefit from the NC.

CHAPTER 2

NC Specifications

Although no official standards body has produced a specification for network computing, industry leaders have produced several guidelines. Considering the young age of network computing, it is impressive that guidelines even exist. Specifications will evolve as new products hit the market. Compare the first desktop PC to the PCs in the market today and you get a feel for how technology and standards change. This chapter discusses the major NC specifications to date and looks at some implementations.

NC Reference Profile 1

The NC Reference Profile 1 was the first attempt at a standard by industry leaders such as Oracle, IBM, Apple, and Sun Microsystems. The standard was presented in July 1996 and officially accepted in August 1996. This particular specification has been criticized for being very general and following the "anything goes" policy. Although the generality of the standard cannot be debated, generality is perhaps one of the standard's strengths rather than weaknesses. By providing a less specific guideline, the Reference Profile allows different vendors to transform their products to meet the standard rather than design a brand-new one. This was a smart move on part of the NC "founding parents" to get support for the idea and, more important, get products out there.

NOTE *The NC Reference Profile does not specify an implementation for an NC. It merely states requirements for an NC device and leaves implementation details open.*

Hardware for the NC

The specification requires that an NC be equipped with a monitor with minimum screen resolution of 640×480 (VGA). The monitor can be built into the device and does not have to be a separate unit. The NC must also support a pointing device such as a trackball or a mouse. This is probably in anticipation of using a graphical user interface (GUI) for NC applications.

The specification does not require a keyboard. Instead it states a more general requirement: "text input capability." Although the most common method for inputting text into a computer is the keyboard (which is how this book was written), the NC leaves this open. The keyboard could be a touchscreen on the monitor. Or it might be a voice recognition system in which you talk away and the computer translates your words into text.

The requirements also call for an audio output device. Again, none of the specifics are mentioned. The next guideline is perhaps the most controversial. The specification states: "persistent local storage not required." In other words, neither a disk drive nor a hard drive is required for an NC. Given what you know about the network-centric model, this should make sense. Applications are downloaded from an application server. Files are stored in a file server. Data is stored in a database server. The operating system is implemented at the hardware level or downloaded. Does the NC really need a local drive? Perhaps not, but in actual implementations, some vendors include a local drive to act as a cache. This increases the price tag on the NC, but promises to increase performance. By not requiring a permanent storage device, the designers of the NC were able to expand the NC market substantially by capturing the so-called device market as part of the NC market.

Based on the hardware requirements, the NC doesn't look much different than a desktop PC. After considering the software requirement, the difference becomes more apparent. The NC does not run any software that a desktop cannot run, but the NC was designed from the bottom up for the network-centric model, whereas the desktop PC was not.

Note that no mention of processor type, memory size, or even an operating system is made in the specification.

Internet Protocol

Regardless of the networking hardware, the NC operates on top of IP, the well-known Internet Protocol upon which the Internet is built. Following the layer model, several protocols are built on top of IP. The specification has a list of required protocols for the NC:

- TCP

- UDP

- SSL

- FTP

- Telnet

- SNMP

- HTTP

- NNTP

- SMTP

The first protocol is Transmission Control Protocol (TCP). TCP is responsible for creating a stream-based network on top of the IP layer. TCP along with IP forms the basis for almost all the major Internet applications, such as the Web, email exchange, and remote login. The other protocol on top of IP is User Datagram Protocol (UDP), which is also supported by the NC. UDP is used for "connectionless" communication between client and server software, providing a more efficient but less reliable compromise. Finally, for secure transmissions, the Secure Socket Layer (SSL) is supported. This protocol is already widely used for secure transmissions of Web data, and can be incorporated into any TCP application as needed.

Another protocol required by an NC is File Transfer Protocol (FTP). This protocol makes sense for NCs that have some sort of local storage capability and allow reading and writing to the file system. FTP is one of the products that is directly supported by the URL addressing scheme. For example, the URL `ftp://www.xyz.com/filename.exe` points to the file `filename.exe` on the server `www.xyz.com` via FTP.

To get a prompt on another computer on the network, you would use the Telnet protocol. UNIX machines usually run the Telnet server (**telnetd**) and thus clients can access a particular machine by telneting to their address. Of course, you must have an account on the machine you are trying to access. With an NC, you should be able to get a prompt on different machines running **telnetd**; that is why this protocol is a requirement for the NC.

In a network-centric model, you can have data files scattered throughout the network. You could use FTP to access these files, but that would be cumbersome. The UNIX solution to this problem is distributed file systems in which you address files in different locations on the network the same as if they were on your own local file system. One such solution is Network File System (NFS); support for this protocol is a requirement. To understand NFS, you have to understand the file system philosophy in most modern operating systems.

The operating system is told where to look for files through a collection of *mount points*. That is, physical disk drive space is assigned to a position within the file system hierarchy. In UNIX, these mount points look like any other directory to the user (for example, **/usr**, **/opt**, **/home**), whereas in Windows 95, the mount points are assigned unique *drive letters* (for example, **C:**, **D:**).

Under NFS, different remote file systems can be mounted to the local file system. For example, assume a machine called MARS is on your network and you want to mount the **/oradata** directory on that machine. In your local NFS configuration file, you would specify **MARS:/oradata** and map that to a directory name such as **/usr/oradata**. When you change directory to **/usr/oradata**, you are actually looking at the content of the **/oradata** directory on the machine named MARS, but it looks as if you are looking at the **/usr/oradata** directory on your local drive. That is the biggest advantage of NFS; file systems are accessed in the same way regardless of where they physically reside. NFS is an open standard and has been supported by all major operating systems.

Management of networks has become more and more complicated as networks have become more complex. Simple Network Management Protocol (SNMP) is a popular protocol for managing networks. NCs are required to support SNMP, which eases their remote administration and the overall management of the network. This requirement should come as no surprise.

Recall that NCs do not have to provide local storage. One way to compensate for this is by having the NC boot over the network from a server. In UNIX, the BOOT Protocol can been used to perform this function, and NC inherits the same functionality. So NCs must support BOOTP. Another protocol is the Dynamic Host Configuration Protocol (DHCP), which enables a client to boot itself from a server, dynamically be assigned an IP number, and establish a communication channel over which configuration information can be transmitted. By requiring both DHCP and BOOTP, the standard reiterates the fact that NCs rely on servers.

The success of the Web has led to the popularity of the network-centric model. The NC requirement specifically supports several Web protocols. The first is Hypertext Markup Language (HTML), which is the language used to create Web pages. The version of the language is not mentioned in the specification. The current version is HTML 3.2. This requirement is likely to be fulfilled either by supporting a built-in browser as part of the operating system or by being able to download one from the network. The Web browser implementations at the OS level are not as sophisticated as popular browsers such as Netscape and Internet Explorer, but they nonetheless perform the basic functions a browser must perform.

To support HTML, the NC specifications also require support of the Hypertext Transfer Protocol (HTTP), which is the protocol behind the World Wide Web. The NC will get many of its resources, including applications, in the form of Java applets from a Web server and therefore it must be able to support HTTP. No particular version of HTTP is mentioned. The current version is 1.0, but version 1.1 is not very far away.

The Network News Transfer Protocol (NNTP) facilitates network-based discussion groups organized by newsgroups. Each newsgroup is typically dedicated to a particular topic. Users post messages to one or more newsgroups. These messages can be seen by other subscribers who can then respond to the news postings.

The final Web-related requirement is the ability to support Java applications. Java promises to be the foundation behind NC applications. In addition to the Java virtual machine (JVM), the Java class libraries must be supported. Java is an evolving language currently in version 1.1. The specification does not state a version of Java that must be supported. It will be a challenge for NCs to conform to the latest Java specifications, because most will likely implement Java at the hardware level. In a distributed environment, Java classes can reside on other machines connected to the network and accessible to Java applications. However, the core Java classes and packages such as java.lang and java.net must be available as part of the local JVM.

The most widely used application on the Internet is email. The NC Reference Profile requires support of no less than three email protocols. The first is Simple Mail Transfer Protocol (SMTP). This is by far the simplest of all mail protocols. An email message contains some header information that states who the message is from and who it is going to. With the help of the lower layers (IP and TCP), the message is delivered to the recipient.

Another popular email protocol is Post Office Protocol, Version 3 (POP3). This protocol is modeled after the post office for regular mail. Mail from the sender is collected in a post office and postal carriers deliver the mail to each recipient. With POP3, the mail is delivered to an email post office and kept there until the recipient retrieves it. After retrieval, based on the configuration, the message or just a copy can be transferred to the recipient's machine. The latter is the appropriate approach for NC machines because some may not have local storage capability. The NC is also required to support Internet Message Access Protocol, Version 4 (IMAP4), which is similar to POP3 but provides more advanced features.

The most likely approach for handling email is by providing an email program as part of the operating system. Another approach is by downloading an email reader application from the network. This can be a Java applet. Regardless of how the email reader is stored, users will most likely want to be able to store their messages in folders and keep them on a file server, which is the reason for POP3 and IMAP4.

Multimedia

The Reference Profile 1 has a small section that states that certain audio and picture formats must be supported. These formats are very popular on the Web already. They are JPEG (images), GIF (images), WAVE (sound), and AU (sound). Any Web browser that was released since 1996 supports JPEG and GIF image formats. Most browsers leave the task of playing sound files to helper applications on the platform on which they are running, however, because playing sound files requires an interface to the audio hardware that is dependent on the operating system.

Security

As was mentioned earlier, the NC must support SSL for secure transmission of network packets, which provides communication security at the software level. The NC requirement states two optional hardware security features. The first is ISO 7816, commonly known as *smartcards*. These cards are like credit cards, but have a built-in chip that stores security information such as a digital signature. Cryptographic algorithms use digital signatures for authentication and encryption of data. A digital signature is similar to a handwritten signature. Rather than using paper as the transport means, digital signatures are transported using smartcards. Smartcards add a powerful level of security at the hardware level. Their main function is to help authenticate users before they gain access to a system.

In the electronic business world of the (not-so-distant) future, consumers will use smartcards to authorize purchases and payments over the network. The smartcard not only uniquely identifies the user to the vendor, it also keeps the transaction private from any "observer" on the network. The NC will be able to serve as a universal ATM on your desktop (or laptop), capable of facilitating business transactions securely anywhere on the network.

Support of the Europay/MasterCard/Visa specification is also recommended. Along with the smartcard technology, NCs can shape the future of catalog shopping by bringing the vendor, the warehouse, the shipping company, and your wallet together for a completely paperless transaction. Won't that be interesting?

Miscellaneous Comments

"NC" is actually a trademark. Devices complying with the NC Reference Profile 1 will be able to carry the NC brand. The logo is shown in Figure 2-1. Also, Web sites that provide content suitable for viewing from an NC are considered "NC friendly" and can use a logo specifically designed for this purpose.

The NC Reference Profile is an industry-led effort. The standard will be revisited regularly and modifications will be made accordingly. By being very general, the NC standard can apply to a broad market; this explains why a number of companies, large and small, have endorsed the NC initiative. At the end of this chapter, you will find a list of some of these companies.

The latest information on NC Reference Profile 1 is available from `http://www.nc.ihost.com`.

Net PC

With the largest install base among the various operating systems, Microsoft Windows continues to play an instrumental role in the way we do computing. The move to a network-centric environment can only go so far without the support of the most popular operating system in the world. Fortunately, Microsoft has initiated a transformation to network computing, called Net PC. Although it is centered around Microsoft's own Windows operating system, it merits a closer look. Net PC is a variation of the Windows 95 and Windows NT Workstation operating systems and is considered a direct competitor to the NC Reference Profile standard. It addresses some of the same issues that justify a shift to

Figure 2-1 The NC logo

network computing, namely, cost of ownership, ease of management, and application maintenance. The differences are in the specific hardware and software requirements. This section takes a closer look at Microsoft's Net PC specification, Version 1.0.

System Requirements

The Net PC guideline contains very specific requirements. At a minimum, a 133-MHz Intel Pentium processor or compatible processor is required. The specification also allows other kinds of processors that support the Windows NT system, for example, the Digital Alpha processor. At least 256K of level 2 (L2) cache is required for Pentium systems, but this requirement is waved for Pentium Pro systems because the cache is built into those processors. Finally, a minimum of 16 MB of memory is required, although 32 MB is recommended. These requirements are consistent with the system needs of the Windows operating system and some typical applications. The specification does leave the door open for upgrade capabilities of RAM and CPU, but it does not allow such capabilities to be accessible to the end user. This is consistent with one of the main goals of the Net PC, which is to ease maintenance and management of multiple workstations.

Central management is an important theme in the Net PC specification. Central management can occur once the operating system is loaded, but the specification requires security precautions to be in place so that users cannot alter the capabilities of the system before the OS loads. It is not clear exactly how this will be done. The system BIOS (basic input output system) must be based on the COMPAQ, Phoenix, Intel BIOS Boot Specification (version 1.01 or later). This is especially important because Net PCs must be able to boot remotely from another machine. Dynamic Host Configuration Protocol (DHCP) and Trivial File Transfer Protocol (TFTP) are the two main protocols responsible for remote boot capabilities of Net PC, and they are both required. Net PC must also support some form of a storage device such as a hard drive. It also must support universal serial bus (USB) keyboards. In order to upgrade the system or change its behavior, it is sometimes necessary to upgrade the BIOS itself. The Net PC specification requires that this task be automated and that BIOS ROM be updated remotely.

Power

Power consumption is an important topic when dealing with network devices. Net PC machines will automatically shift to a low-power state when they are not in use. This behavior is similar to how notebook computers conserve power. But just because the user is not typing does not necessarily mean the machine is not being used. It may be downloading or uploading data from or to servers on the network. Because the Net PC depends heavily on the network, it must be able to receive "wake-up" calls not only from the user, but also from the network. The requirements state that a Net PC system must support the Advanced Configuration and Power Interface (ACPI) Specification, Version 1.0 or later. The systems must also support the OnNow initiative as outlined in the *PC 97 Hardware Design Guide*. This ensures coordination among the operating system and individual device drivers as far as power management is concerned.

Platform Management

As mentioned earlier, a major reason for moving the Windows operating system is to provide a centralized management solution for a large number of Net PCs. The specification states: "The management solution must ensure that the Net PC is manageable in heterogeneous networking environments and that there is a basic set of management information that is guaranteed to be available for management applications."

In a basic sense, platform management has three key parts:

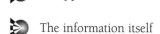 A device that provides information about itself

An application that accesses the information provided by the device

The information itself

Many devices have remote management capabilities. A simple router, for example, can provide information about its activities and state. Applications can access this information by means of a standard protocol. The router information has a defined structure, and the intent is to apply the same concepts to a Net PC computer.

A number of management technologies are mentioned in the Net PC specification. One is the common information model (CIM), which is the data structure for WBEM (discussed later). By design, CIM can be implemented on a variety of operating systems by extending its core functionality. Another management technology is desktop management interface (DMI), an industry standard. HyperMedia Object Manager (HMOM) is an application component that can communicate with a number of devices and provide a consistent view for administration purposes. Microsoft plans to incorporate HMOM into Windows NT 5.0. Web-based enterprise management (WBEM) is another standard aimed at providing a seamless and consistent interface (using the Web) to network-based devices and equipment. Through WBEM, you can get information about devices that support SNMP, CIM, or other management protocols. Some of the standards mentioned previously are still under development, but they all should be available with

Windows NT 5.0. They all address the basic need for simplified and effective management of a large number of Net PCs in an organization, both from a cost perspective and from a technical point of view.

Physical Attributes

Although seemingly trivial, the following requirement is part of the Net PC specification. At a minimum, systems must have a power light indicator. It may have other indicators of disk activity or network traffic, but they are not required. This requirement is probably geared toward simplifying user interaction with the Net PC. Another such requirement is that the Net PC should not have any internal expansion slots that are accessible by the user. In other words, there is no reason for the user to open up the box and configure boards or add new internal devices. Such tasks are to be performed by qualified service personnel only.

There are also stringent requirements for device drivers. Aside from passing the Windows Hardware Quality Labs (WHQL) tests, all configuration information must be stored in the registry that is part of the operating system. Device drivers are needed to support almost any peripheral device connected to the computer. Conflicts among device drivers can lead (and has led!) to hours of head scratching by system administrators. By checking that device drivers conform to a universal standard, most of the incompatibilities should be eliminated.

Net PC also requires that all attached devices comply with the Plug and Play specifications. Plug and Play automates much of the configuration and resource allocation issues when a new device is installed. Also, since each device provides a unique Plug and Play device ID, there will be no conflicts among the devices.

I/O Devices

The Net PC specification requires a keyboard as well as a keyboard connection. Even systems with a built-in keyboard must be able to support an external keyboard. The keyboard connection can be a PS/2 style port or wireless. Similarly, the specification requires a pointing device connection and a pointing device. Interestingly, parallel and serial ports are considered optional. If a parallel port is present, it must be an extended capabilities port (ECP). A serial port must be implemented using a 16550A serial port or equivalent.

Another important device is the network card. This device must meet the PC 97 requirements such as remote control and configuration. The network card is the main link between the Net PC and the network; thus it is important that this element be based on a set standard. The specification also allows for other communication devices such as modems or ISDN cards as long as they meet the PC 97 guidelines.

Multimedia

Although the Net PC is not specifically designed for graphic-intensive applications, it must support minimum multimedia capabilities. The Net PC display supports a minimum resolution of 800 × 480 and a color depth of 16 bits per pixel. It must also operate with the default VGA mode driver, because that is the mode used during operating system installation. So generally, the graphics requirements for a Net PC are consistent with an ordinary PC configuration. The specification does not require NTSC or PAL television support, but if present, they must meet the PC 97 requirements. The actual monitor connected to the Net PC is Display Data Channel standard 2.0, level B (DDC2B) compliant. This standard controls how the monitor device and the computer communicate. A CD-ROM device along with audio and video capabilities are optional, but if they are present, then the specification states a number of guidelines such as support for Microsoft ActiveMovie and DVD playback.

Storage Components

Unlike the Reference Profile 1, the Net PC specification allows a variety of storage and related peripherals. Common standards such as IDE (integrated drive electronics), SCSI, or IEEE (Institute of Electrical and Electronics Engineers) 1394 are supported. Typically, devices such as hard drives, tape drives, and CD-ROM use the above standards. In addition, there are several requirements regarding storage devices outlined in the PC 97 guidelines that must be adhered to. This is mostly to ensure that devices from different manufacturers function the same and that they can be controlled by the operating system. The specification also recommends that traditional floppy drives not be included with the Net PC.

Hardware Security

We have already covered some security features at the BIOS level. There are also physical security features in the Net PC, such as lack of user access to components inside the machine. In a large network environment, there is a greater need for security. Smartcards are an ideal choice when it comes to device security, especially for authorization purposes. If smartcard support is present in a Net PC, then it must comply with the *Interoperability Specification for ICCs and Personal Computer Systems Guidelines,* which is a document published by several industry leaders such as Hewlett-Packard, Microsoft, and Siemens. Information about this publication is available at `http://www.smartcardsys.com`. Additionally, the smartcards must be Plug and Play compliant and adhere to the Win 32 smartcard specifications.

The Net PC guidelines not only require that the machine as a whole be secure, but that each device attached to it also have security capabilities. For example, an external device, once removed from the system, should become disabled. The machine itself should have locking capabilities. These points are consistent with the goal of the specification to provide a simple, "one-box" solution to network computing.

Further Information

Throughout this section, references were made to a number of other specifications and standards. The following provides a listing of Web sites that contain additional information about some of these standards.

- Intel developer information (`http://developer.intel.com`)

- Information on Net PC, Zero Administration Windows (`http://www.microsoft.com/windows`)

- Information on hardware development on Microsoft Web site (`http://www.microsoft.com/hwdev`)

- Windows Hardware Quality Labs (WHQL) (`http://www.microsoft.com/hwtest`)

- WBEM information (`http://www.microsoft.com/management/wbem`)

- Windows management instrumentation (WMI) information (`http://www.microsoft.com/management/wbem`)

- Information on Desktop Management Task Force (DMTF) (`http://www.dmtf.org`)

- Common information model (CIM) (`http://www.dmtf.org/work/cim.html`)

- Advanced Configuration and Power Interface Specification, Version 1.0 (`http://www.teleport.com/~acpi`)

- CIM specifications (`http://www.dmtf.org/work/cim.html`)

- Desktop Management Interface Specification, Version 2.0 (`http://www.dmtf.org/tech/specs.html`)

- Device Bay Interface Specification, Version 1.0 (`http://www.device-bay.org`)

- Device Class Power Management Specifications (`http://www.microsoft.com/hwdev/onnow.htm`)

- Intel/Duracell Smart Battery System Specification (`http://developer.intel.com/ial/powermgm/specs.htm`)

- International Color Consortium Profile Format Specification (`http://www.color.org`)

- Interoperability Specification for ICCs (integrated circuit cards) and Personal Computer Systems Guidelines (`http://www.smartcardsys.com`)

- PC 97 Hardware Design Guide (`http://www.microsoft.com/hwdev/pc97.htm`)

- PCI Bus Power Management Interface Specification (`http://www.pcisig.com`)

- Plug and Play specifications (`http://www.microsoft.com/hwdev/specs/pnpspecs.htm`)

- Universal Serial Bus, Version 1.0 (`http://www.usb.org`)

- Universal Serial Bus PC Legacy Compatibility Specification, Version 1.0 (`http://www.teleport.com/~usb/data/usb_le9.pdf`)

- WBEM Specifications (`http://wbem.freerange.com`)

- WMI Specifications and Win32 Extensions Schema (`http://www.microsoft.com/management/wbem/`)

Odin Reference Platform

Odin is a hardware platform based on the NS486 chip from National Semiconductor. You can learn more about this standard from `http://www.national.com/appinfo/ns486/odin.html`.

WebRef Reference Platform

WebRef is similar to Odin. It is specific to a particular processor (Motorola PowerPC series). The effort is led by Motorola. Additional information can be found at http://www.motorola.com.

Implementations

This section provides some specifics about some of the implementations of the above standards. Chances are, by the time you read this book, many more new products will have hit the market. Where applicable, a URL is provided from which you may get the latest information on a particular product.

@workstation

HDS is a leader in NC technology and markets its family of @workstation products as the "world's first network computer." It supports Java applications, Web applications, Windows applications (via technology from Insignia Solutions), and legacy terminal-based applications. Figure 2-2 shows a picture of @workstation.

Figure 2-2 @workstation from HDS

One of the unique features of @workstation is its operating system, netOS. netOS has implemented JVM at its core level. This means that Java applications are executed just like other applications built on top of the operating system. The major benefit of this approach is speed. netOS was originally developed on the Intel x86 platform, but it has since been ported to the Intel 960 and the Motorola PowerPC. The majority of the code is written in C language, so it is portable.

@workstation can be booted from the network or from local storage such as flash memory, ROM, or local disk. The main interface is an X-like window manager. From there, you can launch the HDS Explorer Web browser and surf the Web. From the Web browser, you can launch other applications. You can access distributed file systems using either NFS or NTrigue. NTrigue is also used to access Windows applications. It functions in a manner similar to Citrix Winframe.

@workstation has powerful audio and video capabilities. It can provide CD-quality audio and supports live video signals. @workstation has been a very popular and successful product in the enterprise market. For the latest information, go to `http://www.hds.com`.

JavaStation

Sun Microsystems is the main force behind Java. It would only make sense that Sun would enter the NC world with a Java-based machine. Sun was one of the early supporters of the NC Reference Profile 1, and its NC meets that standard. JavaStation (see Figure 2-3) is based on a 100 MHz microSPARC II CPU from Sun. It supports VGA and super VGA (SVGA) displays with enhanced graphics. It can boot either from flash memory locally or over the network from a server.

Figure 2-3 JavaStation from Sun Microsystems

The operating system for JavaStation is JavaOS, which consists of a small Java kernel, an embedded JVM, a Java user environment, and a number of device drivers written in Java.

The user environment for JavaStation is customizable. You can have JavaStation configured to run only one application, such as your order-processing program. As soon as the user logs in, he or she is presented with that application. On the other hand, you can use the HotJava Browser, which is a Web browser, to run a variety of Web and Java applications. There is a third alternative called HotJava Views, which gives you a desktop-like environment. Here you have access to basic programs like email, Notepad, and Calendar. These programs are all part of the desktop (Sun refers to desktop as *webtop*). From the webtop, you can launch other applications.

JavaStation supports all the popular terminal emulators for accessing mainframe applications. Additionally, it uses software from Citrix to provide an interface to Windows applications. One of the drawbacks of JavaStation is that it relies on a Netra J server, which is not surprising, because Sun also manufactures the Netra J. JavaStation and the products (both hardware and software) built around it are bound to improve in the coming months. For the latest, check out `http://www.sun.com`. Sun regularly updates the pages related to JavaStation. One interesting section is the one that lists commercial applications written specifically for a Java-based NC such as JavaStation.

Network Computer XL & XLC

Boundless Technologies has targeted the enterprise market with two models of its NC. These NCs (see Figure 2-4) are geared more toward Windows applications, but Java support is being added to the system so that it can run Java applications as well.

The system is based on an Intel i960 CA RISC processor with speed of 25 or 33 MHz, depending on the model. Although the board supports 32 MB of RAM, the system can function with as little as 4 MB of RAM. The display can be a color or a grayscale monitor, based on your preference. Several different keyboards are supported, including PC style, 3270, Sun, VT-220, and DEC LK411 keyboards. A mouse also ships with the product.

TCP/IP, PPP, and SLIP are supported communication protocols. You can connect a modem via the serial port or use the Ethernet controller to link directly to the network. There is also a parallel port that you can connect to a local printer.

Figure 2-4 XL from Boundless Technologies

Windows applications are supported using WinFrame technology. The server for these applications is Windows NT with the WinFrame server. The NC boots from the NT server and the server is also responsible for application and user storage needs. As of writing this book, Java applications were not supported yet on the NC, but you could run a Java application on the NT server and see the result (similar to how X Window servers operate).

The system also has audio and telephony support. Optional features include the ability to support TN3270, Motif Window Manager, OPEN LOOK Window Manager, and RS-232 window. The XL and XLC products fall in a gray territory. They are not Net PC-compliant because they are not based on the Intel architecture (although they use a chip from Intel, that chip is different from the popular Pentium and Pentium Pro chips upon which the Windows operating system is based). On the other hand, until adequate support for Java and Internet protocols is provided, the Reference Profile 1 requirement is not fulfilled. So for now, we have to place XL and XLC in their own category. Additional information about these products is available from **http://www.boundless.com**.

NetStation

IBM has positioned itself between the terminal market and the desktop personal computer market with its network computer called Network Station, or NetStation. The product is really an addition to the existing IBM product line. NetStation requires an IBM AS/400, PC Server, RS/6000, System/390 mainframe, or compatible non-IBM system.

As for hardware, NetStation complies with the Reference Profile 1 standard. It is based on the IBM PowerPC architecture and comes with 8 MB of RAM that is expandable to 64 MB. There is no local disk, but a network card, serial and parallel ports, and a VGA display are supported. Monitors with higher resolutions (SVGA and SXGA) are also supported.

NetStation has a small part of the operating system stored in ROM. The remaining pieces are downloaded from the server. The following pieces of software are downloaded from the server:

- IBM Network Station Manager: The remaining part of the operating system to manage the NetStation and devices attached to it.

- Terminal support software: This piece differs based on the server. For RS/6000 and UNIX servers, an X Window emulator is provided. For S/390 servers, a 3270 emulator is downloaded. AS/400 servers are supported by a 5250 emulator.

- IBM Network Station Browser: A standard Web browser for accessing Web resources.

- IBM Network Station Support for Java: Support for the JVM.

After the system boots, it prompts for a user name and a password. This information is sent back to the server for authentication and then the user environment and preferences stored on the server are used to set up the environment on the client.

IBM has used its expertise in the server market to create a powerful NC. By taking a multilayer approach to the operating system, the NetStation can be modified at runtime to work with different servers. Further information is available at `http://www.ibm.com`.

Explora

Network Computing Devices (NCD) entered the NC market with Explora. Explora is based on the NCDware operating system, which is proprietary to NCD. In addition to supporting Java applications, Explora has the capability to support Windows applications.

NCD's focus is the corporate market, and therefore the ability to support enterprise and office applications is a top priority.

Explora is based on the reduced instruction set computer (RISC) architecture (32-bit) and uses a 28 MHz PowerPC chip. It comes with 4 MB of RAM that is expandable to 36 MB. The display supports up to a SVGA resolution. Explora communicates with the network via its 10Base T network adapter and can also connect to devices through its serial and parallel ports.

Explora uses the NCDware operating system. Its standard user environment is based on the X Window system. Explora can execute Windows applications using a software called WinCenter (from NCD). In addition to X Window and Microsoft Windows applications, Explora supports 3270/3179G, TN3270, and VT320 applications that allow it to be used as a client to legacy system in the enterprise.

Audio capabilities and local storage via a floppy drive are optional. The following Internet protocols are supported:

- TCP/IP

- NFS

- Telnet

- DNS/BIND

- X11

- XDMCP

- LPD

- DHCP

- BOOTP

- RARP

- ARP

- SNMP

- PING

- TFTP

The following management protocols and functions are supported:

- FlexLM

- Remote reboot

- Network diagnostics

- Remote control via SNMP and ConfigD

- Secure boot monitor

- Persistent and secure boot

Explora does more than merely follow the NC Reference Profile; it provides support for non-Java applications as well as Java applications. NCD has many years of expertise in providing enterprise solutions, and Explora is a continuation of that tradition for corporate intranets. Execution of Windows applications requires special software on both the client and the server, and that software is provided by NCD. Additional information about Explora and network software solutions is available from **http://www.ncd.com**.

Internet Client Station

Internet Client Station (ICS) is a classic implementation of Reference Profile 1 by I.D.E. Corporation. ICS implements a built-in shell that includes a Web browser and serves as the main GUI to other applications. An ICS is connected to a network in a manner similar to other clients. It has an IP number and uses TCP/IP for its networking communications. It supports all the Internet protocols required by Reference Profile 1. The Web browser is HTML 3.0 compliant and supports HTTP, Gopher, FTP, and proxy servers.

A useful feature of ICS from an administrative point of view is its ability to support a number of email servers, including Lotus cc:Mail, Oracle InterOffice, HP OpenMail, and MS Exchange. New users of ICS will also appreciate the fact that the user interface is not much different than what they are used to.

ICS can be used to access text-based 3270 applications via a TN3270 emulator. It also supports 5250 IBM host applications. Access to UNIX machines is provided via Telnet. ICS does not support X applications. The built-in browser does support Java, so ICS can be used to download and execute Java applets.

ICS requires a UNIX server to function. It depends on the server for authentication, booting, applications, and file storage. In that regard, it is similar to traditional UNIX clients.

According to the specification from I.D.E. Corporation, ICS is equipped with 4 MB of ROM and 4 MB of RAM. The ROM size is probably the result of the built-in shell. The RAM is expandable to 16 MB. The CPU is a 40 MHz ARM7500FE based on the RISC architecture. Network connection is made via a 10BaseT adapter. The display supports a resolution of up to 1024 × 786 (SVGA), which is more than what the NC Reference Profile calls for. Additionally, ICS has a 101-key keyboard, a mouse, a printer port, a 25-pin serial port, and a built-in speaker. As for security, ICS supports the ISO 7816 standard (smartcard).

ICS is a classic example of an NC. It uses the network to perform its tasks. It also provides an interface to the Web via a built-in browser with Java support. Additional information can be found at `http://www.idea.com`.

Winterm

Wyse Technology has been known for its terminals; with the NC revolution, it has introduced the Winterm 4000 series. The NCs come in different models and follow their own standard. Winterm can be used not only for Internet and Java applications, but also for MS Windows programs (using technology from Citrix).

Winterm is based on the Java operating system and comes with a browser that is HTML 3.2 compliant. It supports TCP/IP, DHCP, HTTP, NNTP, SMTP, SNMP, BOOTP, RARP, and UDP/IP. Support for PPP will be available later in 1997. Winterm is a completely Internet-ready machine.

Winterm can run Java and Web applications using its built-in Web browser. It runs terminal applications using popular emulators such as TNS270 and TN220. The interesting fact about these emulators is that they are written in Java and are in fact Java applets. MS Windows applications are supported because Winterm can be a Citrix ICA3 client. X applications will also be supported when X capabilities are added to Winterm in the future.

Winterm is another classic example of an NC. With no local storage, it can be used to access a variety of applications using the network and application servers. One of its strengths is that its operating system is JavaOS. Winterm is targeted for the enterprise.

By providing a robust and easy-to-maintain machine, Winterm has already fulfilled many of the promises of the NC. Additional information about this product is available from `http://www.wyse.com`.

AcerBasic

AcerBasic from Acer is a Net PC-compliant NC built around the AMD 5x86/133 MHz CPU. In addition to supporting VGA, AcerBasic has built-in video capability for both PAL and NTSC formats. The base model comes with 4 MB of memory, serial and parallel ports, a keyboard, and a mouse. It also supports the popular zip drive from Iomega.

Acer is targeting three different markets with its NC. The education market is served with the Education PC, which is a multimedia PC with hard drive, floppy drive, CD-ROM, and audio capability. The home market product is Internet PC, which can be used to surf the Web and send and receive email. This product is also equipped with a modem, hard drive, and zip drive. Finally, there is the Application-Specific Computer (ASC), which can be customized for specific applications. For example, if call center personnel use a special application, you can use the ASC in that environment.

Additional peripherals are available from Acer to customize the NC for your needs. BIOS is made by Acer itself, and the base operating system is MS-DOS 6.22. There is also optional support for Windows 3.11. Additional information about this product is available at `http://www.acer.com`.

Other Products

It is impossible to include the latest NC-related products in a book. The industry is very young and it is changing rapidly with advances in both the hardware and the software markets. Following is a list of companies that have endorsed the Reference Profile 1. All have products related to the network computer industry.

- Acron Computer Group

- Adobe Systems

- Advanced RISC Machines (ARM)

- AirMouse Remote Controls

- Akai Electronic

- ALCATEL Business Systems

- ANT Limited

- Axis Communications

- BT

- Cable & Wireless Innovations

- Canon

- Cirrus Logic

- Corel Corporation

- CSK Corporation

- CTC Laboratories

- Digital Semiconductor

- Eidos Technologies

- France Telecom

- Fujitsu

- Funai Electric

- Hitachi

- Hyndai Electronics

- IDEA

- IPS

- The Japan Research Institute
- Japan Telecom
- Justsystem Corporation
- K.K. Ashisuto
- Lexmark International
- LG Electronics
- Lite-On Technology
- Lotus Development
- LSI Logic
- Macromedia
- MasterCard International
- Matsushita Electric Industrial
- Mitac
- Mitsubishi Electronics America
- Motorola
- NEC Corporation
- Neighborhood Global Network
- Nippon Steel Information & Communication Systems
- Nippon Telegraph and Telephone Corporation
- Nokia Group

- Nomura Research Institute

- NTT Data Communication Systems

- Olivetti

- Otsuka Shokai

- Pyramid Technology

- SABRE Interactive Division

- Samsung Information Systems America

- SanDisk

- SGS-THOMSON Microelectronics

- SOFTBANK

- Sourcecom

- SunRiver

- Tatung Company

- TECO Information Systems

- Toshiba Corporation

- Toyo Information Systems

- TriTeal Corporation

- Uniden Corporation

- VeriFone, Inc.

- VISA International

- VLSI Technology

- Voxware

- Wearnes Technology

- Weitek

- Westell Technologies

- Wyse Technology

Similarly, a number of companies have endorsed the Net PC Reference platform. Here is a partial list:

- COMPAQ Computer

- Dell Computer

- Digital Equipment

- Gateway 2000

- Hewlett-Packard

- Intel

- Microsoft

- Packard Bell

- NEC

- Texas Instruments

Summary

The first industrywide standard for network computers came from a group of industry leaders comprising IBM, Sun Microsystems, Oracle, Apple, and Netscape. This standard is known as Reference Profile 1. Although it avoids specifics, the standard outlines general requirements for an NC. These requirements include the ability to support Internet protocols, to execute Java applications, and to function without a local storage device.

Another major standard is the Net PC Reference Profile, which was drafted by Microsoft and Intel. The Net PC is based exclusively on the Windows operating system and Intel processors. It supports Java, but at the same time it requires support of Windows applications.

A number of NC products have hit the market. This chapter included a brief description of some of these products. Although the hardware industry will continue to introduce new products, the software industry will also bring out a number of applications written specifically for the NC.

CHAPTER 3

Software for the NC

The NC represents a change not only in computer hardware but also in software. Applications developed for the computer-centric model have their own distinctive attributes. Programmers will soon find out that some of the techniques they have used for development of client/server applications on the desktop will not apply to the NC, although most will continue to be useful. The NC encourages the design and development of applications that are downloadable over the network, object based, and component based. This chapter focuses solely on what makes an application NC friendly. Because Java is one of the primary languages used to develop software for the NC, I will make some references to the language, but a complete treatment of the Java language as it relates to the NC is postponed until Chapter 5, "The NC and Java."

Operating System

The software abstraction closest to the hardware is the operating system. Operating systems are usually highly compact, efficient, and robust; one of their major tasks is to provide an interface between the hardware and applications. Applications access the hardware through the operating system, as shown in Figure 3-1. As a result, applications do not have to be rewritten for each type of hardware. A good example is accessing a file

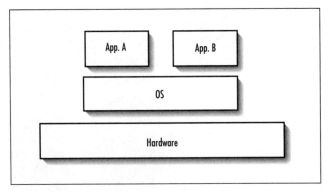

Figure 3-1 Applications access hardware through the
operating system

on your disk drive. The operating system provides a series of Application Programming
Interfaces (APIs) for reading and writing a file. Your application simply uses the
services provided by the operating system. It is up to the operating system to make sure
data is read and written properly on the particular type of disk drive on your computer.

The NC also has an operating system (OS). To provide cross-platform compatibility,
all the features of the operating system are specified in the NC standards, with the implementation details left to the platform developers. Many existing operating systems can
be used to support the NC operating system, such as the popular Windows operating
system from Microsoft and the UNIX operating system. Several operating systems are
specifically designed for the NC, such as JavaOS. JavaOS has a built-in Java virtual
machine (JVM), so it is ideal for supporting Java applications. Another such OS is netOS,
developed by HDS for its @workStation NC. Figure 3-2 is an example of a typical NC
based on the Reference Profile 1 standard.

Figure 3-3 shows how a typical NC based on the NetPC standard may look.

The primary challenge faced by OS designers is that the NC specifications do not
require a permanent storage device. Because the OS may not be stored locally on a disk
drive, it must either be stored in the hardware (Java-enabled chips take this approach)
or be downloaded from a server. This process is commonly known as *booting*. On your
desktop computer, you install the operating system on the local disk drive. Every time
you turn on the machine, the operating system is loaded from the hard drive. This is a
relatively fast operation because disk speeds have increased substantially over the past
few years. After loading, the main part of the operating system (commonly known as the
kernel) stays in memory and basically runs your computer until you turn it off. The
process of booting an NC is similar to that of booting a conventional PC. The main

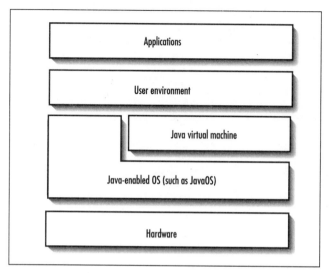

Figure 3-2 Software layers for Reference Profile 1 NC

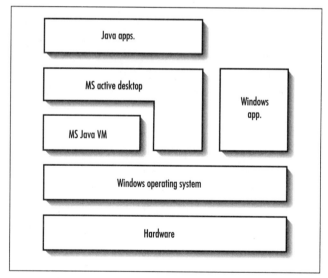

Figure 3-3 Software layers for NetPC NC

difference is that the source of the boot process might not be a disk. This is especially true for the NC devices. Smartcard technology is widely regarded as an appropriate boot device for NC.

NOTE *The NC specification does not require a local storage device.*

Due to space limitations, the NC cannot have a large kernel. Because the OS must be loaded every time you turn on an NC, a large kernel would be counterproductive. That is why most OS designs rely heavily on the server and the network. The initial kernel will get things started, but subsequent operations may have to be forwarded to the server. So it is safe to say that a typical NC OS is smaller than a typical desktop OS. This is particularly true in the case of Internet-ready devices that also fall under the NC category.

I should mention that the idea of downloading the OS from a server or implementing the OS at the hardware level on a chip is not new. Embedded devices such as camcorders have been around for a long time and they have an OS built into them. Networking hardware such as routers also use embedded OSs. An X terminal usually boots from a server and provides the user with a graphical user interface (GUI). A UNIX workstation typically either boots off a server or depends on the server for many of its operations. Such implementations have only recently begun to take hold in the PC mass market, however, and thus seem more revolutionary than evolutionary.

The NC OS must also provide an interface to accessories connected to the NC, such as the modem, the mouse, the monitor, and perhaps even a sound card. Again, these tasks are typical of an operating system. The challenge is that the NC OS has to do it in a more compact environment and across all hardware platforms.

User Environment

You turn on the computer and after initial hardware checks, the operating system takes over and the system is booted. Now what? Desktop users are so accustomed to environments such as Windows and the Mac desktop that they consider these environments part of the operating system. They are not. They are one layer above the operating system. For example, in Windows 95, there is the Start menu in the lower-left corner. There is wallpaper in the background and users can set the look and feel of the rest of their desktop. These elements really are not part of the operating system (kernel). Designers of the NC have taken this into account and have come up with different user environments.

User environments are similar to window managers in the X Window terminology of the UNIX world. A user environment is responsible for providing the user with an initial environment through which the user can interact with the system and particular applications. Typically, after you enter the user environment, you launch an application and do your main work.

A typical user environment includes some basic programs such as a notepad, a clock, and an email program. Again, due to lack of local disk space, a decision has to be made as to where to store these applications. Some NC implementations have gone the hardware route, as the NC has done with its operating system. NC devices typically implement the hardware solution. Other NC implementations download these applications like other applications from the server as needed. Sun Microsystem's JavaStation uses the HotJava user environment, which includes the following:

MailView: Electronic mail

CalendarView: Electronic calendar

NameView: A phonebook-type application

InfoView: A Web browser

Selector: A "push-button" GUI

NC implementations based on the Net PC standard have adopted the look and feel of the familiar Windows operating system. Regardless of how things look, all NCs have a user environment. You will not find an NC with a DOS-like interface, where typing commands at a prompt is the only way you can interact with the system. All NC implementations support a GUI.

Application

Aside from the operating system and the user environment, the other important software on the NC are the applications themselves. As the NC market grows, so will the application market. In the PC world, applications run in two different ways. One method is to load the application on the local hard drive and then execute it from there. This is very common in the consumer market (that is, home computers). The application loads into memory and begins execution. If it needs another module, it will go to the hard drive and load that part into memory. This approach is depicted in Figure 3-4. The second method is used by operating systems such as NetWare and Windows and involves network file servers. In those cases, the server interacts with the client and together they execute the application. Usually, a client piece resides on the desktop that manages the

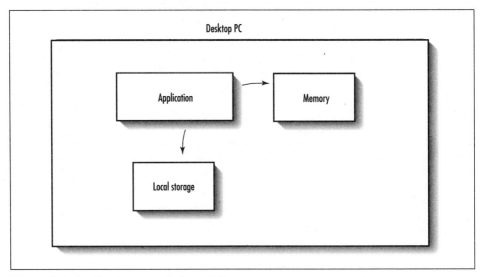

Figure 3-4 Application on a desktop PC

communication between the server and the client. This client piece is stored on the hard drive. A variety of approaches is possible. The server may execute the application and the client will see only the results. Another approach is that the client will download part or all of the application from the server and execute it locally. More recent versions take an approach that uses both of these options.

The network-centric model takes a different approach. The most common approach is that the client downloads the components of an application from the server as needed and executes them using its own local processing power. In cases where the application must access a database or perform huge calculations, the client will directly or indirectly establish a connection to the appropriate database server and ask it to perform the necessary tasks. This approach is shown in Figure 3-5.

Whereas the traditional client/server uses two pieces (client and server), the network-centric model usually deploys three pieces. The first is the client. The second is the application server, which sends out the application to the client to be executed. The third piece is the server in its traditional role such as a database or a file server. Because the focus of the majority of software developed for the NC is the application market, I will focus on how an application works on the NC.

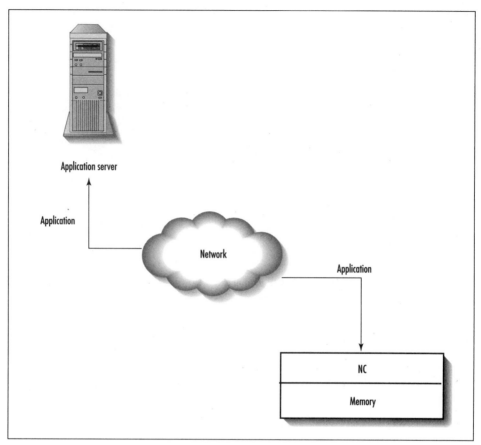

Figure 3-5 Application on an NC

The Client

An application designed for the NC has a client piece that is downloaded by the NC and executed on the NC. This piece is relatively small and performs very specific tasks. In the PC model, you have the entire client application installed on your PC. An application may contain individual pieces such as inventory, order entry, billing, and shipping forms. All of these modules make up an application. In the NC model, it doesn't make sense to spend time downloading modules that you are not going to use. So the first task for designing NC applications is to divide the application into small, independent parts. Only the needed parts are downloaded. Component technologies such as JavaBeans and ActiveX are ideal for this type of design and are discussed later in this book.

In a client/server model, you can expect the client to perform the following tasks:

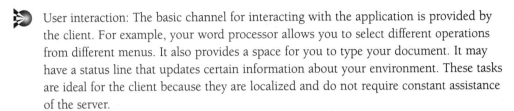

Display management: This is what the user environment does; every NC supports it.

User interaction: The basic channel for interacting with the application is provided by the client. For example, your word processor allows you to select different operations from different menus. It also provides a space for you to type your document. It may have a status line that updates certain information about your environment. These tasks are ideal for the client because they are localized and do not require constant assistance of the server.

Generate requests: A client must take user input and generate a request to the server. A good example is a database application. You select a query in a very high abstraction level using menus and lists, but the actual SQL commands for the query are generated by the client and sent to the server. When you use a Web browser, each link you click on generates a request that is sent to the Web server. The process of transforming your request into a lower-level protocol is done by the client.

Data validation: The client can do initial data validation of user input. For example, in an order-entry form, the client can check and make sure the phone number is indeed ten digits. The client would not validate whether the phone number is already in the system or not. That would require the assistance of a database on a server.

The software client in a network-centric model is not much different than the client in the client/server model. It performs similar tasks, but it is smaller, specific, and component based.

The Application Server

The design of NC requires a relatively new component known as the *application server*. Recall that, aside from some basic programs that may be embedded in the NC, all applications must be downloaded from the server. The server responsible for sending application components to the NC is called the application server.

The traditional client/server model does not have such a component (and doesn't require one either). In that model, the entire application resides permanently on the client after the initial installation. You have already used an application server if you have used any Web applications. When you view a Web page with an applet, you are downloading the applet (which can be the application) from an application server. In this particular case, the application server is more commonly known as the *Web server*.

Application servers must be equipped with fast processors and network cards. They don't need to store terabytes of data, as a traditional database server must, but they do need to be very responsive to clients requesting application pieces. Some designs require the application server to execute part of the application; in those cases, the machine must be equipped accordingly.

With an application server, you can immediately realize several important benefits. First of all, by storing all the applications in a central place, you have more control over them. You know who is using what and to what extent. You also eliminate long and expensive software upgrades necessary for desktop PCs. With an application server, you can put up a new version of the application and instantly all your NCs use the upgraded version.

Another advantage of application servers is that they fit the distributed model very well. You can have several application servers serving the same or different applications. You can easily scale your system based on your needs. The Java programming language offers several important pieces for deployment under this model. Whereas applets are Java applications running on the client, *servlets* are Java components of the application running on the server. The application server is discussed at length in Chapter 4, "Servers for the NC."

There is another variation of the application server. In some NC configurations, the application executes on a server and only the output is shown on the NC. A good example is the product from Citrix Software. Using a protocol called ICA, an NC can execute programs on a Windows NT server and see the result on the NC monitor. This configuration puts a heavy load on the server because it has to execute all of the applications requested by clients. On the other hand, there is less of a burden on the NC itself. This configuration works with less memory and less processing power on the NC as compared to the conventional NC model. The real advantage of network computing is the ability to download components of an application and execute them locally.

The Web is another example of an application server where the application is executed on the server. When you access an online catalog, your browser sends the request and processes the response in an appropriate manner, such as placing graphics on the monitor or tabulating the pages. The Web server uses common gateway interface (CGI) technology or a server-specific API to process the information you provide and to interact with the database to place your order. Web servers at high-traffic sites are very expensive, and fast machines are needed to be able to handle the total number of client requests that they receive. Technologies such as JavaScript and Java attempt to shift most of that burden to the client, which is where the NC is well suited.

The Data Server

From the NC point of view, the data server continues to play a traditional role. Data warehouses, distributed databases, and transaction servers form the third piece of the network-centric model. The client gets its application from the application server and starts executing it. The application may need to access a database; that is where the data server comes into play.

Data servers are good at storing information and providing a fast and reliable method for retrieving that information. Relational database management systems (RDBMs) have done just that for the past few years. Oracle, Informix, Sybase, MS SQL Server, and CA Ingres all fall into this category. Recently, new object-oriented database systems have hit the market and promise to make multimedia data storage and retrieval even easier. The NC will certainly benefit from that.

An important point must be made here. Many database vendors already allow developers to embed applications within the database server itself. Such applications are generally called *stored procedures* and provide a great deal of flexibility, security, and performance when you are developing database applications. In the client/server model, the concept of stored procedures is similar to that of the application server. By allowing code to be stored as part of the database, a data server could play the role of application and data server at the same time. The drawback of this approach is that the stored procedures are database specific (unlike the application server in the network-centric model). Although we will continue to see stored procedures in data servers, they should not be confused with what application servers do. The network-centric model has extended the concept of stored procedures to the client (applets) and the application servers (servlets). An application designer has the flexibility to distribute the processing and execution burden among the different components. The concept of stored procedures is depicted in Figure 3-6.

Generally, you want your data and your application to be separated. You also want to have an open architecture where you don't have to depend on one vendor and one technology for everything. As databases begin to support additional data types such as audio and video, there will be a need for specific applications to handle the new data types. The best way for this to happen is to allow developers to create their own data types and their own applications to handle the new data types. That is the basis of the object-oriented paradigm; the database industry is showing signs of moving in this direction by offering object-based databases such as Informix's universal server.

Java provides a tool called Java database connectivity (JDBC) that links data servers and Java applications. Depending on the design, the application residing on the server can directly open up a connection to the data server and perform the necessary operations. This approach is shown in Figure 3-7.

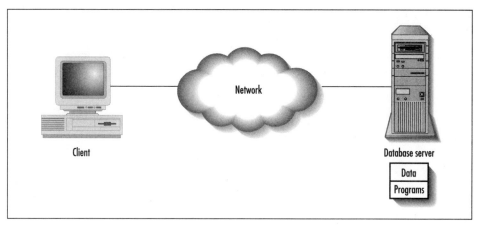

Figure 3-6 Stored procedures

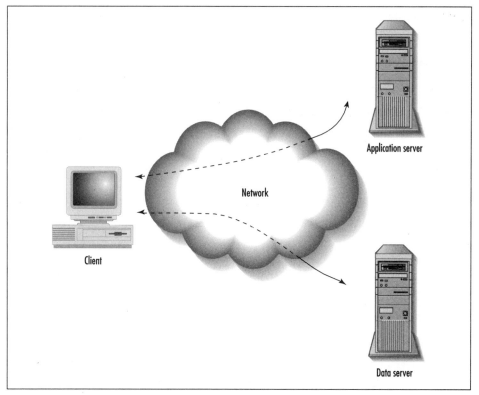

Figure 3-7 Client accessing the database directly

Another approach is for the client application to access the data server through the application server. This is shown in Figure 3-8. This design is particularly useful in large organizations where a firewall blocks direct access to internal network resources, including the data servers. JDBC is discussed in Chapter 6, "The NC and Databases."

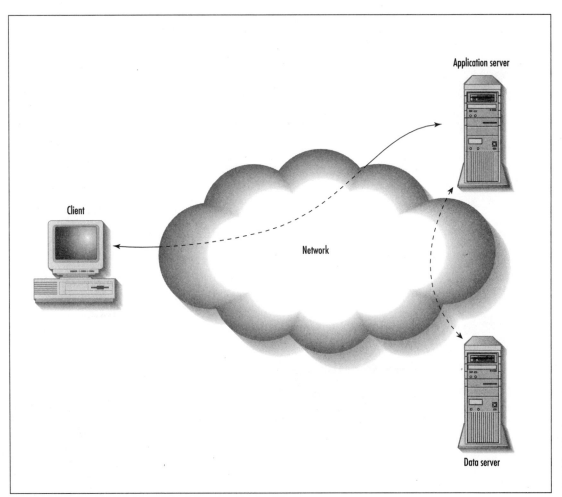

Figure 3-8 Client accessing the database through the application server

Communication

Communication between the client and the server is accomplished over a TCP/IP network. This is the type of network that already supports all the computers connected to the Internet. It makes sense that the NC is built on top of the largest network in the world. TCP/IP is not a proprietary network protocol, and as a result many different applications can be built on top of it, as shown in Figure 3-9. Many such standard application protocols are already in existence. Some of the most commonly used ones are

- FTP: The File Transfer Protocol is commonly used to transfer files between two remote machines.

- Telnet: This is a standard protocol that allows a user to log on to a remote machine; it is terminal-based access, not GUI based.

- SMTP: The Simple Mail Transfer Protocol is the protocol used for sending and receiving email.

- NFS: The Network File System is a protocol for distributed file system implementations. It creates an environment in which users can access files on different machines as if they all belonged to a central file system.

- SNMP: The Simple Network Management Protocol allows computers to be managed across a network.

- HTTP: Hypertext Transfer Protocol is the standard Web protocol for sending multimedia documents over a network.

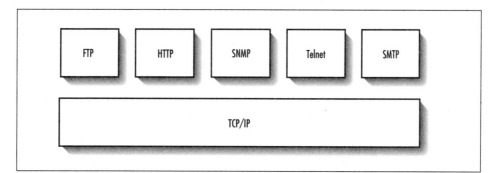

Figure 3-9 Application protocols on top of TCP/IP

The NC counts on a reliable network for its smooth operation. Technology has been very responsive by providing a number of potential hardware and software solutions for faster networks with more capacity. Cable modems, ISDN, high-rate digital subscriber line (HDSL), and asynchronous transfer mode (ATM) are some examples.

It is beyond the scope of this book to discuss the details of networking protocols, but one of the most important steps in moving to the network-centric model in any organization is the design of the network. You must have a reliable infrastructure in place before you can successfully deploy NCs and take full advantage of the potential they offer. If you are already heavily invested in a client/server system, chances are your network can support deployment of NCs with little or no modification.

Security

In the desktop days, you would lock up the office and that was sufficient security that your data was safe. In the early network days, you would connect machines via the network and wouldn't connect the network to anything else. Unfortunately, such strategies no longer work. Welcome to enterprise networks and the Internet. Today, networks are so large and complex that distinctions between what is and what is not connected to the network are sometimes very hard to find.

Two prevalent models are in existence today. One is the Internet, which is a conglomeration of public networks and is shown in Figure 3-10. The other is an intranet, which is a closed network modeled after the Internet and is shown in Figure 3-11.

Many applications require a bridge between these two models. Consider the example of an online catalog. The Web server that interacts with the browsers is on the Internet. The data about the customer, the order, inventory, and shipping is stored in a database inside the company intranet, which is protected by a firewall. To make the application work, there must be a connection between the Internet and the intranet. Several technologies provide this service.

The NC can operate within each model or a combination of two. It has no direct affect on your Internet/intranet security. Whatever security mechanism you are deploying for your existing Web applications can continue to exist. The NC affects security at the application level.

With the NC, you have more control over the application. You store applications in a centralized place. And because NCs have no local storage capability, you don't have to worry about users introducing viruses into the network by using an infected disk. You also have more control over licensing issues surrounding your applications and can protect against unauthorized usage of applications.

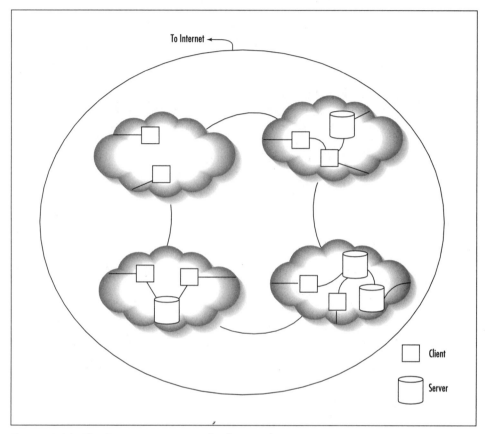

Figure 3-10 The Internet is a network of networks

NOTE *Scope of Security*

Security is and must be implemented at several levels. Secure applications will be only as effective as the operating system and hardware they are running on. Similarly, there are different levels of security within an application. The traditional user name/password approach may or may not work in your case. Generally, security should be implemented specifically for the application it is intended for.

Certain implementations of the NC include a smartcard that authorizes the user to use the machine. This is more secure than the standard user name/password combination. Such added security is important if NC devices are going to be used for electronic commerce. As you design your applications, you have to assess their security requirements. Most likely, you will have some security-specific code at the application level.

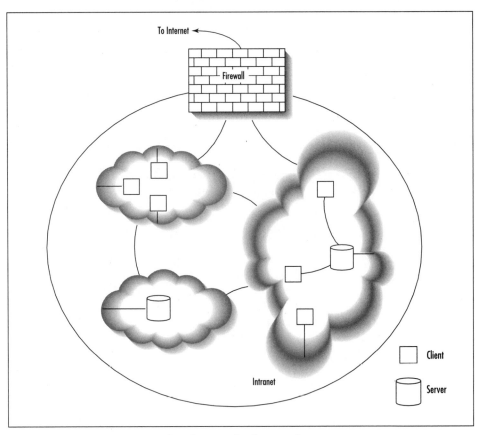

Figure 3-11 An intranet is a closed network of networks

The Java language provides a mechanism by which you can sign your applications. Malicious applications, although not a concern in a corporate environment, are a threat in the Internet world. Application signatures, digital certificates, and encryption schemes can work together to provide a safe environment for the consumer NC market.

Documents and Applications

For the most part, the NC eliminates the distinction between an application and a document. We have learned to organize our documents in a directory structure and then open an application to access our documents. The NC, with its object-oriented nature, provides a different perspective. Everything on your screen is an object. You have no way of "interacting" with an object unless you open the appropriate application. This is similar to double-clicking on an icon and launching the application associated with that document type.

The NC takes this approach further by applying it globally to all applications, big and small alike. Your documents are stored in a server. A document may contain documents of a different type. That is OK as long as the application to view the different documents is available from the application server. The NC will take care of storing and associating documents with applications. You get only a very high-level view. These concepts will become more clear when I discuss JavaBeans, ActiveX, and CORBA in later chapters.

An Example

To provide a perspective on what software is like on the NC, let's use an example. Figure 3-12 shows Quicken, a popular desktop application from Intuit Software. The application comes on disks or a CD-ROM. All the components are installed on your hard drive. The application runs independent of a local network and stores its data (documents) locally. There is a clear distinction between the data and the application.

Quicken is not a client/server application, but it can dial into a network and get information about your financial accounts and download that information. Of course, you have to have the proper authorization first. In addition to offering password protection, Quicken encrypts data during transmission using an RSA-based encryption algorithm.

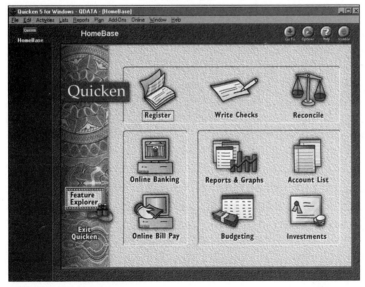

Figure 3-12 Quicken main screen

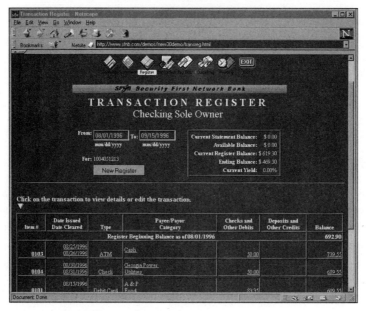

Figure 3-13 Web page from SFNB

Figure 3-13 shows a Web application. It is a banking application from Security First Network Bank (SFNB) (**http://www.sfnb.com**). The application itself is running on a Web server connected to the SFNB network. Your computer acts as a client and uses the browser application to access and interact with the banking application. The Web server most likely accesses the information about your transactions from a database server inside the SFNB network protected by a firewall. This type of application can be used by the NC. The NC will have a browser application that in turn points to the appropriate Web site. The only difference is that on a desktop, the browsing application is stored on your local drive; on an NC, the browsing application must be downloaded or it is embedded at the hardware level.

Neither of the above scenarios is what NC is really about. NC encourages the use of applications that are downloaded to the client and executed there. A Java applet that is an interface to your bank account meets the above criteria. Figure 3-14 shows an applet. It is part of the Quattro spreadsheet application from Corel. The applet is a compiled piece of code. It is downloaded to your machine (whether a desktop or an NC) and is then executed by the processing power of your machine. This is the simplest model. More complex applications have different components spread across the network. They may also have a server component for the applications requiring heavy transactions or complex calculations.

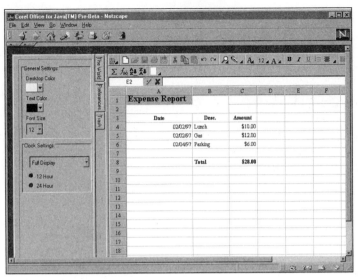

Figure 3-14 Quattro spreadsheet from Corel

Summary

NCs have brought changes to the software world. The NC puts a greater emphasis on object-oriented programming and the tools and concepts that go along with it. NC operating systems can be either downloaded from a server or built in at the hardware level. Obviously, a built-in OS will be loaded faster, although it cannot be upgraded as easily. Several chip makers have already come up with prototypes for Java-based operating systems.

NCs use a GUI for applications and desktop environments. Applications such as email and text editors may be part of the basic operating system environment. Larger or less-used applications for the NC usually are downloaded from an application server and then executed locally using the processing power of the NC. This reduces the burden on the server. Some NC configurations require the application to be executed on the server and only the output sent back to the NC.

In addition to the application, other more specific servers can be incorporated as needed, such as a database server. The client may access this server directly or may have to go through the application server. The architecture depends on security and the networking model of the environment. An important benefit is that all three tiers have processing power and can become active parts of the application. The application design specifies the tasks distributed among the many components.

Communication among NCs and servers is accomplished using the TCP/IP. Application protocols such as HTTP, Telnet, and FTP are layered on top of the TCP/IP itself. An NC must support a series of specific application protocols and some optional protocols. By storing applications on a central server, the NC can provide better security than a desktop computer, where each machine stores its own applications.

CHAPTER 4

Servers for the NC

The network-centric model calls for a collection of clients and servers distributed throughout the network. This chapter concentrates on the servers. In particular, it concentrates on servers with the most broad impact—that is, servers that can serve a variety of thin clients. Whereas an X server can serve X clients or a Windows NT server can serve Windows clients, a Web server can serve any client capable of browsing the Web, and all NCs can do that.

This chapter specifically focuses on the features of the server most suitable for application development and the architectural components of application design. The servers studied are

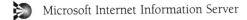 Microsoft Internet Information Server

 Netscape Enterprise Server

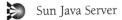 Sun Java Server

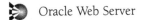 Oracle Web Server

Of course, there are many others, but these four offer a complete network-centric application development architecture most suitable for network computers.

Microsoft Internet Information Server

Known as the latecomer in the Internet arena, Microsoft has quickly come up with a complete set of tools for all aspects of Internet development. The main advantage of the Internet Information Server (IIS) is its tight integration into the Windows NT operating system, although that tight integration also can be viewed as a disadvantage, especially from a security point of view. Because of this integration, IIS offers some unique capabilities. For example, the security model of IIS is identical to the one for Windows NT servers.

IIS supports the Hypertext Transfer Protocol (HTTP) 1.0 standard in addition to File Transfer Protocol (FTP) and Gopher. It also supports Secure Socket Layer (SSL) 2.0 and 3.0 for secure transmission of data over the Internet. A definite plus for IIS is its tight integration with not only the NT operating system but also Microsoft's suite of Office products, including Microsoft BackOffice. BackOffice offers a rich set of applications, and so its integration with a Web server makes sense. The ability to publish an Excel spreadsheet over the Web instantly is an important asset in team projects where document and data sharing is crucial. IIS also has built-in database connectivity. This is in addition to open database connectivity (ODBC), which makes access to almost any database possible.

ISAPI

As for application development, IIS supports the usual common gateway interface (CGI) and WinCGI specifications. It also supports a native set of Application Programming Interfaces (APIs) called ISAPI (Internet server API) that allows you to extend the Web server capabilities easily. These programs are generally written in C++. ISAPI gives you control over the way the server works. You can intercept specific HTTP traffic and headers and perform additional tasks to handle them. There are also a large number of server extensions available from third parties.

In general, ISAPI extensions are similar to CGIs in functionality, but they have a lot less overhead. ISAPI extensions are written as dynamic link libraries (DLLs) and therefore are loaded into memory at runtime. They execute under the address space of the server itself, so, unlike with CGIs, spawning a separate process is not required. This reduces overhead substantially.

Because ISAPI gives you control over the way the Web server functions, you can also use it as a powerful filter for both incoming and outgoing HTTP messages. For example, the IIS creates logs of HTTP requests in a predefined format. By using ISAPI, you can customize that format and extend it to include storage of access logs in a database of your choice. Other possible filters include

- Customized authentication

- Compression and decompression of data

- Encryption/decryption

Complete documentation of ISAPI can be found as part of the Win32 API. The Microsoft Web site also has a number of good examples. Although ISAPI gives you a very low-level control of the Web server, this may not be what you need. IIS 3.0 also supports a different application architecture called Active Server that is more suitable for business application development.

Active Server

As a counterpart to Microsoft's ActiveX technology on the client (see Appendix A, "A Guide to ActiveX"), Active Server pages provide an extensive and rich environment for application development on the server. Active Server pages (ASPs) have the ASP file extension. They combine VBScript, JavaScript, and ActiveX technologies to produce rich and dynamic Web pages. Because the application is executed on the server, any browser can be used (unless the output page includes ActiveX controls; in that case, the browser must support ActiveX).

Active Server technology takes IIS a step closer to a distributed object model. ActiveX technology offers a component model for the clients. Active Server does the same for the server. They both support the Microsoft component object model (COM). They can be written in a variety of languages including Visual Basic, C++, and Java.

A powerful component of Active Server pages is database connectivity. IIS 3.0 ships with Active Data Object (ADO), which contains the database application logic. For example, a VBScript application can make a request to the ADO to retrieve some data from a database. Once the data is retrieved, VBScript formats it and displays it in the browser in Hypertext Markup Language (HTML) format. ADO supports all ODBC-compliant databases.

Another feature of Active Server is automatic compilation. Because the active scripts are part of the Windows NT operating system, their last modification date is known. When a request to a script is made, the server checks that date and compiles the application so the clients always get the latest version.

Both Active Server and ActiveX technology tie nicely into the distributed component object model (DCOM), which is discussed in Chapter 8 "The Distributed Object Model." These technologies are complemented by Microsoft Transaction Server and message queue technology. By putting the pieces together, you can create a rich environment for developing business-oriented applications using the Web environment and the network-centric model. Ideally, these will be the applications that your network computers will use. One of the drawbacks of IIS is that it runs only on the Windows NT server and most of the pieces such as Active Server and ActiveX are limited to computers running the Windows operating system. For IT shops that have heavy investments in one operating system, this may not seem like a drawback at all. It should be noted that the network-centric model encourages open standards and environments. Microsoft's approach has been criticized as one that favors (or forces) a particular operating system (Windows). A true distributed and scaleable environment should support components from different vendors.

Netscape Enterprise Server

Netscape does not have a long history, but in its short life it has become a major player in Internet/intranet and Web technologies. Netscape has a variety of Web servers and other Internet-related servers in its product line. This discussion is about Netscape Enterprise Server 3.0, which should be out by the time this book hits the market.

Traditionally, Netscape has offered flexible and high-performance Web servers for a variety of platforms, including different UNIX flavors. It has complemented its Web server by a number of other servers for newsgroups, mail, and security certificates. For a successful deployment of the NC, you do not need all the servers. You just need the servers for which you will have clients. It is important to define what you will be using NCs for before planning the server infrastructure.

One of the new features of Enterprise Server is superior capability to publish and manage site content. Authors of Web pages can easily publish the pages they have developed from their browser. There is a version-control mechanism as well as an access control system that specifies what pages can be changed or viewed and by whom. Another new feature is the incorporation of the Verity search engine into the server, giving your visitors instant search capability.

Application Platform

Enterprise Server really stands out as a server for the NC in its support for Netscape's open network environment (ONE). This consists of three different parts:

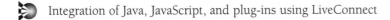

Integration of Java, JavaScript, and plug-ins using LiveConnect

Internet foundation classes

CORBA/IIOP support

Netscape introduced LiveConnect as part of version 3 of its browser. LiveConnect allows for three-way communication among client-side application components, as shown in Figure 4-1. The Netscape server takes that same concept and replicates it at the server level.

Internet foundation classes (IFCs) are extensions to Java classes. At its first release, the main parts of IFCs were extensions to the Java Abstract Window Toolkit (AWT) package. Some user-interface components that were not directly supported by AWT could be created easily with IFCs. Enterprise Server takes the same concept and applies it to its server. A series of IFCs on the server extends the capabilities of Java and integrates it with Netscape's applications.

The missing piece becomes the connection between the Java applications on the client and the server: This is where common object request broker architecture (CORBA) and Inter-ORB Protocol (IIOP) come into play. The details of these new technologies, which should flourish in the NC paradigm, are discussed in Chapter 8, "The Distributed Object Model."

Netscape has integrated an object request broker (ORB) into its Web server. Using the IIOP, browsers can directly communicate with the ORB. Each ORB can have an application associated with it in the form of a server plug-in that can be written in Java. The server plug-ins can complement (and in some cases replace) CGI and NSAPI technologies. NSAPI stands for Netscape server API and is very similar to ISAPI (discussed

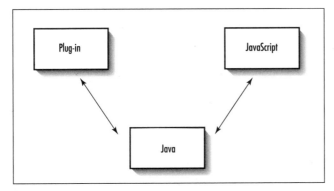

Figure 4-1 LiveConnect

earlier). NSAPI is a set of API libraries that extend the functionalities of the server. CORBA-based communication between the client and the server is shown in Figure 4-2.

Another standard supported by Enterprise Server is the Lightweight Directory Access Protocol (LDAP). This protocol can be used to manage users and groups at a network level. In other words, instead of having user and group information at each server,

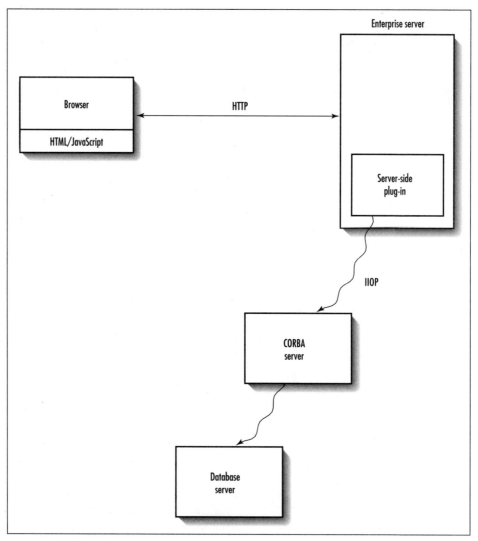

Figure 4-2 CORBA/IIOP in Enterprise Server

you can centralize that information. LDAP is the means by which centralized information can become available to clients that request it.

You can remotely configure the Web server itself using a browser. You can also manage the Web server using Simple Network Management Protocol (SNMP). This is a great plus for any server in a network-centric environment. As you may recall, the ability to support SNMP is part of the NC Reference Profile 1. Additionally, the Java management API will enhance management of network resources.

Enterprise Server supports HTTP 1.1. This is the latest version of HTTP. HTTP 1.1 is able to support byte ranges. With HTTP 1.0, if you request a file, the entire file is served back to you regardless of its size. If what you need is at the end of the file, you must download the entire file before getting the end part. HTTP 1.1 allows you to specify a particular range of bytes and servers; it will serve out only those bytes. A good example of the application of byte serving is serving Adobe PDF files. The latest PDF specification makes it easy for the client application to make a translation from the requested page number to the byte range needed. As a result, you can specify that you want to see a particular page of the document, and only that page will be served to you.

Intelligent agents are another new feature in Enterprise Server. Users can create agents that monitor the server and send email notifications of updates and changes. The following types are already supported:

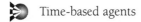 Time-based agents

 Document-based agents

 Application-based agents

Time-based agents are triggered by a timing event. For example, every Monday morning, they send out the team activity schedule for the week to members of a group. Document-based agents are triggered based on certain changes in the documents on the Web server. For example, if a page that lists new product offerings changes, subscribers to that agent will get a notification. Program-defined or application-based agents are triggered based on certain events on a server-side program such as a server-side JavaScript code.

LiveWire is Enterprise Server's solution for database connectivity. LiveWire applications are written in JavaScript or Java. In a manner similar to ASP from Microsoft, LiveWire can be used to generate dynamic HTML pages whose content may be coming from a database. LiveWire has native libraries for connecting to Oracle, Sybase, and Informix. It uses ODBC for other databases. It now supports stored procedures, allowing you to keep your application logic on the database server itself. Additionally, a single application can connect to multiple databases. The LiveWire application architecture is shown in Figure 4-3.

The NC is about the network. It brings together servers and clients from across the network and makes them work together. By supporting many of the open standards upon which NCs are built, Netscape has positioned its server products for the network-centric Enterprise Server. This is perhaps the main divider between supporters of Netscape and Microsoft visions. Extensions such as ORB/IIOP support and server-side plug-ins complement the technologies Netscape pioneered on the browser side. NC applications will be written in Java; Enterprise Server offers the right infrastructure to bring together Java on the server with Java on the client. As for accessing databases, LiveWire and its components satisfy the needs for most applications. By using an object-oriented application development model involving Java, JavaScript, and IFCs, you can create rich database applications.

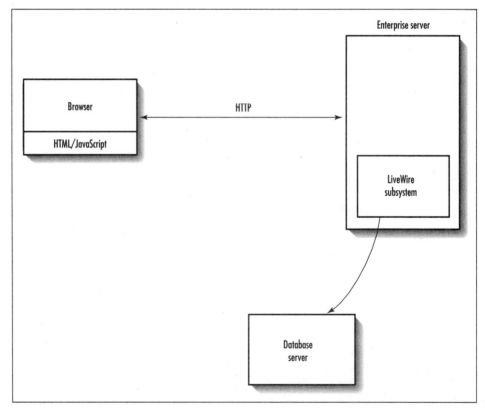

Figure 4-3 LiveWire application architecture

Sun Java Servers

Java *applets* are applications written in Java that download to your browser and are executed within the Java virtual machine (JVM) provided by your browser. What if there was a Java application that stayed on the server and executed under the JVM provided by your Web server? What would you call that kind of Java application? The answer for now is *servlet,* which leads me to the next discussion about deployment of Java applications on the server.

Simply put, servlets are Java objects that extend the functionality of the Web server. Both Microsoft Internet Information Server and Netscape Enterprise Server have server-specific APIs; this is similar to what servlets do. The main difference is that servlets are written in Java and are independent of the server, whereas the server APIs are written in C and C++ and are server specific. Another difference is that a servlet can act as an independent object after it is invoked by the Web server. It can establish a direct connection back to the client that requested it and continue its communication that way. Also, whereas server API applications reside on the Web server locally, servlets can be scattered throughout the network and be downloaded when they are needed. Servlets are considered an advocate of open server standards. There is a culture that promotes the server as the center of computing and places the highest cost on the server. With a true network-centric model, this view changes. Both the client and the server become important, and both must support open standards. Applets bring this type of openness to the client; servlets do the same to the server. Figure 4-4 shows the architecture of servlets.

The Java servlet API is the standard to make servlets work in all platforms and with different Web servers. This assures that once you write a servlet, it will run on any Web server that supports servlets. Currently, the only Web server that fully supports the standard is the Java Web server. This server is written in Java and so integration with servlets makes a lot of sense. Netscape is moving in the servlet direction and hopes to support the entire API soon.

The servlet API is divided into four different categories:

 Initializing the servlet

 Processing the request

Accessing information about the servlet

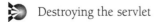 Destroying the servlet

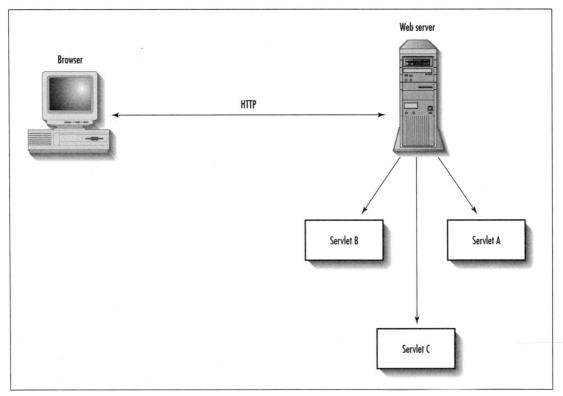

Figure 4-4 Servlet architecture

A servlet object must implement the servlet interface. Rather than doing the full implementation yourself, you can simply extend the **GenericServlet** class or the **HttpServlet** class (for servlets designed to work with an HTTP server). Now that you have a servlet, the question becomes how will it communicate with the server. This is done by implementing the following interfaces:

- ServletRequest

- ServletResponse

- ServletContext

Through these interfaces, the servlet can accept requests from the server, create responses to those requests, and interact with the server environment. A package called **java.servlet.html** can help generate dynamic HTML pages for your applications.

Just as downloading applets from the network created a security frenzy, servlets have led to some of the same concerns. The current security model revolves around the distinction between two classes of servlets: trusted and untrusted. It is entirely up to the server to decide which servlets it will trust and which ones it will not.

Servlets provide a good mechanism for database access, which is one of the main applications for NCs. Although Java database connectivity (JDBC) allows an applet to communicate with a database directly, there are many instances where you may not want to follow this architecture or it simply is not feasible due to firewall and other security constraints. Servlets can become very helpful in those situations. The Java applet or the Web client can make a request to the Web server regarding specific data from the database. That request is passed on to a servlet after it is initialized and the servlet takes care of connecting to the database and retrieving the needed data. It will then format the data and send it back to the client. This is shown in Figure 4-5.

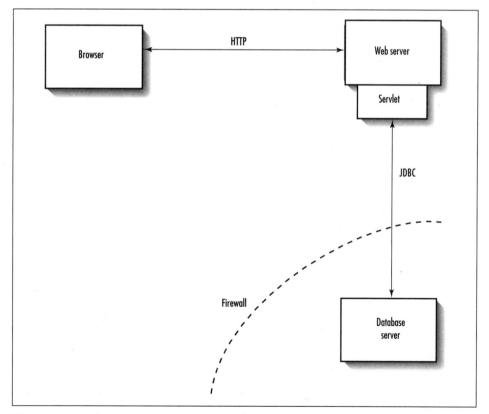

Figure 4-5 Database connectivity using servlets and JDBC

To give you a taste of how a servlet code may look, Listing 4-1 shows a simple HTML servlet that prints out the message **Hello World**.

Listing 4-1 A simple servlet

```
Import java.servlet.*
public class HelloServlet extends GenericServlet
{
    public void service(ServletRequest req,
                        ServletResponse res)
    {
        res.setContentType("text/html");
        ServletOutputStream out;
        out = res.getOutputStream();
        out.println("<H1> Hello World! </H1>");
    }
    public String getServletInfo()
    {
        return "My Hello World servlet";
    }
}
```

You may notice the similarity between servlets and CGI applications. Although they are similar in functionality, they do have differences. Servlets are more tightly integrated with the Web server and can directly interact with it. CGI relies on environmental variables for that kind of interaction. Servlets can become independent objects after they are initially invoked. A CGI application is invoked by a request and dies after it completes its tasks. The next request requires a second invocation. A servlet can stay alive and even establish direct communication back to the client. Finally, servlets can be downloaded from the network at runtime, whereas CGI applications must be physically residing on the Web server before they can be started. From an NC point of view, servlets are a better fit, especially when you consider the huge potential of the NC device market. The ability to load applications at runtime regardless of platform and operating system is very important for the success of NC devices. Currently, if you release a new version of a CGI program, it must be installed on all the servers running it. With servlets, this task is more seamless.

Oracle Web Server

Oracle has long been known for its database servers and related products. During the past year, Oracle has also become a major proponent of the NC and its deployment for enterprise applications. Although Oracle is a software company, it is working very closely with hardware vendors to build and market enterprise solutions based on the NC. On the software side, Oracle has developed an entire architecture based on the network and the NC called network computing architecture (NCA).

NCA is based on CORBA and HTTP/HTML. If you are not familiar with CORBA, you may want to refer to Chapter 8 for an introduction to distributed object models. HTTP is the standard Web protocol and it will remain so in NCA. Oracle's product line includes a Web server that is tightly integrated with the Oracle database server. You saw the integration of a Web server and a database server in the discussion of Microsoft's Information Server and its Structured Query Language (SQL) server. Oracle's architecture is similar, but it also uses CORBA-based technologies.

CORBA is the link between application-level objects. Traditionally, objects reside within one application running on a single machine. The next phase is interaction between objects from two different applications, similar to how object linking and embedding and COM work under the Windows operating system. CORBA takes this to a higher level and allows for objects residing on different machines to communicate with each other. NCA is based on a three-tier model and has the following components:

 Client

 Universal application server (Web server)

 Universal server (database server)

This is shown in Figure 4-6.

You may ask what makes Oracle's three-tier model different from similar architectures. The answer is nothing! Oracle's equivalent to server APIs and servlets is a pluggable object technology called a *cartridge*. A cartridge is an object that you write or purchase from a third-party vendor. You can write cartridges in a variety of languages including Java, C++, and PL/SQL (Oracle's procedural language used to write stored procedures). Recall that the main purpose of CORBA is to allow objects to communicate with each other across the network. To achieve this goal, CORBA uses an Interface Definition Language (IDL). As an object developer, you need to expose portions of your object using IDL. These are properties and methods that you want other objects to have access to so they can use your object.

One piece of the puzzle is missing. Suppose you write a cartridge using C++. The cartridge exposes its properties and methods using IDL. There needs to be a link between IDL and C++. This link is called an interface binding. C++ already has one and Java will have one very soon. The architecture of CORBA-compliant objects is shown in Figure 4-7.

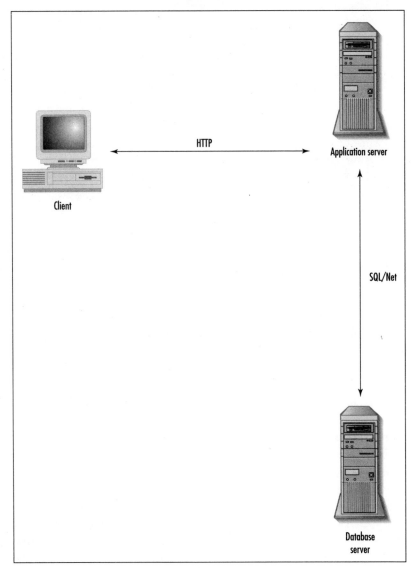

Figure 4-6 Three-tier model of NCA

How do these objects communicate? The intercartridge exchange layer (ICX) is the underlying communication medium. It is a CORBA-based object bus that acts as a broker among all the objects connected to it. It is based on Inter-ORB Protocol (IIOP), which is the communication part of the CORBA standard. The three-tier NCA now looks like Figure 4-8.

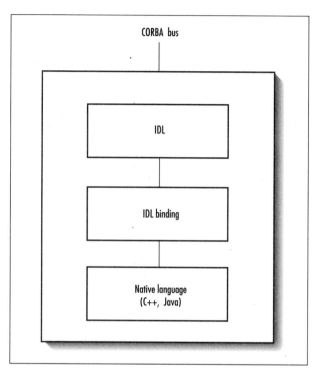

Figure 4-7 CORBA-compliant objects

Based on the design, you can create the user interface of your application using client cartridges written in Java, JavaScript, VBScript, or other common client-side languages. Your application server will serve out application cartridges. These are specific applications such as credit card verification or inventory control. Finally, you can have cartridges on the database server itself. These can extend the capabilities of the database server similar to the way stored procedures work. The effect, however, is more broad because cartridges can define entire new data types and implement them as independent objects. For example, a data cartridge can define a new data type for audio data. It would define how audio data is to be stored and retrieved in the database. Additionally, it can define methods to search a collection of audio objects.

In an effort to support a broad market, Oracle plans to make available a bridge that connects CORBA to DCOM. DCOM is the distributed object technology from Microsoft. This would allow an ActiveX client cartridge to access a Java-based application cartridge.

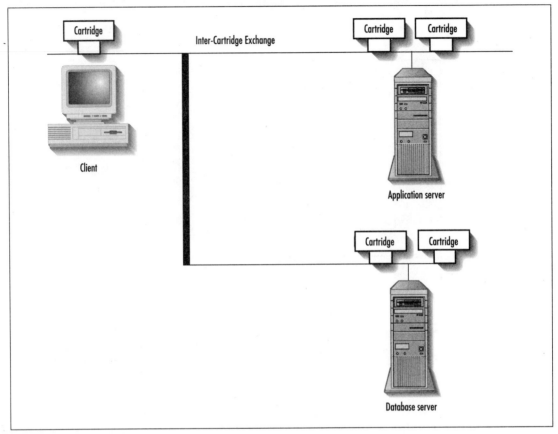

Figure 4-8 CORBA-based three-tier design of NCA

The Application Server

The Oracle Web server that is part of the application server is composed of two parts:

 The Web listener

 The Web request broker

The listener is the basic HTTP engine that listens for HTTP requests from clients. It then hands off the HTTP request to the Web request broker (WRB), which serves the request. A typical Web server would either serve out a static HTML page or execute a CGI- or API-based program. The WRB can route the request to the appropriate service handler, which is a cartridge. If the request is for a video file that matches certain characteristics, the WRB would hand it off to the video cartridge that has the capability to understand the request and make an appropriate response.

Java and Oracle

Oracle has incorporated Java in almost all its products. Traditionally, PL/SQL was Oracle's choice for developing stored procedures, triggers, and methods. Oracle has extended that capability to J/SQL, which is a Java-based language for server-side application code. On the client side, J/SQL uses a standard JDBC driver to connect to a database. This enables universal clients to access a database in a direct manner.

NOTE *Universal Clients*

Oracle uses this term to refer to any database client, including workstations, network computers, and network devices.

Oracle's development tools, such as Oracle Developer/2000 and Oracle Designer/2000, also support application development using Java. They are used to create Java-based cartridges to support NCA.

The Lesson Learned

The architectures of the server products are all very similar. NSAPI, Oracle cartridges, ISAPI, and servlets all enhance the server in a manner consistent with the network-centric model. This is good news for the NC as it becomes a major component of the computing world. The adoption of similar architectures can be viewed as a sign that the industry is riding the new wave of network computing and that vendors are competing for market share under the new paradigm.

As application architects pave the way for transforming Enterprise, it is important to view the different solutions at a higher level than an architectural point of view. You must first choose the architecture and then the product that implements the chosen architecture. Fortunately, more and more products are supporting network-based approaches, so your choice might be easier.

Summary

Successful deployment of the NC depends on a close integration of client and server technologies. The Web has emerged as the predominant application interface. Technologies such as Java, JavaScript, VBScript, and plug-ins enhance the functionality of the browser. Your infrastructure must also include Web servers with enhanced functionality to support rich and complex applications.

Microsoft information server runs on the NT platform and provides close integration with other Microsoft products on the NT platform, such as SQL Server and Back Office. It supports dynamic generation of HTML pages via Active Server technology. You can write your back-end programs in many languages, including Java, Visual Basic, and C++.

Netscape Enterprise Server supports multiple platforms, including most popular UNIX flavors. Its back-end technology is based on Java, server plug-ins, and ORB. It also supports agents that notify users of specific events. LiveWire is Netscape's solution to Web applications and database connectivity.

The Java servlet API from Sun brings the functionality of the applet from the browser to the server. The servlet API allows you to create objects on the server that are invoked upon request from the client. These objects in turn can connect to a database or other resources to fulfill the request. They can also establish a direct link back to the client, thereby eliminating the server as the middleware. Currently, the Java HTTP server from Sun is the only Web server that supports servlets.

Oracle's network computing architecture brings the client, the application server, and the database server together using CORBA technology. The application components are distributed across the network as cartridges. These objects communicate using the intercartridge exchange layer (ICX). Oracle also supports Java in most of its products. J/SQL is equivalent to the popular PL/SQL language, which can be used to develop JDBC-compliant client applications, as well as server-side programs such as triggers and stored procedures.

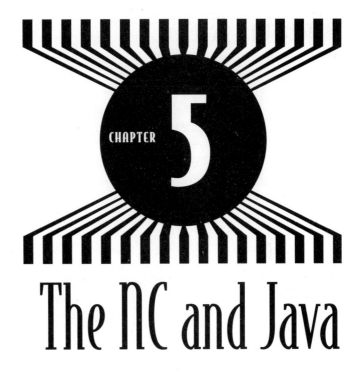

The NC and Java

The NC and Java complement each other—the NC provides a standard hardware environment for the execution of client applications, whereas Java provides a standard software environment for the development and execution of applications. Almost all NC specifications require the Java virtual machine (JVM) so that Java applications can be executed locally on the NC. Considering the requirements for a network-centric model, Java is currently the only language that can fulfill the needs of such an environment. In fact, Java is one of the primary reasons the NC has received so much interest in recent years.

The Java language is a widely accepted technology. Perhaps no other language comes close in the speed of adoption by both the computer industry and the consumer market. No other software product has received the attention given to Java both inside and outside the computer software industry. Java is simple, but it can be used to write complex applications.

Numerous sources cover the Java language and its details. Rather than providing another tutorial on Java, I focus here on the features of the language that make it a perfect fit for the NC.

Object-Orientation

Java is an object-oriented language. It focuses attention on both the data the application must manipulate and how that data is manipulated. That is, both data and processing are embodied within the same object. The rest of the application is built around that. Another popular object-oriented language is C++. Java has some of the same constructs as C++, but generally the language is simplified and more robust due to the introduction of automatic garbage collection and the elimination of pointers.

In an object-oriented environment, the basic modeling tool is called a *class*. A class has some *properties* or data associated with it. For example, a car has a color and a model name. A class also offers *methods* to manipulate its properties and data. For example, a car can go forward and backward and it can stop. You can think of methods as the behavior associated with a class.

NOTE *A class has properties that describe its state and methods that control its behavior.*

A particular instance of a class is called an *object*; hence the name *object-oriented*. A 1990 white Geo Storm is an instance of the car class and therefore is an object. A 1997 Lexus ES400 is also an instance of the car class and is thus an object. It is important to understand the difference between an object and a class. In the above example, both cars belong to the car class, but they are different objects (for one thing, the Lexus is more expensive than the Geo Storm!). The difference between a class and an object is depicted in Figure 5-1.

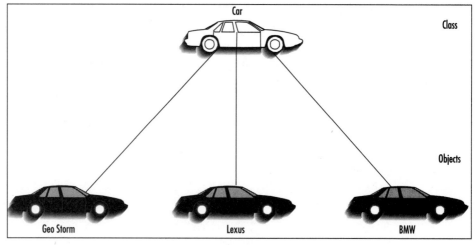

Figure 5-1 Difference between a class and an object

Object-oriented programming views the world as people usually do. It is more structured than our view, but it resembles our view in many ways. Another characteristic of classes is that they can have parent and child classes. A car, for example, can belong to a higher class called vehicles, which also includes motorcycles, trucks, and bicycles. That would make the vehicle class the parent class and the car class the child class. What is interesting is that the child class can modify the properties and methods associated with its parent class. After all, what makes a car different from a truck? Or a bicycle different from a motorcycle? They all have their own unique properties.

Object-oriented programming provides significant benefits for software development because it provides a clear framework and structure for the application. Think of an application you have used lately and try to identify the different objects in that application. Next, think about how the different components interact with each other. Object-oriented programming encourages building applications based on components and interactions among objects.

Another powerful concept in Java is that of *interfaces*. An interface is like a class, except that it can define only abstract methods. In other words, it specifies a name for the method, but it doesn't specify how the method should be implemented. A car has a license plate. A useful method is one that can validate the license plate number. Each license plate object is derived from the parent class. Each has different properties; that is why license plates are different in each of the 50 states. As each class extends the license plate class to make up its own characteristics, it also implements the validation method specific to that state's license plate numbers.

Java classes offer a lot of flexibility. The full potential of objects and object-oriented languages cannot be exploited unless we look at the role of objects in a networked environment: Let's look at a distributed network such as the Internet. What if there were a standardized way for any object on the network to communicate with any another object? Let's take this a step further. What if a given object were able to find other objects on the network, decide whether they were suitable for the task it needed, and, if appropriate, establish a connection to those objects? Java is moving toward that direction and the NC can guide that effort because it encourages the creation of distributed object-oriented applications.

Consider a simple notepad application. It, in itself, is an object. If you need to print the contents of the notepad (which is a property of the object), the notepad object communicates directly with the printer object on the network and sends that request. The printer object accepts the request and prints the data on the printer. If you need to save the contents of the notepad, the notepad object contacts the file storage object and sends the necessary information to that object. This is shown in Figure 5-2.

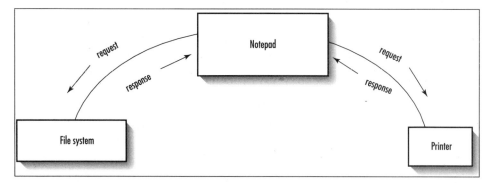

Figure 5-2 Notepad object in communication

Technologies such as object linking and embedding (OLE) provide some of these capabilities to objects running in the same environment on the same machine. Java takes those concepts and applies them to objects across the network, thus creating a more powerful architecture.

Another benefit of object-oriented technology is that objects break down the application into smaller chunks. NCs can download the main object for an application to start the application. After that, the main object either can communicate with other objects on the network to accomplish specific tasks, or it can request additional objects whose code is then downloaded to the NC for instant execution. The network-centric model wouldn't be practical without this breakdown, because the long delay in downloading applications in their entirety would be very unproductive.

Threads

Java supports a multithreaded architecture. Whereas *multitasking* is used extensively in the client/server model, *multithreading* plays an equally enormous role in the network-centric model. Before jumping to details, let's discuss what threads are.

In the single-tasking operating systems such as DOS, you are allowed to run one application at a time. The operating system folks refer to that one application as a *process*. Your operating system handles one process at a time and gives that process all its attention.

On the other end of the spectrum is a generation of operating systems (OSs) able to handle more than one application (process) at a time. UNIX, Windows NT, and Windows 95 are examples of multitasking operating systems. In Windows, it is perfectly normal to have your word processor, your clock, your calendar, and your spreadsheet applications open all at once. Each application is viewed as a process by the operating system. The OS has to divide its resources among all the running processes. The different flavors of the UNIX operating system also understand processes and are able to manage more than one process. Multitasking is shown in Figure 5-3.

Soon after Windows and UNIX became widely used, it became apparent that there was a need to go a step further. The operating system manages multiple processes. A single process, however, sometimes has more than one task to complete. So there was a need for another level of depth: a single process to start and stop other processes within its own context. These secondary processes are called *threads*. You see threads in many applications. Your spreadsheet application is one process. Within the application, you can have multiple threads working simultaneously. For example, two separate threads recalculate two different worksheets, another thread redraws a graph, and a fourth thread sorts items in a list. The important thing to remember is that these tasks are performed under the umbrella of the spreadsheet process. The concept of threads is depicted in Figure 5-4.

The JVM and the Java language both support threads. The concept of threads combined with the object-oriented nature of Java provide a very powerful environment. In a distributed network, one of the important goals is balanced distribution. Objects can run on different processors and they can have their own threads running under them. These objects can then communicate with other objects (which in turn are running their own threads) over the network.

The **Thread** class is part of the **java.lang** package and is the basis for using threads in a Java application. There are two ways to create a thread; depending on the circumstances described below, use one way or the other.

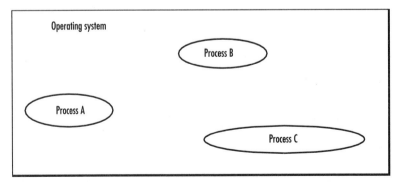

Figure 5-3 Multitasking and multiple processes

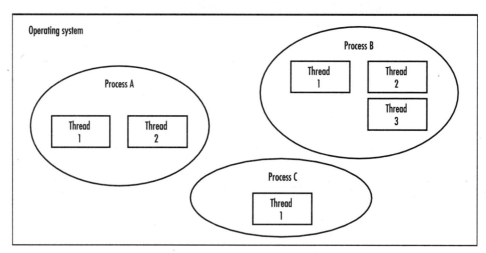

Figure 5-4 Threads exist within a process

Suppose you have a class **X** that is not derived from another class. To add thread support to this class, use the following definition:

```
public class X extends Thread {
   public run() {
//   task to be completed as a thread
   }
}
```

The class **X** is a subclass of the **Thread** class. By providing the method **run()** within the class **X**, you are specifying the tasks to be completed as a thread. You can instantiate the class **X** and create an object with the following line:

```
X myThread = new X();
myThread.start();
```

By invoking the **start()** method, you automatically execute the **run()** method specified in your class. The Java documentation indicates several other methods provided by the **Thread** class. They are

stop: Stops a thread that is running. If you have to do any cleanup work after the thread is stopped, this is one place you can place that code.

suspend: Temporarily halts a thread.

resume: Brings a suspended thread back to life.

As you can see, using threads in an application is not very difficult. There is another scenario where the above example will not work, however. In the example, the class **X** extends the **Thread** class. What if the class **X** needs to extend another class? You can't have a class extending two classes simultaneously. This is called *multiple inheritance*, and Java has no direct support for it. If you recall the discussion on the object-oriented nature of Java, I introduced the concept of interfaces. That is what we use to create threads in classes that must extend another class beside the **Thread** class. Let's look at an example.

Suppose you have a class **Y** that requires a thread. This class is an applet, so it is normally defined as follows:

```
public class Y extends Applet {
// class information
}
```

To add a thread to the above class, implement the **Runnable** interface, as follows:

```
public class Y extends Applet implements Runnable {
    public run() {
//   task to be completed as a thread
    }
}
```

To use the class **Y**, you first have to instantiate it. Here is the code:

```
Y myClass = new Y();
```

Unlike the previous scenario, you still need access to the thread, so you have to instantiate the thread inside the **Y** class.

```
Thread myThread = new Thread(myClass);
myThread.start();
```

When you have to implement the **Runnable** interface, the process of creating and using the thread becomes a three-step process.

Synchronization

Threads are interesting, aren't they? It is possible for a process to start several threads. That is fine as long as the threads don't interfere with each other's operations. A simple example of where an interference might occur is when two threads attempt to access the same piece of data. Without a careful design, you can create deadlocked situations where two threads will wait for each other indefinitely to complete their data access. Software designers have studied this phenomenon for more than 20 years and have come up with a number of different solutions to this problem.

Java also has a solution to the interference problem. It uses the keyword **synchro-nized** to distinguish critical parts of an application. Here is an example:

```
public class ID {
    public synchronized Boolean changeID() {
    // threadsafe code goes here
    }
}
```

The above example restricts access to the **changeID** method. Only one thread at a time can execute the **changeID** method. This way you can be sure that two different methods will not change the same ID at the same time, because that will likely diminish the integrity of your data.

Actually, almost all database servers already have built-in mechanisms that protect data integrity similar to the above example. By using synchronized threads on the client, you prevent deadlocking among threads in clients. Understanding threads and synchronization raises your awareness of the distributed environment your applications are running in. In the desktop model, you have more control over what processes are running and what threads are associated with those processes. Within a network, you could have multiple processes running on different clients, each producing a thread that needs to access a common piece of data. Threads are powerful and help you develop robust and balanced applications, but you also need to spend some time at the design stage to make sure threads don't run around unsupervised and create resource problems.

Scheduling

An NC has a single processor. How can that single processor manage multiple processes? Furthermore, how can each process manage multiple threads? The secret lies in Java's scheduling and thread priority mechanism. Although an operating system might seem to you to be executing several processes simultaneously, it only looks that way. Inside, the processor is busy juggling instructions belonging to different processes. By giving each process a split second of execution time, the OS manages to provide a look and feel that we perceive as multitasking.

In any design, some processes will require more attention than others. System processes are usually high on the priority list. A graphing process in a spreadsheet can wait a bit, if the system's garbage collection process needs to free up more memory. This is exactly how Java manages threads. Rather than giving each thread equal attention, Java looks at their priorities and executes them based on that. There are three main priority levels in Java:

MIN_PRIORITY

 NORM_PRIORITY

 MAX_PRIORITY

If you have a thread **myThread**, then you can use the **setPriority()** method to specify its priority explicitly. Otherwise it will get the same priority as its parent. You can also use the **getPriority()** method to find out what the priority of a thread is. If two threads have the same priority level, they are executed one after the other. Otherwise, all threads must yield to threads with higher priority.

Unless you have good reasons, you should stick with **NORM_PRIORITY** for all the threads created by you. **MAX_PRIORITY** is usually for system-level threads. On the other hand, specifying **MIN_PRIORITY** may affect the performance of your application because it must delay execution until higher priority threads are done.

You can find a complete discussion of threads with all the related API in the Java documentation under **java.lang.Thread**.

Exceptions

No matter how good the design is and how reliable your hardware is, there is always the possibility of something breaking along the way. What distinguishes great programs from good ones is their capability to encounter unexpected breakdowns and deal with them in an effective and gracious manner. In a distributed network, your application not only may have to worry about its own environment, but it must also consider the possibility of breakdowns in the network, in server processes it is communicating with, and in other processes on the network on which it relies. Fortunately, Java has a solution for dealing with the unexpected: *exception handling*.

Let's start with a simple example. Your application is writing to a file byte by byte. Unexpectedly, the disk on which the file resides becomes full and so there is no more space for that file. Java refers to this situation as an *exception*. The mechanism used to detect and respond to an exception is called exception handling. The concept of exceptions and exception handling is not unique to Java. It is common among many languages, notably ADA and C++. However, Java has added its own twists.

Java classifies exceptions into three separate categories. The first are *normal exceptions*. These are exceptions that occur in a specific and sometimes predictable part of the code. Consider the situation in which your application needs to open a URL but cannot find it. This is considered a normal exception. The line of code in which the exception occurred is obvious.

The second category deals with *runtime exceptions*. These are exceptions such as division by zero. Any part of the code performing arithmetic division could produce such as exception. These exceptions are less predictable than normal exceptions and they are harder to find. They also are usually more serious than normal exceptions.

The third category of exceptions is called *errors*. They are mostly server type exceptions, and your program probably cannot do much to deal with them. The Java environment must handle such exceptions and it usually does so without your intervention.

Exceptions, when used properly, lead to robust and reliable code that keeps an application operating smoothly. Because NC applications may affect other applications on the network, their reliability is important. Let's discuss how exceptions are used in Java.

Java uses a simple code structure, shown here, to manage exceptions:

```
try {
// code that may throw an exception
}
catch(Exception A) {
// code to deal with exception A
}
catch(Exception B) {
// code to deal with exception B
}
finally {
// code to execute regardless if an exception was generated or not.
}
```

Notice that we had to identify the part of the code that may throw an exception in advance. Then we had to write routines to handle each type of possible exception that might be thrown. The **finally** clause is executed regardless of whether or not an exception was generated and/or handled. This clause is generally used to perform cleanup operations.

In the Java documentation, each package lists its exceptions. There are many exceptions, and not every single one has to be handled by your code. What you catch really depends on your application. A neat feature of Java is that if the current class does not handle the exception, the class is automatically propagated up the calling stack to the method that called the current method. In most cases the default behavior is that the exception is ignored, unless, of course, it is a severe exception that must be dealt with to maintain the integrity of the Java environment.

One final word about exceptions. Exceptions are not cheap. They convey a certain amount of overhead. Keep that in mind as you design your application. Don't get carried away and try to catch every single exception. You will be writing code for a long time! Find a balance that meets the needs of your application and stick to it. On the other hand, don't completely ignore exceptions either. They are a powerful tool that add to the robustness of your application and at the same time provide a structured method for dealing with the unexpected.

Graphical Interface

Recall that one of the requirements for an NC is its ability to support a graphical user interface (GUI). The Java language provides a rich set of graphical elements that can be used to develop attractive and effective user interfaces for applications. The model used by Java for development of GUIs is similar to those used in other systems. You design an interface using the many elements available to you, such as buttons, lists, menus, and drawing tools. You respond to the events associated with each of the items and provide the code to perform specific tasks. For example, selection of the File-Open menu would draw the dialog box for opening a file. Clicking on the Save button would save the contents of the buffer to a file.

JVMs that run on top of another operating system rely on the underlying OS to draw the graphical elements on the screen. That is why the same Java application looks different on a Macintosh compared to a Sun Workstation. In the NC, how the graphical elements look depends on the JVM implementation. Although the user interfaces may not be identical, they will provide the same functionalities because they are based on Java.

General Java components are customizable and extendible. The latest major release of Java (version 1.1) has added some nice features to the toolkit. If you don't find the exact element you need, chances are someone has built the class that has the look you want. It is also fun to experiment with the basic elements and combine them to make new and innovative user interface elements. Although you can write very "innovative" code, the user interface is all that the user can see, and many users will judge your application based on how it looks and feels. So do spend some time designing the user interface. You may want to consult some of the literature detailing the research done in the area to help you decide on effective interfaces for your particular application.

The **java.awt** package Abstract Window Toolkit (AWT) is the heart of what Java has to offer when it comes to graphics and GUIs. It is one of the more complex packages in Java, with many subclasses associated with it. Following is an overview of the type of classes and methods available in AWT. For a complete description of these classes and their corresponding syntax, please refer to the Java API documentation distributed with the Java Development Kit.

Graphics Class

The **Graphics** class is the basic class for anything you draw on the screen. An instance of this class contains information necessary for performing drawing operations. As a result, you will see a graphics object passed to methods responsible for drawing and painting. The information contained in a graphics object includes

- The current clipping region

- The current color

- The current font

- The current logical pixel operation function (XOR or Paint)

- The current XOR alternation color

- The component to draw on

- Information about the coordinate system (usually a translation origin)

The coordinate system used by the graphics object places the origin in the upper-left corner, as shown in Figure 5-5. This is common among most programming languages. Similarly, the unit of measurement is a pixel.

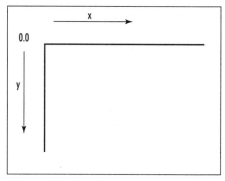

Figure 5-5 Coordinate system in Java

Colors

Java allows you to define your own color model. It comes with two models, which are sufficient for most purposes. They are **IndexColorModel** and **DirectColorModel**. The first uses a lookup table to find out what color a given pixel is. The second model uses a 32-bit integer to hold the color value. If you need to define your own color model, you can use the abstract class **java.awt.image.ColorModel**.

You can define colors using the standard RGB method, where you define a color by its red, blue, and green (RGB) components. Different bits of an integer are assigned to hold values for each of the three components of RGB. Most often, you refer to a color using an instance of the **java.awt.Color** class.

The other method for specifying colors is the HSB model. A color is represented by a hue, saturation, and brightness (HSB) value. These parameters are described below:

- Hue: The value runs from 0 (red) to $\frac{1}{4}$ PI (violet).

- Saturation: The value runs from 0 (gray scale) to 1 (color).

- Brightness: The value ranges from 0 (black) to 1 (brightest possible color given the current hue and saturation).

The HSB model is ideal when your application must do image processing. It lets you easily gray out or bring color to an image. Although most NCs will be equipped with a color monitor, some (particularly the smaller NC devices) may use a gray-scale presentation unit. Keep this in mind as you develop your applications.

Geometric Classes

Most drawing applications take advantage of geometric properties. Many geometric manipulation routines have already been written for other languages. Java provides a number of classes that correlate to geometric figures and concepts. It also provides a number of routines for manipulating these geometrics. It should be very straightforward to translate geometric manipulation routines from other languages to Java (if you have some code and want to reuse it) because they all deal with one geometry. Specifically Java has classes for representing a **Dimension**, **Point**, **Polygon**, and **Rectangle**.

Drawing

When it comes to drawing, you will be drawing either interactive objects such as buttons and menus or noninteractive objects such as images or filled rectangles.

NOTE *Using the location of the mouse and the events associated with it, you can make a noninteractive component interactive. Regardless, there is a fine boundary between the two types of components.*

One of the simplest things to draw is text. Given a string and location, you can use the **drawString()** method to draw text. Java supports a limited number of fonts compared to the existing desktop systems. The fonts currently supported by Java are

 Monospace

 SansSerif

 Serif

To specify a font, create an instance of the **Font** class and assign it to a font object, as shown below:

```
Font myFont = new Font("Serif", Font.ITALIC, 14);
```

The above line defines a font of type **Serif** with size **14** and italicized. Once you have a font, you can use the **setFont** property of your graphics object to set the font for the current graphics context.

Aside from text, you many need to draw shapes and figures. Before you reinvent the wheel, make sure you have studied the methods supplied by the **Graphics** class. You may find out that Java already supports the type of figure you want to draw. Examples of these methods are **drawRect()**, **drawOval()**, and **draw3Drect()**.

Whereas most other languages rely on static drawing methods for animation, Java provides a series of classes and methods devoted to animation. As a matter of fact, the capability of Java to do animation and add "life" to static Web pages is a great part of its success. To understand animation, you have to understand the **paint()**, **repaint()**, and **update()** methods. These methods are often used in applets and other graphics-oriented applications.

- **paint()**: If another window uncovers a graphics component, that component must be redrawn. The **paint()** method performs the drawing. Anything that can be displayed in Java has the method **paint** via inheritance from the parent class, which is usually **java.awt.Component**.

- **repaint()**: After repainting a drawable, Java calls the **update** method.

- **update()**: By overriding this method, you can control what **repaint** does.

By using threads and double-buffering techniques, you can create impressive animation in Java. Before you create an animation using high-resolution images, consider the fact that some NC users may have to download all the images before they can see your animation. Animations that draw figures and text should have a better performance than ones using static images. Of course, the speed of the local processor, the implementation of Java (interpreter or Just In Time compiler), and the speed of your video board affects performance also.

Components

The **Component** class in Java is the parent of all of the interactive user interface elements. There are many variations of GUIs, such as MS Windows, Macintosh, and Motif. Although they all look a bit different, they have many common elements. For example, they all have an object that represents a button. They all have an object that looks like a list. Other common elements are check boxes, text fields, radio buttons, and text areas. Java supports all the common elements and adds some of its own.

If you look at the definition of any of the GUI elements, they all extend the **Component** class. That is why it is very important that you understand the **Component** class and its methods and properties. For example, the **enable()** and **disable()** methods are used to control whether a GUI element can be used or not. These methods belong to the **Component** class and thus all the descendants inherit them. The **Component** class is the heart of Java GUI.

Containers

So far, I have talked about individual elements such as buttons and lists. These elements need a place in which to exist, and that place is a *container*. There are many variations of containers; depending on your application and the purpose of your GUI, you have to choose the best one for you. Some containers are Windows, dialog boxes, frames, panels, and, of course, applets.

Frames are a variation of windows that support traditional menu bars. They are usually used for a main view of the application. Menu bars are also supported in Java by the `MenuComponent`, `MenuBar`, `Menu`, `MenuItem`, and `CheckBoxMenuItem` classes. Dialog boxes are useful when you need to inform the user about something or get some specific information from the user.

To aid you in the arrangement of GUI elements within a container, Java supports several layout managers. When you have to arrange several elements in a container, you can specify their absolute positions within the container. A better and more flexible way is to specify their relative positions and use an appropriate layout manager to take care of the arrangement automatically. For example, `GridLayout` uses a matrix and places the GUI elements in a grid whose dimensions are specified by you. Layout managers are flexible and provide methods and properties that allow you to customize for your needs. You can also create your own layout managers.

A canvas is a plain drawing board. If you want to implement buttons that display a picture, then you want to use a canvas to draw the picture and provide an event handler that responds to the `click` event.

Enhancements to AWT

Java 1.1 introduces several enhancements to the AWT. The more important ones concern the capability of separate components to communicate with each other and to transfer data using a common clipboard. Other enhancements include printing and popup menus. This section discusses the enhancements in detail.

Security

Java takes several approaches to security. The first approach is the *sandbox model*. Under this design, each Java application is given its own space under the JVM. It is limited to resources within that name space.

The sandbox model is the simple solution. It is also generic. To take full advantage of Java's capabilities, a mechanism is needed to treat certain applications as trusted and allow them to access system resources outside their name space. Java Development Kit (JDK) 1.1 partially delivers on this premise: It allows you to sign a Java archive (JAR) file. The client can check that signature and upon verification relax the sandbox security restrictions.

In JDK 1.1, you will find four security-related functionalities:

 Support of digital signatures such as DES. A digital signature has two functions. First, it can be used to verify that a certain piece of data has not been tampered with. This is important in application downloads because you want to be certain that the application is what it says it is.

 Digital signatures can be used (in conjunction with public/private keys) to verify the source of the data. If an applet has been signed by company XYZ, using a digital signature, you can be sure that it really came from company XYZ.

 JDK 1.1 also supports a number of encryption algorithms. The architecture is flexible enough that new or modified algorithms can be integrated fairly easily.

 To facilitate key-based encryption schemes, JDK 1.1 provides a set of key management APIs. This allows an application to manage its own users, their keys, and digital certificates.

Enhancements to the Windowing Toolkit

The user interface is one of the most important parts of an application. Users expect sophisticated interfaces such as those of Windows and X applications. Early versions of Java were not a match for such levels of complexity. The new JDK makes a giant leap toward providing all the common elements of a GUI. A major addition is the Application Programming Interface (API) to support clipboard-like operations by which users can cut, copy, and paste data among different applications and widgets.

Another enhancement is the ability to access and customize the coloring scheme for the objects your application creates. This ability is crucial for visual consistency. For example, when you create a new widget, you may want the font and the background to match the coloring scheme of the desktop. The new JDK provides a simple set of APIs for doing such operations.

All the modern GUIs are based on an event model. JDK 1.1 adopts a new event model necessary for the adaptation of JavaBeans. In JDK 1.0, the event model is based on the class hierarchy. An event works its way up the ladder until some class "consumes" it or it reaches the top. With that model, you can either have each widget handle all its own events or let the events propagate up and capture all of them at a higher level. In the latter case, you then go through a decision-making routine to decide what event you are responding to. This model does not work well for large and complex applications.

The new event model is fundamentally different. An event is generated by a `Source` object. The content of the event is passed on to a `Listener` object by invoking a method on the listener. Typically, the listener defines different methods for the different events it is interested in. It registers these methods with the source. With JDK 1.1, the listener is notified only when an event that it is interested in occurs.

Events are encapsulated in their own class. A listener can read and in some cases modify some of the properties of the event. Your programs can define their own events. The new event model should pave the way for GUI design programs in which you can write code snippets for the events associated with each widget.

Java now allows you to write popup menus. Scrollbars are easier with the introduction of a **ScrollPane** class. **ScrollPane** provides a container that implements automatic scrolling for a single component child. Printing is now also supported.

JAR

Distribution of applications is another area that JDK 1.1 addresses. With simple applets, the base class and its children are downloaded to the client and executed from there. Many applets consist of only a handful of classes. Larger applications not only have more class files, but they may include other file types such as images and audio. JDK 1.1 provides a platform-independent file format called Java archive that packages all the related files for an application in compressed format into one file. It can even digitally sign the JAR file. The goal is to pave the way for software distribution over the Net.

RMI

Despite its label as the premier network programming language, earlier versions of Java do not include a standard mechanism for interapplication communication. The code is downloaded over the network and it can access data and network resources, but it cannot systematically use the functionality of other existing Java applications. JDK 1.1 addresses this issue by introducing Remote Method Invocation (RMI).

If an object **X** has methods that can be invoked by other objects, then object **X** is referred to as a *remote object*. It has certain unique properties. For example, a remote object must implement the **Remote** interface. It also needs to define a class that implements that interface. You can then generate stubs and skeletons for the client that will be calling the remote object's methods. A program called **rmic** is provided for this purpose.

Reflection

Sometimes an object must be able to discover certain information about another object and its class at runtime. The reflection API provides a standard mechanism for just this purpose. Through this API, an object can

Construct new class instances and new arrays

Access and modify fields of objects and classes

Invoke methods on objects and classes

Access and modify elements of arrays

These operations follow the restrictions imposed by the security manager. In a component model such as Beans, introspection is done primarily using the reflection API. Applications that need runtime information about an object such as debugging tools are also included in JDK 1.1.

Object Serialization

Objects are dynamic and change throughout the application's life. Object serialization is a mechanism that allows the application to save and restore the states of its objects, therefore introducing persistence. You can use the **readObject** and **writeObject** methods to read and write objects to the stream. Because a variety of objects can be written and read from a stream, the object stream can be viewed as a container, just as ActiveX is a container. This is a fundamental element of the JavaBeans component model.

With serialization, you can create a bytestream of objects, send that bytestream over the network to another machine, and recreate an equivalent set of new objects with the same states using deserialization. An important security issue arises here. Once you have created the bytestream and sent it across the network, you will lose control over those objects because they are now in a different environment. To address the issue, Java restricts serialization to only those classes that implement the **java.io.Serializable** or **java.io.Externalizable** interfaces. Additionally, a mechanism allows an object to limit which parts can and cannot be serialized. Deserialization always leads to the creation of a new object with the state of the serialized object. It will never recreate the serialized object.

JDBC

The Java language has evolved in stages. One of the first requests from the programming community was a standard for linking Java and databases. JavaSoft responded by introducing Java database connectivity (JDBC). JDBC is very similar in functionality to the popular open database connectivity (ODBC) standard. It is a programming-level interface for database communication. An application based on JDBC will work the same regardless of what database server is used. This is ideal for general applications, where you do not know in advance under what database server the application will be deployed. The details of JDBC are discussed in Chapter 6, "The NC and Databases."

JavaBeans

JavaBeans is an object-oriented component model for Java. Beans are an important addition to Java because they provide the means for making powerful applications using Java. JavaBeans is discussed in detail in Chapter 7, "Distributed Applications on the NC."

Networking

By now it should be clear that the network plays an important role in successful deployment of NC devices and applications. It should come as no surprise that the application language is network friendly. Java has an entire package dedicated to network-related classes and methods (**java.net**). Network programming can be done at several layers. The least common denominator is socket programming. All Internet protocols are implemented using sockets. Java also supports access to Internet resources using URLs. There are also provisions for applet-to-applet communication and object-to-object communication using Beans components.

Socket Programming

Socket programming is used to implement client/server applications. There are two distinct programs you have to write. One is for the server and the other is for the client. Typically, the server starts up and listens to a port. As soon as it encounters a message on the port, it spawns another process and hands off the task of communicating with the client. This process is shown in Figure 5-6.

To implement the server functionality, Java has the **ServerSocket** class. First you request that you want to listen to a particular port (9876 in this case):

```
try {
  myServer = new ServerSocket(9876);
} catch (IOException e) {}
```

Now that you have a port to listen to, use the **accept()** method to monitor that port constantly and listen for any incoming requests.

```
Try {
  Socket s = myServer.accept();
} catch (IOException e) {}
```

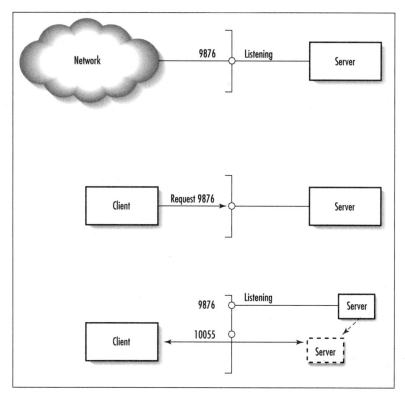

Figure 5-6 Server handling request

If a request does come through, you have an instance of the **Socket** class in the variables that contains all the necessary information to communicate back to the client. You can then continue with handshaking and application-specific communications.

The second part of a client/server application is the client. The client is the initiator of communication, so it must know where the server is and to what port it is listening. This information is usually stored in a local configuration file. The client needs to instantiate the **Socket** class and start up a connection. Here is an example:

```
Try {
  Socket s = new Socket("110.98.78.9", 9876);
} catch (IOException e) {}
```

The above will initiate a request to port **9876** of the server located at the address **110.98.78.9**. If the server is listening, it should respond with a message and the client and server can then establish communication.

Once the communication channel is established, you can use the **getOutputStream()** and **getInputStream()** methods of the **Socket** class to send information back and forth.

The networking discussion is not complete without mentioning the **URLConnection** class. Due to tight integration of Java applets and the Web, the ability to work with URLs becomes important. The **URLConnection** has a method called **openConnection()**. The parameter passed to this method is of type URL and is the URL of an Internet resource. You can open up that URL just like your browser does for you and use the **getInputStream()** method to read its contents. You can then implement your own filtering to get the data you want. The **HttpURLConnection** class is an HTTP-specific subclass of **URLConnection**.

Security

Java integrates nicely into a networking environment. At the same time, it must address a class of security issues that desktop applications usually do not face. For example, you may require a password before the user can be allowed to change customer records. These security features must be programmed into your application just like other features. The kind of security this section is concerned with is specific to the nature of Java, such as signed applets or the ability to download applications over the network.

Let's start with the latter. A user with a Java-enabled browser can point to an applet and download it to his or her machine. The local JVM will then execute that applet. What if the applet is malicious? The approach taken by Java is commonly referred to as the sandbox approach. An area of the system is devoted to executing the downloaded applet. The applet is limited to this area only and cannot intentionally or unintentionally damage the rest of the system. This is in contrast to desktop operating systems, where an application has access to almost all system resources. Viruses have been in existence almost as long as PC applications have; despite sophisticated virus detection and prevention programs, viruses remain a threat. Java's sandbox approach is a definite plus, especially in a more hostile environment such as the Internet, where large and small networks are subject to attacks from anywhere.

The first layer of defense in the sandbox approach is the *class loader*. One of the functions of the class loader is to assign a unique space to downloaded applets and prevent them from interfering with other spaces that may be dedicated to the JVM system classes.

The second layer of defense is the *verifier,* which checks the code downloaded from the network. The verifier looks for common language violations that may be disruptive to the execution environment. Examples include memory leaks, stack manipulation, and illegal type casts.

The verifier then passes the code to the JVM and the code begins to execute. If at any time the JVM has a question about the operation requested by the applet, it consults the security manager, which is part of the JVM. Depending on the answer it gets, the security manager may or may not allow the requested operation. There is only one security manager, to assure that decisions are made from one authority only. The security manager may allow a trusted applet to open up a connection to a database server, but it will not allow an untrusted applet to perform the same operation.

The Java language has some other features that enhance its security. For example, Java does not support pointers as they are used in C and C++. Pointers give an application access to areas of memory that really were not intended for application usage. Even honest mistakes in pointer operations could cause system crashes and headaches for both developers and users. Java addresses that problem by eliminating pointer operations.

The new version of JDK supports digitally signed applets and JAR files. In the same way that you can trust shrink-wrapped software from reputable vendors, you can trust signed applets and applications.

Summary

The NC and Java complement each other to provide a foundation for network computing. Java answers almost all the needs of a networking application language. Because it is object oriented, Java encourages an object-based design of applications that can lead to interobject communication across the network.

Java supports threads, which are processes within a process. By controlling threads, an application can balance its work load and perform multiple operations at once. Java can provide a robust execution environment by supporting exceptions. You can write code to recover from minor errors, but most likely you will let the JVM handle the more severe system errors. By supporting a hierarchical structure, the JVM passes the exception on to the parent classes until one of them decides to handle it.

The AWT brings graphics to Java. It supports basic drawing routines for both interactive and noninteractive elements. The **Component** class is the parent to almost all the common GUI elements, such as buttons and lists. As in other languages, an event model is used to handle user input.

Java also has extensive support for networking and security. It supports the basic socket programming elements on top of which you can build your own client/server protocols. It also supports accessing Internet resources via a URL. Java supports security at several stages, from the time an applet is downloaded until it is removed from memory. These layers of security verify the integrity of the code and keep the code in a limited space so it cannot interfere with the integrity of the rest of the system. Signed applets and the JAR format enhance secure distribution of applets and applications across the network.

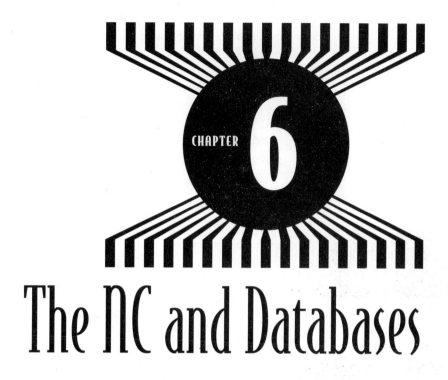

The NC and Databases

Computers are very good at information storage and retrieval, and databases are the main tool used for information management. Nearly all enterprise applications have some sort of database on which they depend. The network-centric model creates a very powerful environment for databases. Within such an environment, databases can be scattered across the network, yet clients can view them as one resource. It is not unusual for an application to access several different databases. Furthermore, these database engines can be from different vendors. In the network-centric model, databases are viewed collectively as one unit of information. This chapter discusses several methods NCs can use to access databases on the network.

What Is a Database?

Information is basically an interpretation of data. Computers are good at storing and retrieving data, but the interpretation is left to humans. Conceptually, we organize data into different units that are in some sense related. For example, we may put all customer information in a database by itself. We may have another database that holds information about our inventory, while a third database may contain shipping information.

As far as the computer is concerned, all databases are just raw data. It is the interpretation layer imposed by humans that makes information out of raw data. This concept is shown in Figure 6-1.

As databases became more widely used, there was a need to create a standard for data storage, manipulation, and retrieval. Such a standard would allow for all data (regardless of its purpose) to be treated in a general manner. The most successful and widely used standard for accessing databases is the Structured Query Language (SQL), which is based on the relational database model.

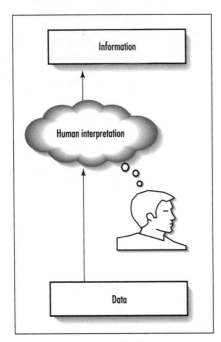

Figure 6-1 Data and information

Relational Databases

In a relational database, data is divided into units called *tables*. Each table has a number of columns. Collectively, these columns present a coherent piece of information. For example, a customer table may have the following columns:

- First name

- Last name

- Address

- City

- State

- Zip code

- Phone number

The power of relational databases lies within the fact that tables can be "related" in several different ways, as shown in Figure 6-2.

By creating these relations, you have a powerful collection of information that can grow quite large while remaining consistent. Relations also can be used to eliminate redundancy in a database. This concept can be difficult to grasp, so let's look at an example.

Going back to the customer table, it is possible for a customer to have two or more phone numbers. Because there is only one column for phone numbers, we can store only one phone number per customer. One solution for storing multiple phone numbers is to add another column to the table. This solution would make sense only when a large number of customers has two phone numbers; otherwise, the extra space is wasted. The limit is now set at two phone numbers per customer.

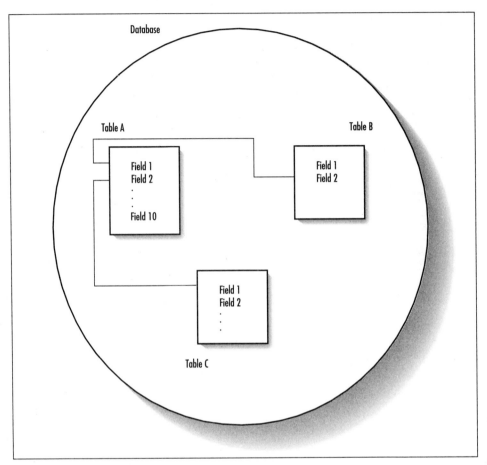

Figure 6-2 Tables in a database have relations

A more elegant solution is to create a second table and create a relation between that table and the customer table. To do that, we first change the columns in the customer table as follows:

- First name

- Last name

- Address

- City

State

 Zip code

 ID

We then create a second table with the following columns:

 ID

 Phone number

Note that both tables have the ID column. That is how they are related. You will see this type of relation in all relational databases. Each customer has a unique ID. That ID field is used in the second table to associate a customer to a phone number. If a person has three phone numbers, then there are three rows in the second table, each listing the customer's ID along with the phone number.

Creating a relation between two tables causes some extra work. For example, if we delete a customer from the first table, then all related records in the second table must also be deleted. Fortunately, most relational database systems have mechanisms to perform such functions, an action that is commonly referred to as *maintaining referential integrity*.

The language of relational databases is SQL, itself a very simple yet expressive language. But database vendors have added their own enhancements to the language, and therefore different dialects of this language exist today. You should refer to your specific vendor's manuals for information about the SQL implementation it uses. Following is a very general treatment of the language to serve as a reference for the remainder of the chapter.

The major functions of SQL commands can be broken down to the following:

 Creation of database entities (tables, columns, references)

 Insertion of data

 Retrieval of data

 Modification of data

 Deletion of data

SQL performs many other functions—otherwise we wouldn't have the thick database manuals. For the purposes of this discussion, however, concentrate on the above functions.

Creation of Database Entities

Aside from the database and the tables that go inside it, you may need to create many other elements. Examples include stored procedures, indices, triggers, devices, users, and groups. Table creation uses a relatively standard syntax across all databases, whereas other elements are database specific.

To create the customer table discussed above, use the following syntax:

```
create table customer (
    firstname     char(30)     not null,
    lastname      char(30)     not null,
    address       char(40)     not null,
    city          char(20)     not null,
    state         char(2)      not null,
    zip           char(12)     not null,
    cust_id       char(10)     not null)
```

Note that each field is specifically defined. You need to specify the type of the field and whether a value for the field is required or not. In this case, we have set all fields to be of type **char** but other types, such as **number**, **date**, **Boolean**, and **currency**, are also available.

Designing the tables in your database is one of the most important steps in database design. A large database can become very complex very quickly, especially when you consider the relationships that exist among the many tables. Many software tools can help you with the design of your database, but they all attempt to do one thing: help you model your real-world information needs within the relational model.

Insertion of Data

After creating the database, you need to populate it with data. Let's insert a record in our customer database:

```
insert into customer (firstname, lastname, address, city, state, zip, cust_id)
values ("Jim", "Jones", "876 Middle Road", "Middletown", "NJ", "07748", "123456")
```

Typically, you would present the user with a form and you would insert the data into the table after you validate the form. What the user enters in the form may affect more than one table, so the design of the database and your application again becomes very important.

Retrieval of Data

Having data in a database will not do any good unless you can retrieve it. Retrieval of data is done in a very structured manner. You specify search criteria using SQL, and only the data matching that criteria is retrieved from the database. Your criteria could, and usually do, include several tables because of the relations that exist within the database. When the criteria span more than one table, a **join** operation must be performed to link the tables together. Once again, a good understanding of the database design becomes important when you write your application.

To select the record belonging to a customer with the ID of **123456**, we would use the following:

```
select firstname, lastname, address, city, state, zip
from customer
where customer.id = "123456"
```

The **where** clause is how you specify your criteria. The **from** clause simply states which tables are involved in the retrieval. The **select** clause indicates the fields from the tables whose values are retrieved.

NOTE _The Window_

The **where** clause provides a window through which you can see the data you are manipulating, as shown in Figure 6-3. It may be all the available data; in that case, the **where** clause is ignored.

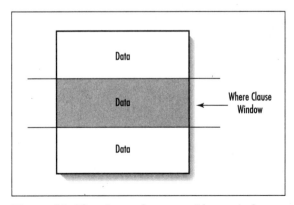

Figure 6-3 The **where** clause provides a window on data

Modification of Data

In any database application, you will have to change data at some point. Suppose Mr. Jones moves to California. His record must now be updated. We can do that using the following:

```
update customer
SET address = "90 Wide Road",
    city = "San Jose",
    state = "CA",
    zip = "87655"
where customer.id = "123456"
```

Deletion of Data

The last operation I discuss is deletion. The syntax is very simple. To delete Mr. Jones from our database, use

```
delete from customer
where customer.id = "123456"
```

Note that a deletion operation could be performed on multiple records depending on the **where** clause.

Database Programs

The purpose of this short introduction to SQL is to familiarize you with the types of operations done by a database application. As you will see, a user interface is typically used to allow the user to specify the type of operation needed and the criteria for the operations. In relational databases, you likely must manipulate tables and data behind the scene to satisfy the operation requested by the user. These manipulations can be done in any or all of the following common layers:

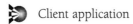 Client application

 Application server

 Database server

These three layers form what is known as a *three-tier application hierarchy*, in which client applications communicate directly with application servers, which use one or more database servers to perform data functions. SQL can be used at any of these

layers, although most application-specific database commands are generated by the application servers and most maintenance processing is done directly by the database server using stored procedures.

Database applications are classic client/server programs. The client consists of the user interface and initial data validation. The client connects to the server via the network and requests that specific operations be done. With the network-centric model, the basic scheme remains the same, but due to the distributed network, many clients may be accessing many servers. Furthermore, the clients can be running different operating systems and processors; however, because the application is the same, they all can access the application or database servers in the same way. This is the true power of the NC: using inexpensive, extremely flexible NCs to serve as client platforms for the relatively expensive and hard-to-maintain application and database servers.

Object Orientation

Remember how object-oriented concepts benefit the network-centric model? Those same concepts have enhanced the database world. For a long time, relational databases were the only players in the market. With the introduction of Informix Universal Server (`http://www.informix.com`), a new class of databases has emerged. These databases apply familiar object-oriented concepts. For example, relational databases had types defined for characters, numbers, dates, and some other types. When it came to pictures and audio, they stored these objects as a big chunk of raw data commonly referred to as the *BLOB type* (binary large object). The database didn't know what the data was, so additional fields were required to describe the blob data. With object-based databases, you can create new types. For example, you can have a picture type that has its own characteristics. These characteristics are data specific. So you may choose to define a color characteristic for the picture type. With that definition, you can search a database for all pictures with a certain color characteristic. This is a very powerful concept and a major step forward for the database industry.

Of course, new data types are not limited to pictures and audio. Any classification you can think of can be described as a new data type. Additionally, inheritance principles still apply, so new types can be formed out of old types.

Efforts are under way to create a standard such as SQL for object-based databases. I encourage you to learn more about these new database servers, especially for new projects, because they usually add to the capabilities of the existing relational databases. Industry leaders in object-based databases include Oracle (`http://www.oracle.com`), Sybase (`http://www.sybase.com`), and IBM (`http://www.ibm.com`).

Terminal Solution

Many of the mainframe databases support a text-based user interface. There are a number of terminal standards for interfacing with these databases. Examples are VT100 or 3270. Fortunately, most NC implementations either directly support terminal emulators or you can run an application that emulates the appropriate terminal for your application. If your users must access a terminal-based database, you should not have much difficulty using the NC for the same task.

The Web Solution

Since late 1993, the Web has emerged as an ideal interface to databases. The main advantage is that the same user interface can be employed across different platforms and users can access database data in the same way that they access documents. In many applications, the user will never know if the documents being viewed are statically stored some place or dynamically generated on demand from a database. As a result, only one client needs to be developed.

You may want to consider the Web solution if you need to develop a new database application. Because all NC implementations support some kind of a Web browser, you can access the Web interface to the database from any NC. So you don't have much work to do if you want your users to access a Web-based database using an NC. You still have to develop the Web database, however; there are a number of methods to do this that are briefly described below.

CGI

The common gateway interface (CGI) is the simplest and most popular method for interfacing database systems and the Web. CGI was created to bring interactivity to the Web. Before the age of CGI, Web browsers requested a specific page from the server and the server would send that page out. CGI merely defined a standard by which a client would request the Web server to execute a program residing on the server. The output of that program is then sent back to the browser as a document. In essence, CGI simply generates a document, as opposed to reading it from a file system. Input to CGI programs is provided using HTML forms. A typical CGI architecture is shown in Figure 6-4.

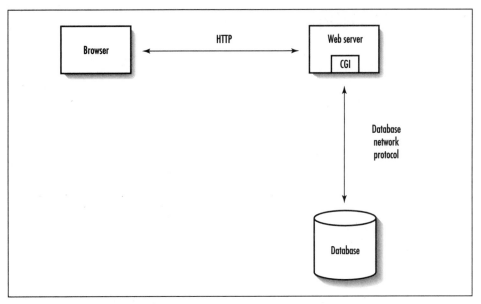

Figure 6-4 Typical CGI architecture

CGI programs are usually written in Perl (Practical Extraction and Report Language) or some other scripting language. Perl is a very mature (over ten years old) and very powerful scripting language specifically designed (well before the Web was invented) to generate reports. It supports all major operating systems and is used for mission-critical applications worldwide. In the Windows environment, Visual Basic seems to be the most popular language. All the script languages are capable of accessing a database using conventional database protocols such as open database connectivity (ODBC).

There are a few problems with the CGI approach. First, it is resource intensive. Busy Web servers may receive multiple requests to execute a CGI program, and that means the operating system must handle several instances of the program at the same time. This can slow down the overall response time of the machine considerably, especially if the machine is not equipped with sufficient memory.

The second issue with CGI regards its inability to keep track of client states. Anytime a browser makes a request, the request is treated independently of all other requests made from the browser. This stateless model works well when all the requests are for static Web pages from clients that come, visit a site, and go. The stateless model becomes cumbersome when the request is not for static pages but for an application. Interaction with an application usually requires hitting a number of pages, executing some programs in the background, and generating dynamic pages in real time. All of these activities are related (usually in a sequential manner). Without distinct states and state management, development of an application becomes a difficult task. When faced with this problem, CGI programmers came up with creative and nonstandard ways to keep track of states as a workaround, but the inherent problem still exists.

Non-CGI

The difficulties with CGI led to several other solutions for connecting the Web and data-bases. Unfortunately, unlike CGI, none of these methods follows a standard, and imple-mentations differ widely. Oracle, a leader in database servers, introduced a Web server. The Web server is completely integrated into an Oracle database server, serving as an agent for each client. The agent is really a CGI program, but because it is implemented specifically for database access, it can overcome the performance shortfalls of the standard CGI approach. Programmers write scripts using the PL/SQL script language, which is standard for all Oracle database applications.

Similarly, Microsoft Internet Information Server provides built-in support for MS Access, MS SQL Server, and other ODBC-compliant databases, whereas Informix, Sybase, and other database vendors have solutions for their product lines.

Netscape uses the LiveWire application server to provide access to ODBC-compliant databases. It also has native drivers for popular databases such as Oracle, Sybase, and Informix. The LiveWire engine keeps track of the database and the Web connections and coordinates the two channels.

Although non-CGI solutions are more efficient and allow for more sophisticated applications, they lack a common standard. Applications developed under one environ-ment may not easily port to another. If you don't foresee migration to a new environ-ment, it is well worth your time to choose one of the non-CGI solutions and make an implementation. The only drawback would be that your application would still be served out of the Web server, and so its performance will depend on the performance of the Web server.

NC solutions work well with non-CGI database applications because all NC imple-mentations support a Web browser. More and more applications are using JavaScript or VBScript to perform some operations on the client and thus reduce the load on the Web server. These applications obviously require Web browsers that support such extensions. Some of the browsers native to the NC may not meet this requirement. For the present time, this seems to be true especially of small NC devices, where the Web browser is very basic in its functionality.

Windows Solutions

The desktop age produced a large number of client/server applications for the Windows operating system. Tools such as PowerBuilder and Visual Basic were used to create powerful interfaces to databases. The investment in this architecture was quite large, and so many NC implementations must coexist with these Windows clients. In those cases, you should make sure that the NC implementation supports a protocol such as ICA from Citrix, where a Windows application can be executed from an NC. You will have to increase the resources of your application server. Other than that, you will be able to use your existing applications without having to rewrite them in Java or change them to a Web-based solution.

Java Solution

The Java language has evolved in stages. One of the first requests from the programming community was a standard for linking Java and databases. JavaSoft responded by introducing Java database connectivity (JDBC). JDBC is a universal database access solution and is very similar to the popular ODBC standard. The layer approach is shown in Figure 6-5.

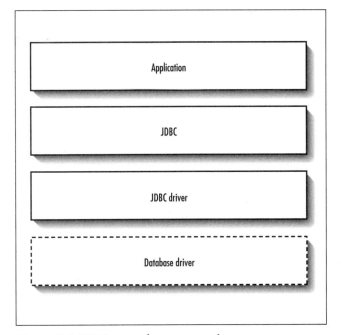

Figure 6-5 JDBC uses a layer approach

A middleware solution provides a consistent Application Programming Interface (API) to different databases, but JDBC is much more than that. It is a major achievement in the database industry because almost all major vendors have adopted the specification in such a short period of time. Additionally, an application based on JDBC will work the same regardless of which database server is used. This is ideal for general applications where you do not know in advance under what database server the application will be deployed. JDBC provides a universal view of the database server to the application.

The following is devoted to a general discussion of JDBC as it is shipped with JDK 1.1.

JDBC API

The JDBC API is what the application programmer uses to open a connection to a database, execute SQL commands, and retrieve results for processing. As an application programmer, you will be mostly dealing with the following APIs, which are documented in the *JDBC API Reference Guide*:

- **java.sql.DriverManager**: Takes care of connecting the application to lower-level database drivers

- **Java.sql.Connection**: Stores information about a connection to the database

- **java.sql.Statement**: Stores information about a SQL command to be executed on the database

- **java.sql.ResultSet**: Stores the result set from the database and provides mechanisms for manipulating it

Recall that there are two ways to request data from the database server. The first way is to prepare an SQL command and send that command to the database. **java.sql.PreparedStatement** takes care of this type of request. The second method is to call a procedure that is stored in the database server. That stored procedure will execute the appropriate SQL commands and return a result set. **java.sql.CallableStatement** is used to call stored procedures on a database.

JDBC is designed to work with both applets and standalone applications. With standalone applications, you have more freedom and can connect to any database on the network. With applets, you are restricted to the applet security model. Furthermore, the particular implementation of the security model in the browser you are using may be more restrictive. In general, untrusted applets cannot access databases residing on machines other than the Web server that serves the applet. That is not a significant limitation given the three-tier hierarchy, because the application server can be located on the Web server, whereas the resource-intensive database server can be located elsewhere.

Additionally, applets using JDBC will download their driver and register that with the driver manager. The security model limits the applet to using only the registered driver. With a trusted applet, you have more flexibility in creating connections across the network, but your applet is still under the control of the security manager.

JDBC Driver

The JDBC driver is responsible for creating a consistent link to the native database drivers. It is because of the JDBC driver that application programmers get a consistent API in the JDBC API. The database driver can be ODBC, SQL NET (Oracle), TDS (Sybase), or any other driver.

The JDBC driver needs to implement the **java.sql.Driver** interface. This is used by the driver manager to find the appropriate driver for the database request that it has received.

Additionally, the JDBC driver must implement the methods provided in the JDBC API based on a particular driver.

Using JDBC

A simple session in JDBC involves the following steps:

- Open a database connection.

- Send an SQL command to the database.

- Receive the results and process them.

To open a connection, you can use **java.sql.DriverManager.getConnection** method and pass a URL, a user name, and a password. The URL convention used in JDBC is similar to the usual URL format. Here is the JDBC URL format:

```
jdbc:<subprotocol>:<subname>
```

The **subprotocol** parameter is the driver type used for accessing the database. **subname** refers to the name of the database. So **jdbc:odbc:mydb** accesses **mydb** using an ODBC driver.

Here is a simple program that selects first- and last-name fields from the customer table.

```
import java.net.URL;
import java.sql.*;
class selectName {
  public static void main(String argv[]) {
  try {
    String url = "jdbc:odbc:mydb";

    Connection con = DriverManager.getConnection(url, "user", "");

    Statement sqlcmd = con.createStatement();
    ResultSet r = sqlcmd.executeQuery("SELECT fname, lastname FROM customer");

    System.out.println("Retrieved result set:");
    while (r.next()) {
      // get the values from the current row:
      char fname[] = r.getVarChar(10).tocharArray();
     char lname[] = r.getVarChar(20).tocharArray();
        // do something with the result
    }
    sqlcmd.close();
    con.close();
  } catch (java.lang.Exception ex) {
    ex.printStackTrace(); }
  }
  }
}
```

After importing the necessary packages (**java.sql.*** is for JDBC), a connection to the database with the URL of **jdbc:odbc:mydb** is established. The variable **con** holds the information about the current connection.

With a connection at hand, we are ready to send an SQL request to the database. Use the **createStatement()** method to create an object that will hold the information about the SQL request. Next, the method **executeQuery** is used to send the SQL command to the database server.

The result of the query is stored in an object of type **ResultSet**. We can then step through each row of the result set using a loop, retrieve the value for each field, and perform some operation on each field. Once we are done stepping through the entire result set, we close the statement and close the connection.

To give you a feel for the data types in JDBC, Table 6-1 lists a mapping between the popular SQL data types and their equivalent in JDBC.

Table 6-1 Mapping between SQL data types and Java data types

SQL	JAVA
CHAR	String
VARCHAR	String
LONGVARCHAR	java.io.InputStream
NUMERIC	java.sql.Numeric
DECIMAL	java.sql.Numeric
BIT	boolean
TINYINT	byte
SMALLINT	short
INTEGER	int
BIGINT	long
REAL	float
FLOAT	float
DOUBLE	double
BINARY	byte[]
VARBINARY	byte[]
LONGVARBINARY	java.sql.InputStream
DATE	java.sql.Date
TIME	java.sql.Time
TIMESTAMP	java.sql.Timestamp

Vendors

JDBC has been endorsed by a number of companies. As you begin your application development, you should use tools from companies that have developed an expertise in JDBC and support it in their products. The following is a list of such companies:

Agave Software Design (`http://www.agave.com`)

Asgard Software (`http://www.borland.com`)

Borland International Inc. (`http://www.borland.com`)

Bulletproof (`http://bulletproof.com/jagg/`)

Caribou Lake Software (`http://www.cariboulake.com`)

Connect, Inc. (`http://www.connectsw.com`)

Cyber SQL Corporation (`http://www.cybersql.com`)

DataRamp (`http://dataramp.com`)

Dharma Systems Inc. (`http://www.dharmas.com`)

Esker (`http://www.esker.fr`)

Gupta Corporation (`http://www.gupta.com`)

IBM's Database 2 (DB2) (`http://www.software.ibm.com/data/db2/index.html`)

IDS Software (`http://www.idssoftware.com`)

Imaginary (mSQL) (`http://www.imaginary.com/~borg/Java/`)

Informix Software Inc. (`http://www.informix.com`)

InterSoft Argentina S. A. (`http://www.inter-soft.com`)

Intersolv (`http://www.intersolv.com`)

Ken North Seminars (`http://ourworld.compuserve.com/homepages/Ken_North`)

NetDynamics (`http://www.netdynamics.com/press/reviews/jdbcfinal.html`)

O2 Technology (`http://www.o2tech.com`)

Object Design Inc. (`http://www.odi.com`)

Open Horizon (`http://www.openhorizon.com`)

OpenLink Software (`http://www.openlinksw.com`)

Oracle Corporation (`http://www.oracle.com`)

- Persistence Software (`http://www.persistence.com`)

- Presence Information Design (`http://cloud9.presence.com/pbj/`)

- PRO-C Inc. (`http://www.pro-c.com`)

- Recital Corporation (`http://www.recital.com`)

- RogueWave Software Inc. (`http://www.roguewave.com`)

- Sanga (`http://www.sangacorp.com/products.html`)

- SAS Institute Inc™ (`http://www.sas.com`)

- SCO (`http://www.vision.sco.com/brochure/sqlretriever.html`)

- StormCloud Development (`http://www.stormcloud.com`)

- Sybase Inc. (`http://www.sybase.com`)

- Symantec (`http://cafe.symantec.com/cafe/`)

- Thought Inc. (`http://www.thoughtinc.com`)

- Thunderstone (`http://www.thunderstone.com/`)

- Visigenic Software Inc. (`http://www.visigenic.com`)

- WebLogic Inc. (`http://www.weblogic.com`)

- XDB Systems, Inc. (`http://www.xdb.com/`)

Drivers

The JDBC API is part of the JDK, so you can immediately begin programming. Your biggest hurdle is going to be finding an appropriate driver for your database. There are four types of JDBC drivers, depending on how you categorize them.

Based on the connection characteristics, drivers fall into two categories. The first kind is drivers that connect directly from the client to the server. Although this approach may provide fast performance, a different driver is needed for each server. Most traditional client/server implementations have taken this approach. Although it is possible to write a database-specific driver in Java, it makes more sense to write that driver based on JDBC so it can be used by other applications.

The other type is when an indirect connection or a middleware is used. This is what ODBC uses to achieve a single point of contact for multiple database access. A client usually is written to connect to a middleware piece, and it is the responsibility of the middleware to perform the necessary translation to the specific database. Usually this approach results in less performance, but the flexibility is its advantage.

Database drivers can also be categorized based on code type. The first type is drivers written in pure Java. This is ideal for the NC environment, because the driver can be downloaded over the network just as the client application is. JDBC supports this type of driver.

The other type is drivers written in languages other than Java. Usually these are existing drivers used in the Java environment. As more drivers are written entirely in Java, this category will probably dwindle.

You will have to decide which type of driver is appropriate for your application. Factors you may consider are performance, flexibility of your database, and whether loading additional binaries under JDBC is feasible. To assist you in finding an appropriate driver, Table 6-2 lists a number of vendors who supply JDBC drivers.

Table 6-2 JDBC drivers

PRODUCT	VENDOR	DBMS TYPE
JDBC Net Server	Agave Software Design (http://www.agave.com/products)	Sybase, Oracle, Informix, ODBC-compliant
Open/A for Java	Asgard Software (http://www.asgardsw.com)	Unisys A series DMSII database
InterClient	Borland International (http://www.borland.com)	Interbase 4.0

PRODUCT	VENDOR	DBMS TYPE
JSQL/Ingress	Caribuo Lake Software (http://www. cariboulake.com)	Ingress
Fast Forward	Connect Software (http://www. connectsw.com)	Sybase, MS SQL Server
Client for Java	DataRamp (http://www. dataramp.com)	ODBC-compliant
DB2 Client for Java	IBM (http://www. software.ibm.com/ data/db2/jdbc)	DB2
IDS Server	IDS Software (http://www. idssoftware.com)	Oracle, Sybase, MS SQL Server, MS Access, Informix, Watcom, ODBC-compliant
mSQL-JDBC Driver	Imaginary (http://www. imaginary.com)	mSQL
Essentia-JDBC	InterSoft (http://www. inter-soft.com)	Essentia
DataDirect	Intersolv (http://www. intersolv.com)	Oracle, Sybase
JDBC-ODBC Bridge	JavaSoft (http://java. sun.com)	ODBC-compliant
JDBC Drivers	OpenLink (http://www. openlink.com)	Oracle, Informix, Sybase, MS SQL Server, CA-Ingres, Progress, Unify, Postgress95
SHARE*NET	SAS (http://www.sas. com)	SAS, Oracle, Informix, Ingres, ADABAS

continued on next page

continued from previous page

PRODUCT	VENDOR	DBMS TYPE
SQL-Retriever	SCO (http://www. vision.sco.com)	Informix, Oracle, Ingres, Sybase, Interbase
WebDBC 3.0 Enterprise	StormCloud Development (http://www. stormcloud.com)	ODBC-compliant
jdbcCONNECT	Sybase Inc. (http://www. sybase.com Sybase)	SQL Server, SQL Anywhere, Sybase IQ, Replication Server, OmniCONNECT-compatible DBMS
dbANYWHERE	Symantec (http://www. symantec.com/dba)	Oracle, Sybase, MS SQL Server, MS Access, Watcom, ODBC-compliant
VisiChannel for Java	Visigenic (http://www. visigenic.com)	ODBC-compliant
jdbcKona	WebLogic (http://www. weblogic.com)	Oracle, Sybase, MS SQL Server
jdbcKonaT3	WebLogic (http://www. weblogic.com)	ODBC-compliant

Summary

Database applications are widely used. Deployment of the NC requires a very good understanding of such applications and making sure that they will continue to work under the network-centric paradigm. Relational databases are the most common type of databases; with the network-centric model, many clients can access many servers scattered throughout the network in a transparent way.

Access to some databases is provided via a text-based interface. Almost all NC implementation has some support for such interfaces. Other databases may have a Web interface via CGI or non-CGI solutions. Because all NC implementations support a Web browser, deployment of such database applications should be seamless with the NC. Another class of database applications is Windows-based programs. If your NC supports a protocol such as ICA from Citrix, then you can continue using such applications.

The Java solution for database connectivity is JDBC. JDBC is a database-independent specification that provides a consistent interface to all databases. At the application level, you typically need to connect to a database, send SQL requests, and retrieve the results.

Distributed Applications on the NC

The network-centric model has changed our concept of an application. An object-oriented application comprises well-defined objects that interact to make an application work. There are several advantages to creating component-based applications instead of monolithic applications—component-based applications can be built faster and cheaper; the code base can be reused; and whenever a new application needs to be built, some or most of the components are already available. With a component model such as JavaBeans, the objects do not need to reside on the same machine: They can be scattered around the network. Objects are downloaded from the network as needed by the application.

This chapter deals with JavaBeans—an architecture for creating and using dynamic Java components that can be composed together into applications by end users. I start off by explaining what components and component models mean. Then I explain how JavaBeans fits the component model. Finally, I talk about the Bean Development Kit (BDK), which contains the BeanBox, example Bean source codes, a demo, and the Beans tutorial. Throughout, I explain the concepts behind JavaBeans using examples. Later on, I compare JavaBeans and ActiveX and raise several issues. I end this chapter by explaining the relevance of JavaBeans technology to network computers. Appendix A covers ActiveX in detail. The underlying object models upon which these component models are based are discussed in Chapter 8, "The Distributed Object Model."

Many of us who use word processors have at some time or another felt the necessity to insert a bar chart or a pie chart or even a spreadsheet into our documents to convey our ideas more effectively. How many of us have wondered how to insert data from one program into another program even when the two programs are totally different?

If you have wondered about this before or if you are racking your brains now, the answer is simple: Component models are used to develop these applications, which means that the word processors and spreadsheets are built as components—and one of the properties of these components is their capability to be placed inside another component. (Strictly speaking, components are placed in *containers*; in this example, the spreadsheet component is placed inside a word processor container. I will look at these concepts a little later.)

What has all this got to do with JavaBeans? JavaBeans is a software component model that describes an architecture and platform-neutral Application Programming Interface (API) for creating and using dynamic Java components. Why should we consider JavaBeans? Because JavaBeans provides a platform-neutral, fully portable, powerful, compact, and network-aware environment. (Like anything related to Java, the JavaBeans documents are full of buzz words.) JavaBeans can do all this because it is written in Java.

Component-Based Software

Bob is a developer whose job is to design graphical user interfaces (GUIs). Being an intelligent developer, Bob quickly finds out that rather than writing code to build buttons and menus each time he needs them, he can write the code once and reuse these buttons and menus whenever he wants them. He calls these objects *components*. Now that he has these components, he finds out that he needs to place them somewhere so that he can assemble them. This he calls a container. Well, these components sit inside a container but they don't do anything interesting by themselves. So Bob comes up with a mechanism by which these different components can communicate with each other. Viola!! Bob has designed a *component architecture*.

The component-based software paradigm is a mechanism in which applications are constructed through the assembly of reusable software components. Products such as Microsoft's Visual Basic and Borland's Delphi have used this methodology to provide developers with an easy-to-use platform to develop applications rapidly.

A software component model has three major elements: components, containers, and a language through which the components can communicate with each other.

Components

Components are the building blocks of the application. Depending on the application, these can be as simple as radio buttons or as complex as spreadsheets. For example, when you are using a paint program, the various tools such as a paint brush or an eraser can be considered components. You use, or assemble, these components to make your application, which in this case is a drawing.

Similarly, when you embed a spreadsheet in a word processor document, the spreadsheet can be considered a component. Components have definite properties and definite actions they can perform. A paint brush has properties such as color and size and it can draw various shapes.

Containers

Containers are objects that hold the components. They are the placeholders where the components are assembled. In the example of a paint program, the canvas can be considered a container because it holds components—paint brush and eraser—that you use to assemble or build your drawing.

Other examples of containers are Netscape Navigator and Microsoft Word. Containers are also called *shells*, *frames*, or *forms*.

Communication

Components sitting by themselves inside a container can be pretty boring. There has to be a means of communication between the components. A scripting language is necessary to provide this communication. For example, when a button is clicked and it has to trigger an action in another component, the two components talk to each other using the scripting language defined for that architecture.

Lest this discussion makes you think that all components are visual things like buttons or menu bars, many components are in fact nonvisual. This means that they do not have a GUI. One example of a nongraphical component is a timer. When the application that uses the timer runs, the user cannot see the timer but the application might be using it for several things. Another example of a nonvisual component is a B-tree. Though such components are not visible to the user, they are extremely useful for rapid application development.

The advantages of creating component-based applications instead of monolithic applications are obvious—component-based applications can be built faster and cheaper and the code base can be reused. Whenever a new application needs to be built, some or most of the components are already available.

Characteristics of a Component Model

There are many kinds of component models; most of them share the following characteristics:

- Component interface exposure and discovery

- Component layout functions

- Event handling

- Persistence

- Application builder support

It is easier to understand these characteristics with the help of an example. Our friend Bob has built an application that lets users view real-time weather for any city in the world. His application uses two components—one component that takes user input and retrieves the current weather data and another component that displays this data graphically. The data retrieval component retrieves current weather data and interacts dynamically with the display component to display weather on the user's screen.

Component Interface Exposure and Discovery

Two things need to be understood here: the mechanism by which components expose or let other components know of their interface (in other words, how they interact with other components) and the discovery of this interface by the other components. When a new component is placed in a container, it registers or publishes its interface with the container framework. As a result, other components know about its existence and how to interact with it.

If we consider the example of providing real-time weather data, the display component provides or announces its interface to the component framework. In other words, it tells the framework that it can take raw data as input and output the data in graphical format. The data retrieval component "discovers" this interface and provides the graphical component with the data it retrieves. Because the display component has exposed its interfaces to the component environment, the data retrieval component need not have prior knowledge of its existence. Thus the components need not be of the same build.

This discussion brings us to an important concept of components: *introspection*. Introspection is the property that allows the properties and events of a component to be discovered by other components.

Component Layout Functions

The layout functions provide a component ways to control its appearance both within its own space and inside a container. For example, a push button can have a default appearance that can change with the state of the button.

Event Handling

Components communicate with each other using events or messages. When a component "raises" or "broadcasts" an event, the component framework notifies the appropriate component. The notified component will then perform some action. For example, in the example of weather-data retrieval, if the user clicks on the Zoom button, the display component is notified, which then displays the zoomed portion of the map. Events can be generated by the system as well as by the components.

Persistence

Persistence is a property that enables nonvolatile storage of state or other information. The information that is stored includes the component state with respect to the container and other components. This means that JavaBeans customized in one session can be retrieved intact during another session. For example, users of an email system might want to save their settings like font, background color, and login ID so that the next time they use the email system, their saved settings/preferences are displayed.

Application Builder Support

There has to be a mechanism by which developers can use the components to build applications. Application development tools like Visual Basic or Java Workshop are generally used. These tools need to know the properties and behavior of the components so that they can be presented visually to the developer. Application builder support interfaces enable the components to expose their properties and behavior to the tools.

JavaBeans

Now that you understand what components and component models are, let's look at JavaBeans. JavaBeans is a set of APIs that makes it easy to create Java applications from reusable components. It is a portable, platform-independent, network-aware component model written in Java for building and using dynamic Java components. JavaBeans has all the characteristics of a component model: interface publishing and discovery, event handling, persistence, layout control, and application builder support.

JavaBeans does to Java what Java did to HTML—it makes Web pages come alive. Although Java has brought life to Web pages through applet animation and the like, the applets are pretty static in the sense that they cannot interact with the page or with each other. JavaBeans provides a mechanism by which the applets can interact with each other as well as with the Web page.

The importance of JavaBeans is that it defines a standard way to encapsulate objects so that they can easily be reused by application developers. It formalizes the applet API across all types of objects, both GUI and non-GUI, to allow you to make robust and reusable building blocks.

The main strength of the JavaBeans component architecture comes from the fact that JavaBeans is written in Java. Let's examine this further.

Portability

Because Java is platform- and architecture-neutral, so is JavaBeans. However, this applies as long as JavaBeans is not embedded in a platform-specific container. When a JavaBean is nested inside another JavaBean, then the functionality is the same on all platforms. But when the main container is platform-specific, like Netscape Navigator or Microsoft Word, then the JavaBeans APIs are integrated into the platform's local component architecture; for example, ActiveX on the Windows platform.

Also, because the JavaBeans framework is distributed as part of the Java platform, JavaBeans exists for all those platforms for which a Java virtual machine (JVM) exists.

Introspection

In the case of JavaBeans there are two ways of inspecting a component: using the reflection API or using the BeanInfo class. If the reflection API is being used, then the methods provided by one class can be determined from the method names. On the other hand, if the BeanInfo class is being used to inspect a class, then "BeanInfo" at the end of the Bean's class name allows other classes to inspect this class.

Default implementations are provided for introspecting a component. This can be used for most of the cases. However, support is also provided for developers to have full control over which properties, methods, and events they want to expose in their components.

Reflection APIs are used to study the methods used by a Bean; *design patterns* are then used to determine what properties, events, and public methods are supported by the method under inspection. Using design patterns means using conventional names for methods and/or interfaces. For example, *get* and *set* methods can be used to retrieve and set the properties of an object. Tools can be written to match these patterns so that their properties, events, and public methods can be studied. If we want to study the properties, then design patterns can be used to locate methods that use get and set, or the keyword *boolean* can be located for studying boolean properties. If we are looking for events, design patterns like *add* and *remove* can be used to determine which events a Bean multicasts, which events a Bean unicasts, and so on. In the case of methods, it is assumed that all the public methods of a JavaBean are exposed as external methods within the component environment for access by other components.

The process described above of determining events, methods, and properties uses reflection APIs. In this case, the events, methods, and properties are not explicitly specified. The BeanInfo interface mechanism provides a way of explicitly specifying which properties, events, and methods a JavaBean supports. While delivering a Bean, the developer also delivers a BeanInfo class, whose name is formed by appending "BeanInfo" to the Bean's class name. It should be noted that the developer can choose to specify only part of the Bean's behavior in the BeanInfo class. Thus, a design pattern search must also be used to obtain complete information.

Network Awareness

The support for a TCP/IP stack that is built in to Java greatly helps in today's distributed computing environment. Extending a component's capabilities by adding networking APIs results in a bloated and less robust API. Because JavaBeans comes with built-in network support, the resulting components are lightweight and robust so they can be downloaded across the network easily and quickly.

Security Issues

Because JavaBeans is written in Java, JavaBeans is subject to the standard Java security model. This means that when a JavaBean runs as part of an untrusted applet, it cannot read or write to the files on the client system; also it can connect only to the server from which it was invoked. But when a Bean runs as part of an application or as a trusted applet, it has full access to files and network hosts.

Distributed Environment and Remote Method Invocation

In today's distributed World Wide Web environment, JavaBeans provides a mechanism to implement distributed systems. This mechanism provides three types of network access.

Java Remote Method Invocation

When implementing an application in a client/server environment, the client might invoke some functions (or methods) on the server and vice versa. Java remote method invocation (RMI) provides a mechanism by which distributed system interfaces can be designed in Java and clients and servers can be implemented against those interfaces. The Java RMI model is shown in Figure 7-1.

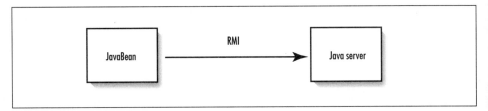

Figure 7-1 Java RMI model

A brief overview of the concepts behind Java RMI follows.

The action of invoking a method of a remote object on a remote object is defined as remote method invocation. In a distributed object system, a remote object is one that resides in a different address space. In the Java distributed object model, a remote object is defined as one whose methods can be invoked from another JVM, potentially on a different host. In Java RMI, a method invocation on a local object and a method invocation on a remote object have the same syntax. It must be noted that the methods on the client and server sides do not talk to each other directly but through interfaces. This brings us to the point of describing the architecture of an RMI system.

An RMI system consists of three layers:

 The stub/skeleton layer: The communication between the remote methods is carried out by the client-side stubs and the server-side skeletons. A client that wishes to invoke a remote object uses a stub to do so. The stub implements the remote interfaces of the remote object; it also forwards any requests made by the client for remote method invocation to the server object. The server, on the other hand, handles requests using the server-side skeletons. This skeleton again serves as an interface to handle the client calls; once it receives a request from a client, it passes the request to the actual method.

The remote reference layer: The communication between the stubs and the skeletons is carried out by the remote reference layer. This layer handles both the invocation semantics and the reference semantics for the server. Invocation semantics deals with determining whether the server is a single object or a replicated object. The reference semantics for the server deals with how to refer to the server objects.

 The transport layer: The transport layer is responsible for connection setup, connection management, and keeping track of and dispatching to remote objects residing in the transport's address space.

Figure 7-2 shows the RMI architecture.

The RMI mechanism implements garbage collection of remote objects just as Java does garbage collection of local objects. Remote objects that are no longer referenced by any client are automatically deleted.

Java RMI provides an RMISecurityManager class that regulates the actions of the loaded classes. The security manager makes sure that the loaded classes conform to the Java model of security and also that the classes are downloaded from a trusted host. Applications are required to define their own security manager or must use the RMISecurityManager; otherwise, classes cannot be loaded from across the network.

Java Interface Definition Language

In a distributed environment, many other component models exist, in addition to JavaBeans. If in an application JavaBeans needs to talk to components written in another language or to components from another vendor, a mechanism must exist for such communication. JavaBeans uses the Java stubs generated from the Interface Definition Language (IDL) interfaces (defined in the industry-standard CORBA IDL) to call in to IDL servers and vice versa. The use of Java IDL allows JavaBeans clients to talk to both Java IDL servers and non-Java IDL servers. The Java IDL model is shown in Figure 7-3.

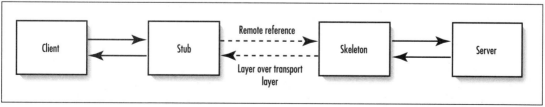

Figure 7-2 RMI architecture showing the three layers of an RMI model

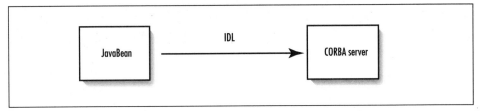

Figure 7-3 Java IDL model

Java Database Connectivity

The database and the client often do not exist on the same server in a distributed environment. Java database connectivity (JDBC), which defines the Java database APIs, provides a means for Java applets or applications to access SQL databases. JDBC provides access to Structured Query Language (SQL) databases even when the client and the database are on the same server. The Java database connectivity model is shown in Figure 7-4.

Persistence

As defined earlier, *persistence* is property that enables non-volatile storage of component state or other information. The stored information includes the component state with respect to the container as well as other components.

JavaBeans uses either serialization or externalization to maintain persistence. Enough information must be stored so that the contents can be restored when a new instance is created. Stored objects repeatedly refer to other objects, which must also be stored and retrieved in a way that the relationships between the objects can be maintained.

The state of the objects is represented in a serialized form for the purpose of storing and retrieving objects. Objects that use the serialization mechanism have enough information in the stream to restore the objects. On the other hand, it is the responsibility of the classes that use externalization to restore the format. For such objects, the container saves only the identity of the class.

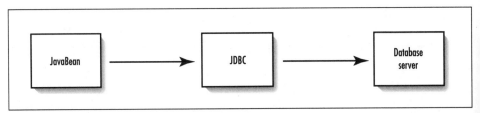

Figure 7-4 Java database connectivity model

Packaging (JAR format)

Many applications have several class files, images, audio files, help files, and other similar resource files. Downloading all these files individually takes a lot of time and also wastes precious bandwidth. For this reason, a file format called JAR (Java archive) was developed. Using this file format, related files (be they class files or image files or any other files) can be bundled as a single file, and this single file can be compressed. The browser can download this file in a single Hypertext Transfer Protocol (HTTP) transaction (rather than opening a new connection for each component of the JAR file), simultaneously reducing download time and using less bandwidth. To address the security of files downloaded over the Internet, the JAR file format also allows the author to sign the individual components of the JAR file, thus the origin of the file can be authenticated.

The JAR format is written in Java and is based on the ZIP file format. The JavaBeans specification does not require the use of the JAR format for archiving and delivering applications. After a JAR file is downloaded, it may be repackaged using any other format.

Manifest Files

In addition to the class files and other resource files, a JAR file may also contain a *manifest* file. Information in the manifest file is stored as name-value pairs. For example, if a JAR file contains a JavaBean, then the section heading for the JavaBean file in the manifest file would contain

```
<name>:Name of JavaBean
<value>:True
```

There is only one manifest file in an archive. The pathnames of a manifest file are of the form

```
META-INF/MANIFEST.MF
```

If the archive is digitally signed (for security reasons), then the pathnames of the security files are of the form

```
META-INF/x.SF
```

where x is a string containing no more than eight characters. Only the characters A–Z, 0–9, dash, and underscore are allowed.

Once a JAR file is signed digitally, the end user can be guaranteed that the file has traveled untampered from its source.

Beans Development Kit and BeanBox

Now that I have discussed various issues about JavaBeans, let's look at designing some Beans components and at the same time some examples. JavaSoft provides BDK 1.0 for the purpose of supporting early development of JavaBeans components.

Note that BDK 1.0 is not a full-fledged application development environment. Also note that when you download Java Development Kit (JDK) 1.1 from JavaSoft's Web site, you get JavaBeans with it. The BDK is a Java-based application whose only dependency is JDK 1.1. The BDK provides support for the JavaBeans APIs, a test container called the BeanBox, sample Beans along with the source code, the JavaBeans specification, and a tutorial.

Where Do I Get BDK 1.0?

To run the BeanBox, you need JDK 1.1. If you have not already downloaded and installed JDK 1.1, go to `http://www.javasoft.com/products/jdk/1.1/index.html` to download it. Also read the `README` file at `http://www.javasoft.com/products/jdk/1.1/README` for instructions on how to install JDK 1.1.

BDK 1.0 can be downloaded from JavaSoft's Web site at `http://splash.javasoft.com/beans/bdk_download.html`. This page provides instructions for downloading and installing BDK 1.0. BDK 1.0 is available for Windows 95, Windows NT 3.5.1, Windows NT 4.0, Solaris 2.4, and Solaris 2.5. BDK 1.0 ports relatively easily to other platforms that support the Java virtual machine.

Downloading BDK 1.0

First I will look at how to download and install the BDK for the Windows platform; then I will concentrate on the Solaris platforms.

To download the BDK release for the Windows platforms:

Type `ftp://splash.javasoft.com/pub` in the Location field on the browser. A list of all the software available for download from the JavaSoft Web site is displayed.

Click on the hyperlink that says **bdk_feb97.exe**. This file is about 1625 KB.

In the Save As pop-up box, select the folder where you want to download the software.

Click the Save button on the pop-up box. The file will be downloaded to that location.

To install the BDK:

Go to the folder where you downloaded the software.

Double-click on the **bdk_feb97.exe** file. This brings up the standard Windows InstallShield installer. Follow the instructions provided by the installer to finish the installation.

You are now ready to play with JavaBeans.
To download the BDK release for the Solaris platforms:

Type **ftp://splash.javasoft.com/pub** in the Location field on the browser. A list of all the software available for download from the JavaSoft Web site is displayed.

Click on the hyperlink that says **bdk_feb97.sh**. This file is about 1511 KB.

In the Save As pop-up box, select the directory where you want to download the software.

Click the Save button on the pop-up box. The file will be downloaded to that location.

To install the BDK:

Go to the directory where you downloaded the software.

Unpack the release using the following command: **sh bdk_feb.sh**.

When you run the above command, the BDK 1.0 license is displayed. Read the license and, if you agree to the terms, type **y** when asked if you agree to the license terms.

The release will automatically be unpacked into a directory called **beans**.

You are now ready to play with JavaBeans.

Running the BeanBox

Before you can run the BeanBox, you need to set **PATH** and **CLASSPATH** correctly.

To set the **PATH** variable under Windows:

1. From the Start menu, select Programs and then Accessories. Under Accessories, choose WordPad or NotePad.

2. Choose Open from the File menu and type **c:\autoexec.bat** for the file name. This will open the file for editing.

3. Look for the **PATH** statement. Add the following line to the end of the **PATH** statement: **;C:\JDK1.1\BIN**.

To set the **CLASSPATH** environment variable, edit the **AUTOEXEC.BAT** file (as in the above instructions) and set the **CLASSPATH** environment variable to the current directory (.) and the directory containing the Java Core Class library file, known as **CLASSES.ZIP**. Separate directories by semicolons: **SET CLASSPATH=.;C:\JDK1.1 \LIB\CLASSES.ZIP**.

After completing these changes to **AUTOEXEC.BAT**, save the file and reboot to make the changes take effect.

To set the **PATH** variable under Solaris, add the following directory to the **PATH** variable: **jdk1.1/bin**. If you use the C shell (**csh**), you can do this by adding that path to your path variable in your **.cshrc** file. If you use the Korn shell (**ksh**), you can do this by adding that path to your path variable in your **.profile** file.

If you have set the **CLASSPATH** environment variable, you may need to update it. You must replace **CLASSPATH** entries that pointed to the **java/classes** directory to point to **jdk1.1/lib/classes.zip**. You can do this by opening the **.cshrc** file (for **csh**) or the **.profile** file (for **ksh**) and making the change to the **CLASSPATH** environment variable.

After completing these changes to **.cshrc** (or **.profile**), save the file and execute the following to make the changes take effect:

```
% source .cshrc (for csh)
$ . ./.profile (for ksh)
```

Now that the installation is complete, you are ready to run the BeanBox. The BeanBox is a container used to test Bean behavior. To run the BeanBox under Windows, go to the folder where you have installed the BDK. Under this folder is a folder called **beanbox**. Double-click on this folder. You will see a file called **run**. Double-click on **run** to start the BeanBox.

On the Solaris platform, **cd** to the directory where you have installed the BDK. Then **cd** to the directory called **beanbox**. In this directory, you will see a file called **run.sh**. At the command prompt, type **run.sh**.

The BeanBox comes up as three separate windows (see Figure 7-5):

The middle window is the main BeanBox composition window.

The left-hand window is the toolbox palette displaying available Beans that can be dropped onto the composition window.

The right-hand window is a property sheet showing the properties for the currently selected Bean.

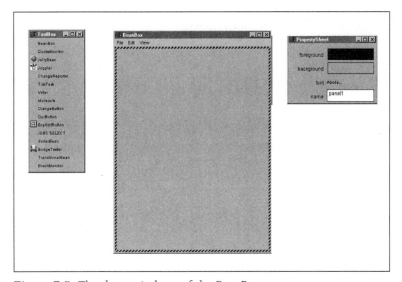

Figure 7-5 The three windows of the BeanBox

Concepts of JavaBeans Explained Through the BeanBox

In this section I will apply several of the concepts of JavaBeans discussed in earlier sections to the BeanBox in order to provide a better understanding of JavaBeans.

Components and Containers

In the toolbox, click on the OurButton Bean and then click in the BeanBox area. In this case, the OurButton Bean is a component that is placed inside the BeanBox container. This is *instantiating* OurButton in the BeanBox. Inside the BeanBox, click on the button. In the property sheet window, you can see the properties of this component, such as foreground color, label, and background color. Change the label of OurButton to Stop. Also change the background color to red. OurButton can be clicked and resized.

Communication Between Components

Let's look at the communication between components. Instantiate Juggler and one more OurButton from the toolbox in the BeanBox. Change the label of the second OurButton to Start and the background color to green, as shown in Figure 7-6.

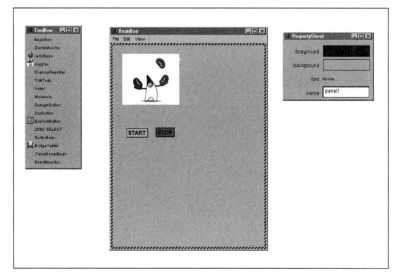

Figure 7-6 Juggler and two OurButtons

Now perform the following steps:

1. Click on the Stop button.

2. From the Edit menu, select Events; under Events, select action; and under Action, click on actionPerformed.

3. Now you can see a red line starting from the Stop button. Connect the line to the Juggler and click the mouse button.

4. An EventTarget dialog box pops up. From this box, select stopJuggling and then click OK.

5. Now click on the Stop button and see what happens. The juggler will stop juggling.

An event from the Stop button has been communicated to the juggler component, which then performs the associated action. In this case, the action is to stop juggling.

Following the above steps, associate the Start button with the startJuggling action. Now, if you click on the Start button, you can see that the Juggler will start juggling again.

Properties

Properties specify the nature and behavior of a Bean. There are many types of properties: **Simple**, **Indexed**, **Bound**, and **Constrained**. Let's look at **Bound** and **Constrained** properties because these can be viewed in the BeanBox.

A **Bound** property notifies other objects when its value changes. If a property of a component is bound to a property of another component, then when the property of the first component changes, the second component is notified of this change and its property changes too.

To demonstrate bound property, let's consider the Start and Stop buttons of the previous example. Let's say that we want to bind the **foreground** color property of these components. Here are the steps:

1. Click on the Start button.

2. From the Edit menu, select and click on Bind property.

3. The PropertyName dialog box pops up.

4. In this box, select foreground.

5. Click OK.

Now you can see a red line starting from the Start button. Connect the line to the Stop button. The PropertyName dialog box pops up again. Because we want to bind the **foreground** property of the Start button to the **foreground** property of the Stop button, select foreground and click OK. Now click on the Start button once again and change the foreground in the property sheet window to blue.

You see that the foreground of the Stop button also changes to blue automatically. This is because the **foreground** property of the Stop button is bound to the **fore-ground** property of the Start button. The reverse, however, is not true. In other words, the foreground of the Start button is not bound to the foreground of the Stop button. So changing the foreground of the Stop button *does not* change the foreground of the Start button. Many other features of JavaBeans can be easily understood by experimenting with the BeanBox.

JavaBeans Versus ActiveX

Just as JavaBeans is the component architecture from JavaSoft, ActiveX is the component framework provided by Microsoft. Like JavaBeans, ActiveX has the characteristics of a component model: component interface exposure and discovery, event handling, persistence, layout control, and application builder support.

ActiveX provides a mechanism by which components can communicate with each other regardless of their implementation languages and platform. Note that this does not mean that ActiveX controls are portable; it just means that communication between controls on different platforms that support ActiveX is possible.

The elements making up ActiveX are ActiveX controls, ActiveX documents, ActiveX scripting, ActiveX server framework, and the JVM. For the following discussion to make sense, you need a thorough understanding of ActiveX. See Appendix A for more details on ActiveX.

Now that you know what JavaBeans is and what ActiveX is, let's see how they compare against each other vis-à-vis portability, security, availability, network support, and other such relevant factors so that you can make an informed decision about which technology to use.

Platform Support and Portability

Because JavaBeans is written in Java, JavaBeans runs on any platform for which the JVM exists. The JVM exists for most operating systems, so JavaBeans components will run across multiple platforms.

On the other hand, Microsoft supports ActiveX on the Windows platform only. Microsoft is working with other companies to provide a port of ActiveX to other platforms, including UNIX. One such company is the German software maker Software AG. ActiveX-based applications run best on the Windows platform because they take advantage of the Windows API. Even if the controls for different platforms are available and even if those platforms support ActiveX, if the application takes advantage of the Windows API, then a fair amount of porting needs to be done to execute it on any platform other than Windows. Thus, ActiveX-based applications are not truly cross-platform because they come with the penalty of having to rewrite at least some portion of the code to port it to different platforms.

Security

Perhaps the biggest area of concern regarding ActiveX is its security—or lack thereof. Anyone who has watched the news over the past few months has seen instance after instance of ActiveX's poor security model. The most famous of these exploits is ActiveX Exploder and the scare caused by the German Chaos Club when it transferred funds from one bank account to another without any clearances using ActiveX controls and banking software on the victim's PC.

To understand why applications written in ActiveX are not secure, whereas those written in JavaBeans are, you need to understand the security models of the two component architectures.

Because JavaBeans is written in Java, the JavaBeans security mechanism is tied to the Java security mechanism. Java provides security in the following ways:

- There are no pointers in Java. This prevents illegal memory access. Also, illegal typecasting is not allowed. Thus, even if the developer has made a genuine mistake, the mistake will be caught before the program is executed.

- Untrusted Java applets originating from the server cannot access the local (client) file system. In other words, applets cannot read from or write to a user's files. Applets can open connections only to the machine from which they originate (server). This model of security is the *sandbox model*.

JDK 1.1, on which JavaBeans is based, introduces the concept of digitally signed applets. Applets are digitally signed at the source; this tells the end user that the applet has come from the source untampered. JDK 1.1 allows digitally signed applets extended access to the user's system resources. As long as the applet comes from a trusted host, the user can run signed applets with the knowledge that they are safe; if the developer of these applets slipped up and the code tries to access memory that it is not supposed to, the Java security mechanism prevents it. Thus there is protection against malicious intents as well as genuine mistakes. And the user can run the downloaded applets with confidence.

On the other hand, the only security mechanism for ActiveX controls is digital signatures. As long as a control is digitally signed, the user knows that it has come from the source untampered; but once they are downloaded and run, these controls have full access to system resources.

ActiveX controls can introduce viruses or Trojan horses, erase the hard drive, and do other mischief. You can read more about some infamous mischief caused by the German Chaos Club in an article in the *New York Times* written by Todd Krieger. The URL for this article is `http://www.nytimes.com/library/cyber/week/021397activex.html`.

Software Distribution

In the case of ActiveX, application servers need to maintain a separate copy of each component for each supported platform. In the case of JavaBeans components, a single copy is sufficient. It will run on any platform.

Thin Client Environment

Because is it compact, JavaBeans can run on such small containers as the Java interpreter or the applet viewer. At the same time, it can run in such heavyweight containers as Netscape Navigator. To run an ActiveX component, you need heavyweight components like Microsoft Word or Internet Explorer. It is very difficult to run ActiveX controls in thin-client environments. The main thrust of network computers or thin clients is to reduce the total cost of ownership. Thus, JavaBeans is the way to go if thin clients are being considered.

Support for Distributed Computing

In a distributed computing environment, network connectivity must be provided for components to interact with components written in other languages. In the case of JavaBeans, CORBA provides this connectivity. Because CORBA is an industry standard object broker architecture, components written in JavaBeans can access components written in many languages hosted on a wide variety of platforms.

On the other hand, ActiveX controls rely on DCOM, which does not provide a linking mechanism to CORBA-based applications. Whereas CORBA is based on open technology, DCOM is not. Thus, applications written in ActiveX are locked up in proprietary technology.

Performance

Because Java-based applications are based on interpreted bytecode architecture, the JavaBeans components do not have the full power of native applications; that is, all the resources of the native platform are not available to the JavaBean components. Though this architecture allows packages to be downloaded and distributed over networks efficiently, because of lack of access to the native APIs, applications written in JavaBeans are slow.

ActiveX controls, on the other hand, have full access to the native APIs, and this is where they derive their power and speed from. Just-in-time compilers are being built to speed up Java applications. JavaSoft has acquired technology to speed up Java by at least twofold without the use of just-in-time compilers. Unless these technologies succeed in speeding up Java applications sufficiently, ActiveX-based applications have a definite edge as far as performance and speed are concerned.

Having said that, I must also mention that in interactive applications, speed is not the overriding concern. What is more important is ease of use, portability, and usability. For example, even though Visual Basic code depends on interpretation (making it slower compared to applications built using compiled code), what has made it so popular among developers is the ease with which interfaces can be built using this language. In the same way, JavaBeans makes the lives of developers and users easier by providing easier and faster ways of developing applications that are friendlier to use.

Availability

Many ActiveX controls currently exist in the market, so developers have access to a lot of controls to build their applications. Application development is fast when building from ActiveX components. Microsoft's Visual Basic 5.0 and Visual C++ 4.2 support ActiveX.

On the other hand, because JavaBeans is very young (it was released in February 1997), few JavaBeans components exist. As far as development environment is concerned, only JDK 1.1 provides support for creating JavaBeans applications. Symantec's Visual Cafe and Borland's JBuilder promise to add Bean support soon (perhaps by the time you read this book).

Interoperability

Bridges between JavaBeans and other existing component models such as Netscape ONE and ActiveX are planned by JavaSoft. In fact, JavaSoft recently provided a bridge between JavaBeans and ActiveX. The bridge can be downloaded from `http://splash.java-soft.com/beans/bridge/`.

On the other hand, because ActiveX controls have full system access, interoperability with almost any system available on the target platform is possible. As of this writing, this means interaction with any system on the Windows platforms only.

Which Technology to Use?

After reading the above sections, if you are unsure of which component model to choose, then read on. If the application will be deployed in a Windows-based environment, where network security is not so critical (say within an intranet) and where Windows is the only platform on which the application will run, then ActiveX is the way to go. On the other hand, if the application runs in a heterogeneous environment consisting of various platforms and security is critical (say over the Internet), then JavaBeans is the obvious choice.

Companies and Products Using JavaBeans

Many companies have announced development tools for JavaBeans. Table 7-1 provides a list of some of the companies and the products they plan to release that support JavaBeans in the near future. For more details on some of these products, refer to Chapter 13, "Java Development Tools."

Table 7-1 Products and companies that support JavaBeans

PRODUCT	COMPANY
SuperCede	Asymetrix
JBuilder	Borland
AppletAuthor	IBM
Mojo	Penumbra
Java Workshop	JavaSoft
Jato	Sybase
Visual Café	Symantec

Summary

The main idea behind network computers is to provide users with a low-cost option without sacrificing any of the existing functionality of PCs. For this to happen, applications need to be written for NCs. JavaBeans provides a framework by which compact, lightweight, platform-independent, and secure applications can be built. JavaBeans is one of the main components that will help NCs become mainstream. Applications written in JavaBeans will run on any platform, including an NC, as long as a JVM exists for that platform.

CHAPTER 8

The Distributed Object Model

The network-centric model is an extension of the client/server model. Objects are a natural fit to this new paradigm, upon which network computers are based. This chapter discusses the distributed object model, which is the underlying reason objects and networks can create a powerful computing environment. Interaction among objects provides a lot of flexibility in a program. The network will take this flexibility a degree further by allowing objects residing on different clients and servers to interact.

The two prevalent models for this type of interaction are the distributed component object model (DCOM) and common object request broker architecture (CORBA). Each model is discussed separately. There is also a section that helps you decide which model is the right one for your applications.

The Problem

Before discussing the details of any distributed object model, you must understand the problem. In a network environment, it is imperative for an application to be network aware and to communicate with the resources it needs via a network protocol. All modern database servers support a network protocol. Your database application uses a set of Application Programming Interfaces (APIs) to connect to a database, send a request, retrieve the results, and disconnect. All these operations require communication between two entities (in this case, a client and a server) via the network.

The same problem exists when you begin distributing objects over the network. Let's consider a simple Java applet that, for the sake of discussion, we consider a distributed object. This object is distributed by embedding it inside Web pages. Once it reaches its destination (which is a browser on your computer), it must connect back to a server to accomplish its task. Let's assume the task is as simple as getting the latest stock quote for a company and displaying it. How would you tackle this problem?

One typical solution is to write a common gateway interface (CGI) program and place it on the Web server. The applet would invoke that CGI program, grab its output (which is the stock quote), and display it. Another solution is for the Java applet to use sockets to open a connection back to the server and invoke a program that is listening to a particular socket port. It can then receive the stock quote and display it. Finally, the applet can execute a method of an object that is located on the server, as defined by the Java remote method invocation (RMI) standard, which might return the desired result. These solutions are shown in Figure 8-1.

What you face here is an array of solutions to a simple problem (an applet receiving data from a server). Different solutions have their own advantages and disadvantages. That's beside the point. What is important is that the solutions are not compatible. If the applet is using the Java socket mechanism to communicate with the server, then you cannot replace it with an applet that uses the CGI mechanism. The implementation is embedded in the object. This does not mean an applet cannot use multiple methods for its communication needs. However, once an applet is designed to use one method, it must be changed before it can use another method.

What is a needed is a standard to oversee object-to-object communication. A given object should be able to access and use services made available to it via the network. Implementation should be secondary. In other words, the object should not care whether the service is implemented in Java or C++ or any other language. The standard should take care of these details.

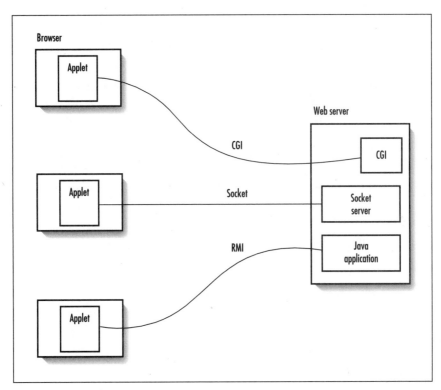

Figure 8-1 Applet-server communication

From a historic perspective, the proposed solution for interobject communication is a steady improvement over what has been happening in the network world. Web browsers provide a universal view of the static resources on the network. You can download an HTML page with some pictures embedded in it, regardless the platform you are in, the browser you are using, or the language your browser was written in. HTML forms give the browser more control over the request it is making. That request can be dynamic and include information specified by the user, such as an account number.

Scripting languages such as JavaScript, VBScript, and Java allow a server to serve out code to a client. This code can be an independent object that can then communicate with other objects and perform the needed task. Network computing and distributed object models build upon this. The next stage is incorporation of these objects into a component model such as ActiveX or JavaBeans (discussed in Chapter 9, "Electronic Commerce"). One standard that makes such a dynamic integration of objects possible is CORBA.

CORBA

CORBA was created by a consortium of more than 600 software companies under the name of Object Management Group (OMG). The initial effort began in the late 1980s, but aside from academic and large corporate IT houses, CORBA didn't gain much popularity. That has now changed. The importance of the network as a part of the computing infrastructure and the introduction of Java has shifted attention to the need for a standard for interobject communication across the enterprise and across the Internet. The commitment to CORBA has been reinforced by the incorporation of CORBA technology into several main product lines from industry leaders such as Oracle and Netscape. Additionally, JavaSoft has made a commitment to bringing CORBA and Java together.

CORBA divides a given object into a client part and a server part (see Figure 8-2). The server includes the actual implementation in whatever language under whatever operating system. The client invokes the methods and properties of the server object as if it were a local object. How is this possible if the client and server are in different languages? The common element among both is an Interface Definition Language (IDL), which is central to the operation of CORBA.

IDL is a declarative specification of the properties, boundaries, events, exceptions, and methods of an object. There are no implementation details and no coding in an IDL specification. You implement the IDL specification in a programming language such as C++, Smalltalk, or Java. The tough part is the creation of a bridge between the native language and IDL.

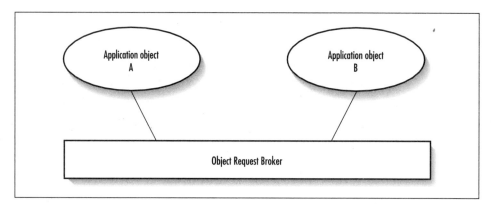

Figure 8-2 CORBA

This approach is not new to the computing world. The remote procedure call (RPC) standard implements something similar at the process level. CORBA is doing it at the object level. The heart of the approach is that you must bring a common factor into the maze and build upon that. The common factor in the case of CORBA is IDL (see Figure 8-3). IDL is similar in syntax to C++. It has some additions for taking care of network and distributed environments.

You can also think of CORBA as a way to manage objects and use them to accomplish a task. If you are managing a company, your employees all have a common factor: They work for your company. Furthermore, you interact with your employees through structures and defined methods. There are organizations with specific missions and responsibilities. All these help you to manage your company and its resources. For CORBA to be successful in managing objects, a similar infrastructure is needed. This is defined in the *Object Management Architecture* (OMA) *Guide*. Let's take a look at each part and see how it fits in the overall model.

Object Request Broker

The object request broker (ORB) is the road that connects objects together. It is a middleware between the client objects, the server objects, and CORBA services. CORBA 2.0 adds a specification to allow inter-ORB communication. Figure 8-4 shows the structure of an ORB.

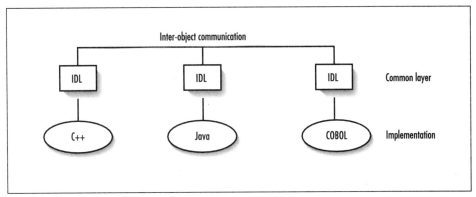

Figure 8-3 IDL is the common factor

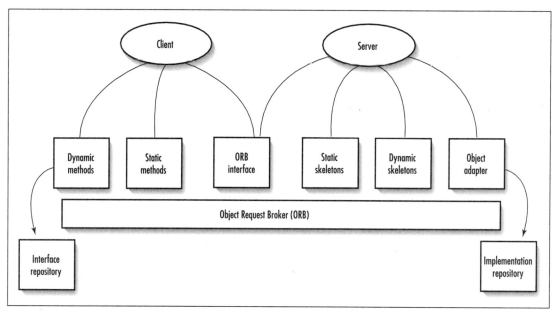

Figure 8-4   Structure of an ORB

An ORB is lot more sophisticated than other middleware solutions or peer-to-peer standards. With ORB, an object can discover other objects on the network and invoke their methods. This is done via an interface repository, which contains real-time information about all server objects. A client can probe this repository and find out how to invoke a certain method on the server object or how to use a particular service it provides.

The ORB also allows you to hide the details of implementation. A typical database vendor offers its API in a variety of languages under different operating system. The ORB treats the objects at a higher level (based on IDL). As far as the ORB is concerned, it is communicating with objects with IDL specifications. Their implementation detail is not a concern to the ORB. Based on this assumption, an ORB can accept requests for services. To understand how the ORB functions, divide its functionality into the client and server sides.

The Client Side

The CORBA client uses IDL stubs that are created at compile time by the IDL compiler. These are the static interfaces the client can use to access the services on the server. That is why IDL is so important. Without an IDL-defined stub, the service is not available to the client.

CORBA also includes the dynamic invocation interface (DII). This standard allows a client object to look for a suitable service at runtime. If such a service is found, the interface to that service, including its parameters, is generated dynamically. To facilitate this type of discovery scheme, CORBA uses an interface repository to store information about the available server interfaces. A set of APIs allows the client object to figure out what it needs to use an interface at runtime by studying the repository database. The interface repository uses repository IDs to identify objects on the network uniquely. This uniqueness is maintained even in systems that span multiple ORBs.

The Server Side

On the server side, skeletons or server IDL stubs are used for static interfaces to the services supported by the CORBA server. These stubs are generated by the IDL compiler.

Similar to the DII on the client, the server side has the dynamic skeleton interface (DSI). Its purpose is to facilitate handling runtime binding to services that do not have a static skeleton. By looking at the request, DSI can figure out which object and which object method must be invoked.

The bridge between a server object and the ORB is the object adapter. By requirement, each ORB must have at least a basic object adapter (BOA). The object adapter intercepts a given request, instantiates the server object for which the message is intended, and passes the request to it. It also acts as the police for the classes that it supports by registering them with the implementation repository. This repository is similar to the interface repository on the client side, except that it includes information about the implementations. The object adapter is responsible for creating an object instance out of the implementation class. The number of instances depends on how many requests the object adapter receives. The object adapter may also advertise the services it provides on the ORB.

Because any object activation on the server must go through the BOA, the BOA must support a variety of activation mechanisms to support different types of server applications. CORBA defines four activation methods. Note that this concerns how the BOA and the server object interact.

 Shared server: The BOA activates the server the first time a request comes in. Subsequent requests are handled directly by the server object. Even if the server implements more than one object, it is initialized only once and directly handles requests for its other objects.

 Unshared server: Under this scheme, each object resides in a different server. Therefore, each request is handled by the server serving the particular object.

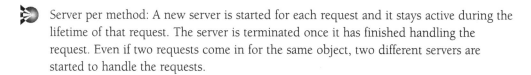

Server per method: A new server is started for each request and it stays active during the lifetime of that request. The server is terminated once it has finished handling the request. Even if two requests come in for the same object, two different servers are started to handle the requests.

Persistent server: With a persistent server, the server takes care of invocation and initialization of the objects when a request comes in. The BOA starts the server initially, but then routes all requests to a single server. This server, in turn, uses a scheduling mechanism to invoke the objects as needed.

For CORBA to be the answer to the global distributed object model, it must be able to handle ORB-to-ORB communication. In other words, the different object buses must be able to communicate with each other. To facilitate this type of interaction, CORBA has introduced the General Inter-ORB Protocol (GIOP). This specification covers the message formats and the data types used for communication between ORBs. It does not specify the underlying medium of communication.

The Internet Inter-ORB Protocol (IIOP) is a specification that deals with GIOP over a TCP/IP network, which happens to be the network upon which the Internet is based. All CORBA 2.0–compliant ORBs support IIOP. There is a third piece to the ORB-to-ORB communication: the Environment-Specific Inter-ORB Protocols (ESIOPs). ESIOPs are specific CORBA implementations over particular networks.

Common Object Services

A collection of 16 services is available to all CORBA objects. These services are not part of the ORB, but they are a complement to the function the ORB performs in the distributed architecture. They are also referred to as *CORBA services*.

Startup

This service allows you to customize the ORB by instructing it to start a request as soon as it starts. This feature comes in handy in ORB-to-ORB communication.

Security

CORBA security is implemented right on the bus. The first class of security is *authentication*. The authentication mechanism is based on a third-party model similar to Kerberos. The authenticated object is called a *principal*. This could be a user or another service. Once a principal is authenticated, a unique authenticated ID is assigned to that principal by the

ORB. This ID is automatically propagated so you can use other services for which you are authorized. Typically, you obtain a ticket for the services you want to use (and are authorized to use). You then present that ticket to the service before usage.

The second part of the security scheme involves checking for authorization. This is done through access control lists (ACLs). Once you are authorized to the system, an ACL can help the system determine whether you have the proper permission to access a particular service. Access controls add overhead to the system. You can generalize access controls by checking permissions for a collection of objects (*low overhead*) or you can invoke detailed permission checking for each method of an object (*high overhead*).

A security mechanism usually includes a logging or auditing facility. This allows a system manager to trace the events leading to a problem. It also has an inherent "go-away" effect if an intruder knows that his or her activities are being logged and perhaps monitored.

The last aspect of the security scheme involves encryption. Standards such as RSA, Kerberos, and NIS+ are supported, among many others. Encryption, along with digital signatures (a variation of encryption), achieves the following objectives:

- It ensures that message A came from party A.

- It ensures that message A was not tampered with.

- It ensures that message A can be read only by party B (the intended party).

Naming

A name is an identifier. Objects are known to the system by their object reference. This is not sufficient from a human perspective, because humans are used to names. The naming service in CORBA maps a name to an object reference. Object references are unique, but names may or may not be unique. CORBA uses the concept of naming contexts to define a boundary within which a given name is unique.

The naming contexts are arranged in a hierarchical structure, with the leaves comprising the actual names. To specify a name, you traverse the hierarchy from the top name context until you get to the naming context that includes the simple name. This combination of naming contexts and the simple name is called a *compound name* and is the basis for object names in CORBA. By connecting naming contexts across different domains, you can have global naming services encompassing more than one ORB.

Persistence

The idea behind the persistent object service (POS) is to provide a standard mechanism by which created objects can maintain their state as they move to different systems. Suppose you have a program that generates picture objects. If the picture it generates is green, then you expect that picture to stay green no matter where it is transported to. In a nondistributed object world, you store the properties of the object with the object itself. In a distributed world, things are a bit different. Maintaining state is still crucial, but how it is done is more complex. The idea of object persistence is depicted in Figure 8-5.

Now that the meaning of persistence is established, let's turn to possible implementations. What you really want to store is the data that describes the state of the object. This data can be stored in many places, including flat files and databases. The philosophy behind POS is that the storage method is transparent to the client. The client simply requests an object and it gets the object with its latest state. The details of storage mechanism are left up to the persistent object.

POS is composed of the following elements:

Persistent object: An object that stores its state is a persistent object. It must be defined as such in its IDL specification.

Persistent object manager: This layer is necessary because different methods of storage can be used to store persistence. To give a uniform view to the persistent object, this layer sits between the persistent object and the persistent data service (PDS).

Persistent data service: Every data source has a PDS associated with it. The PDS is responsible for routing the requests from the layer above it to the datastore.

Datastore: This is where the state information is actually stored. It can be a simple flat file, a relational database, an object database, or some other form. The layers above are used to provide a transparent view of the datastores to the client.

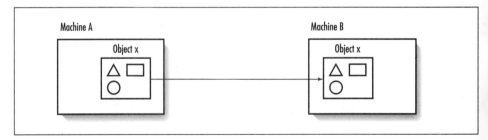

Figure 8-5 Persistent objects

Life Cycle

Objects have an artificial lifetime associated with them. Therefore a systematic service is needed to control the "life" of an object. The life cycle service oversees the creation, movement, and deletion of objects on the object bus. The complexity of this service becomes evident when you consider the relationships among the objects. If two objects have a parent-child relationship, then when the parent's life is terminated, the child must also go away (see Figure 8-6). For example, you may have a container object that holds a number of other objects (a folder with files in it). When the folder goes away, the files must also be removed. In a distributed environment, you can have a large number of objects with very complex relationships among them, making the life cycle service more important and at the same time more complex.

Properties

Properties are attributes of an object. When you define an object (using IDL), you also specify its properties. By changing the properties of an object during runtime, you can change its behavior. For example, the background color may be a property of a text object. Sometimes it is necessary to "attach" a property to an object at runtime. This property was not specified when the object was defined. The property service of CORBA addresses this issue.

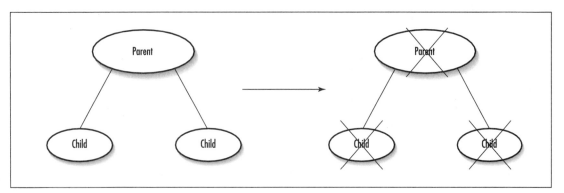

Figure 8-6 Life cycle

When you attach a property to an object, you have to associate a mode with it. Possible modes are

 Normal: There are no access restrictions on the property.

Read-only: The property can be read and removed, but cannot be updated.

Fixed: The property can be modified, but cannot be removed.

Fixed-read only: The property can only be read.

An example of using a dynamic property is when you need to perform a check on a number of objects. You may have a number of account objects and you need to make sure the balance in all of them is positive. You can define an attribute and set it to **TRUE** after you check each object.

Concurrency

Concurrent usage refers to a systematic manner of using a given resource, with one object having access to the resource at a given time. CORBA does not care what the resource is. The resource can be a file, another object, or a stream, among many other things. Control over concurrency is accomplished by using a locking mechanism. A lock is like a ticket that gives an object the exclusive right to use a resource. Once the object is done, it releases the lock (gives up the ticket) and the resource becomes available for another object. This is shown in Figure 8-7.

As with objects themselves, the concurrency control service can manage a group of locks placed on a resource. This group of locks is called a *lockset*.

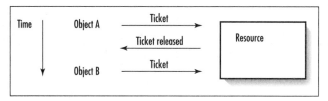

Figure 8-7 Concurrent usage of resources

Collection

Some of the operations performed on objects are group operations. The collection service encompasses these group operations. Examples of groups or collections are structures such as queries, stacks, and sets. The collection service provides a common approach to the creation and manipulation of such groups of objects.

Trader

The trader service allows an object to advertise itself and its services on the ORB. It has been compared to the Yellow Pages phonebook. The exact nature of this service is yet to be finalized.

Externalization

An object is a dynamic entity. It can change. The ability to take an object out of its existing environment and bring it into another is an important part of distributed objects and distributed computing. The externalization service allows you to save and retrieve an object.

Streams are used as the means to save and retrieve internal object data. Most programmers are familiar with streams. The typical externalization operation involves saving an object to a stream, which is stored on a disk, on a network file server, or in memory. That stream can be taken to another environment (even outside the ORB). Internalization then re-creates the original object in the same state from the stream. Streamable objects must implement a number of methods used by the externalization service.

Event Service

An event is an occurrence within an object. In a distributed environment, it becomes imperative for the events to become distributed. CORBA classifies objects into suppliers and consumers of events. A supplier is an object that generates an event. A consumer is an object that has an interest in that event. The consumer usually performs some specific tasks once it is notified of the event. The code responsible for these specific tasks is called *event handlers*. The relationship between the consumer and the supplier is shown in Figure 8-8.

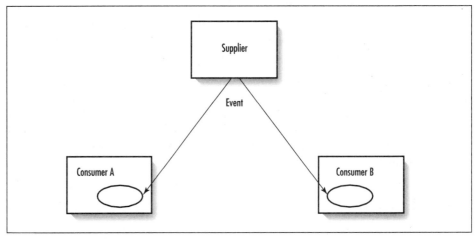

Figure 8-8 Supplier-consumer relationship

The relationship is similar to how objects in an application framework communicate. Almost all graphical user interface (GUI) frameworks such as Windows and Motif are based on the event model. CORBA takes the event model a step further by providing a general event service for all objects on the bus.

Another part of the event model involves the direction of event data transfer. In the push model, the object that generates the event also sends the data associated with the event to interested parties (consumers). This data can be as simple as the fact that the event occurred. It may also have some additional information about the event that is event specific. In the pull model, the consumer must explicitly request the data associated from the event.

Here is a simple example of how an event may work. Suppose there are two objects. One is a spreadsheet object and the other is a graphing object that draws a graph based on the data in the spreadsheet. When the data in the spreadsheet changes, an event is generated by the spreadsheet. The graphing object is a consumer of this event. It receives the event and perhaps checks the data on the spreadsheet and redraws the graph based on the new data. In a distributed environment, you can create complex relationships among objects using the distributed event model.

Transactions

Transactions are important in any business model. CORBA provides the object transaction service (OTS) that combines some of the best features of different transaction systems. A good example of a transaction is using your bank card to receive money from an ATM. The ATM must dispense a certain amount of money and subtract that amount from your bank account and from its own collection. The transaction is not complete unless all the parts verify they have done their part. This is depicted in Figure 8-9. For example, in a broken transaction, your account may be debited, but the ATM machine never dispenses that amount. A transaction model ensures that the above scenario does not happen.

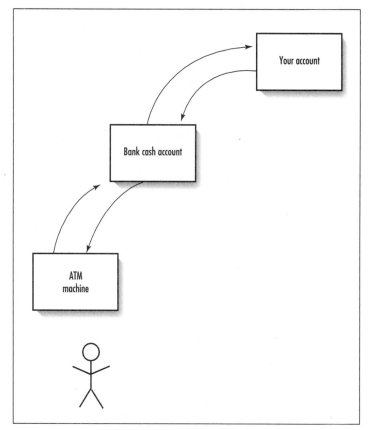

Figure 8-9 A sample transaction

The OTS divides a transaction among three different objects. The first is a transactional client, which is the object initiating the transaction. This could be a Java applet that accepts a merchandise order. The next piece is the transactional server. Objects of this type act as a middleman between the client and the server. Their own resources are not affected by the transaction, but they have the ability to terminate a transaction. The last piece is the recoverable server, such as a database. A piece of data under the control of the recoverable server will change due to the transaction. For example, the bank database will debit your account when you receive money from an ATM.

One more point about transactions. Due to the nature of a transaction, all participants must approve or disapprove of the transaction. A transaction is not complete unless all participants verify they have done their piece of the work. What will happen if a participant does not provide an approval? In a flat model, the entire transaction becomes void and must be reinitiated from the beginning. In a nested model, if a nested transaction fails, only the failed part must be repeated. CORBA's OTS supports both models.

Query

Queries are a standard mechanism to find data matching certain criteria. In the object world, you can query a collection of objects to find the one matching the properties you specify. In a distributed world, you can have several collections subject to your query. The object query service performs the search in each collection and combines the results.

Some of the supported query languages are Object Query Language (OQL) and Structured Query Language 3 (SQL3). The query service not only allows you to search collections, it also allows you to create and manipulate collections. The result of a search can be a collection itself.

In CORBA, a query evaluator performs the evaluation on its objects. A database engine is a query evaluator. The query manager allows you to manipulate (manage) a query object. A query object can perform any of the following four operations:

- Compile a query.

- Execute a compiled query.

- Get the status of the query.

- Get the result of the query.

Queries can be nested. A query selects a number of objects and places them into a collection. That collection itself is then queried. The object that holds the intermediate results is a `QueryableCollection` object.

Relationships

Object-oriented programming is based on the relationships that exist among the objects in an application. Realizing this importance, CORBA has introduced the relationship service. Using this service, you can dynamically link objects together by providing a relationship among them. The objects themselves need not be aware of this relationship.

Relationships can be studied in terms of the roles of the entities involved in the relationship. Two common roles are directly supported by CORBA. They are containment (see Figure 8-10) and references (see Figure 8-11). In a containment relationship, an object is "contained" inside another. Most component models use this type of relationship. In a reference relationship, an object merely makes a reference to another object. For the relationship to make sense, both objects must exist.

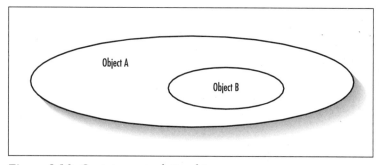

Figure 8-10 Containment relationship

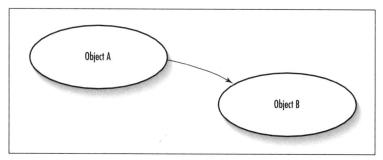

Figure 8-11 Reference relationship

Time

The time service is a service for giving all objects a common frame of reference. Aside from the not-so-simple task of providing the current time to objects that request it, the service is also involved in synchronization and coordination efforts among the objects if such intervention is needed. The most common usage, however, is for a universal service to provide a time to objects.

Licensing

How we buy and use software is affected in a network-centric environment. With the help of technologies such as CORBA and component models such as ActiveX and JavaBeans, you can put together an application by simply connecting the appropriate objects.

To facilitate this type of software development, CORBA provides a licensing service. This service allows you to use a variety of licensing methods for your components. For example, you may want to provide a license based on the number of times your component is invoked or the length of time it was used. A licensed component generates an event when it is being used. This event is consumed by the licensing server. The server can then instruct the client to check the license at certain time intervals or whenever it receives such a request from the server. This allows the server to "keep an eye" on the licensed client. Once the client is finished, the server invokes a method to announce that it is done with the licensed component.

Common Facilities

The common facilities, or *CORBA facilities,* are components that support application objects. The specification divides these facilities into two categories. The first category deals with horizontal interactions among application objects. It includes the following:

- User interface

- Information management

- Systems management

- Task management

The second category deals with vertical applications such as those used in the telecommunication, financial, or retail organizations. The common facilities will continue to be modified and enhanced as more client/server schemes become compatible and interpretable with CORBA.

Application Objects

Application objects are also referred to as *business objects*. These are objects specific to an application that could become available to other objects via the ORB. The OMG is still working on these business objects. Its goal is to come up with some generic business objects that could be used in any application. An object would be a car, a tax form, or a customer. Typically, an application object would fall under one of the following three categories:

- Business object: Encompasses a business model and provides the interfaces to the abstract model

- Business process: Encompasses a business process and the logic associated with that process (when to give a discount on an item is an example)

- Business presentation: Encompasses how a business object is presented visually to the user

IDL

IDL is the link that makes CORBA work. The main concept behind IDL is the use of metadata. This metadata can later be used to find information about the object and use it in a dynamic manner. Some literature refers to this feature as *self-describing* because the IDL definition can be viewed as a description of the object. The metadata is stored in the interface repository.

IDL is based on C++ syntax. It is strictly a declarative language, so don't expect to find control structures and procedure support in IDL. IDL can be used to describe the server object and the client interface. This type of description is useful to both the clients that use the server object and developers who want to extend the functionality of the server object itself.

An IDL file is composed of four parts:

- Module: This is the name space under which the class definitions fall. The keyword **module** is used to denote this section.

- Interface: An interface is similar to a class definition without the implementation. An interface specifies the methods that can be invoked and the properties that can be set or unset. Interfaces also usually define exceptions that indicate the successful or unsuccessful nature of the operations. Inheritance among interfaces is supported using a syntax similar to C++.

Operation: An operation is CORBA's language for what is commonly known as a method in the object-oriented literature. This is the method that can be called by the client. The parameters a method expects and the result it returns are called the operation's *signature*. Each parameter has a mode that can be one of the following. If the parameter value is passed from the client to the server, it is an *in type*. If the parameter value is passed from the server to the client, it is an *out type*. If the parameter value can be passed both ways, it is an *inout type*. Error detection is done by defining exceptions that are raised when an operation fails.

 Data type: This is similar to data type specifications in any language. A data type is a definition of accepted values for an entity. This includes parameters, return values, and exceptions. CORBA supports two levels of data types. The basic types are **sort**, **long**, **unsigned long**, **unsigned short**, **float**, **double**, **char**, **Boolean**, and **octet**. The constructed types include **string**, **struct**, **array**, **union**, **enum**, **sequence**, and **any**.

The metadata described by IDL is stored in an interface repository. The ORB has stubs that are generated at compile time for static method invocations. For dynamic invocation, the interface repository is needed to do type checking of method signatures and provide information about the interfaces at runtime to interested parties. The interface repository is important in the implementation of ORB-to-ORB interfaces.

DCOM

Notably absent from the Object Management Group is Microsoft. That is because Microsoft has its own distributed object model built on top of object linking and embedding (OLE) and the component object model (COM). This section is an overview of this model. It is likely that the gap between CORBA and DCOM will partially vanish via wrappers or translator gateways. However, due to inherent differences within the object models, complete interoperability between the two cannot be achieved.

DCOM is the object bus for OLE objects. It is similar to the ORB. An IDL is used to describe the objects without dealing with their implementations. Microsoft's IDL is not compatible with CORBA's IDL. DCOM supports a second definition language called Object Definition Language (ODL). Support for both static and dynamic method invocation is provided. The type library is similar to the interface repository and contains the description of ODL-defined objects.

The purpose of any object bus is to provide access to the objects on the bus. More specifically, the object bus allows the client to invoke a particular method on the server object. With DCOM, access to server object methods is provided via a table of pointers known as the *virtual table* (see Figure 8-12). This table contains function pointers to the different interfaces available from the server. A client object uses a pointer to the virtual table, which in turn points to a function that is the implementation method for the requested service.

During runtime, all interfaces are known by a unique interface identifier (IID). The server object on the bus is an OLE object or a Windows object. An OLE object is a component that supports one or more interfaces as defined by the object's class. Each class is identified by a unique class ID.

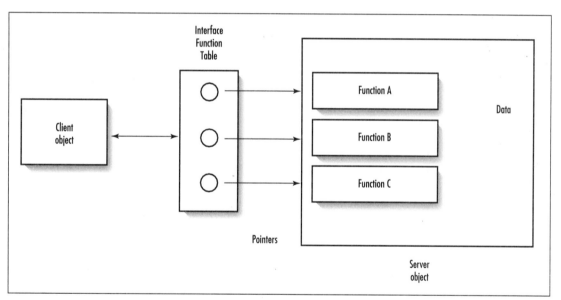

Figure 8-12 DCOM object invocation

DCOM Servers

A DCOM server is a dynamic link library (DLL) or an executable file that contains one or more classes. When a client wishes to invoke one of these object classes, the object bus loads the server, which in turn creates an object of the requested class. After the object is created, a pointer to its interface is sent back to the client. DCOM servers fall into one of the following three categories:

> In-process servers: These servers are executed under the process space of the client that requests the object. Typically they are implemented as a DLL.

> Local servers: The server executes in a different process space than the client. COM's lightweight RPC (LRPC) is used to communicate with the client.

> Remote servers: The server executes on a different process on a different machine than the client that requested it.

You may wonder how a function pointer can span to a different machine or a different process space. DCOM uses a proxy object to handle the translation.

DCOM Services

To support an interface negotiation, every DCOM and OLE object implements the three **IUnknown** member functions. The first of these functions is **QueryInterface**. During the initial object invocation, an interface pointer is returned. Information about additional interfaces is obtained by calling the **QueryInterface** member function and passing the IID as the parameter. If the interface is not supported, a failure code is returned. Another use of **QueryInterface** is compatibility with older objects. A client can ask an object (using **QueryInterface**) whether it supports a particular interface. Depending on the answer, the client knows which version of the object it is dealing with and can adjust accordingly.

The second and third **IUnknown** member functions are **AddRef** and **Release**. These functions are used to manage the life cycle of an object. When a client gets a pointer to an interface, it calls the **AddRef** function of the interface. When the client is done with that interface, it calls its **Release** function.

Another service provided by DCOM involves object creation and licensing. This service is provided by mandating that all DCOM classes implement a class factory. A DCOM server can then use the factory to create an instance of the class. There are two kinds of factory interfaces: **IClassFactory** and **IClassFactory2**. **IClassFactory** has two member functions. The **CreateInstance** function creates an uninitialized instance of the object associated with the class factory. The **LockServer** function allows a client to keep the server in memory, or in effect placing a lock on it. The **IClassFactory2** is an extension of **IClassFactory** that adds three new functions that deal with licensing issues: **GerLicInfo**, **RequestLicKey**, and **CreateInstanceLic**.

DCOM uses connectable objects as the basis for its event model. Through ODL, a DCOM object can define what events it supports. An object can create an event or listen for an event. Objects that create events are called *sources*. Their events are considered outgoing events. Objects that listen for particular events are called *sinks* or event handlers.

Another interesting fact regarding DCOM objects is that they don't directly support multiple inheritance. The ODL does not directly support them either. Two mechanisms allow you to get around this limitation. In both methods, a *parent component* encapsulates a number of inner components and provides an interface to the outside world. In the aggregation mode, the parent component exposes the interfaces of the components it is encapsulating. Clients can directly call the methods of these components. In the delegation mode, the parent component receives all requests from clients and then sends them to the appropriate component inside.

DCOM supports dynamic invocation of object methods. To facilitate that, an object must implement the **Idispatch** interface and its member functions. This will allow a client to access and retrieve information about an object during runtime. The four member functions of **Idispatch** are

Invoke: Maps an incoming dispID to a method call that lets you dynamically invoke the methods exposed by the object. dispID stands for dispatch identifier and uniquely identifies a method or a property. dispIDs are generated by DCOM ODL.

GetIDOfNames: Converts text names of a method to its equivalent dispID, which can then be passed on to **Invoke** to call the method.

GetTypeInfoCount: Returns whether type information is available for this dispID.

GetTypeInfo: Retrieves the type information for the specified dispinterface (dispatch interface).

Microsoft has developed a tight integration of its object model and its operating system. Microsoft will continue on this road and therefore will enhance the services offered by its object bus. It is already setting up the framework for transaction processing. All these services will be supported by the operating system as well as the object model. ActiveX (the component framework based on DCOM) is discussed in Appendix A. As far as users are concerned, ActiveX brings life to DCOM as the underlying object bus. ActiveX to DCOM is what OLE is to COM.

DCOM ODL

Just as CORBA-compliant objects do, DCOM-compliant objects require that you write an interface definition. The specification language is called ODL. The structure is similar to IDL.

The library section defines the name of your library. This is a library of objects and therefore exists under the defined name space. Each library has a global unique identifier (GUID). The **importlib** section allows you to specify another library whose content you want to import into the current library. To use OLE's standard automation types, you usually import **stdole32.tbl**.

The interface section defines the signature of the member functions. Each signature includes the name, the return type, and a list of parameters that it expects. A variable number of parameters is supported. To handle dynamic interfaces, the **dispinterfaces** section lists the properties and methods of these "dispatchable" interfaces.

The last section is the **coclass** section, which is merely a listing of all interfaces for a class. The class is identified by its GUID. This is the place where you specify the class type. For example, a class can be an application object or a control object.

Using the MIDL compiler, you can compile your ODL file and generate a type library file that is then used by the object bus during runtime to access the information about the different interfaces and their properties.

Summary

In a world of distributed objects, it is essential to define standards of communication among the objects. Two leading standards are CORBA and DCOM. Although they attempt to solve the same problem, their approach and implementation are quite different.

CORBA provides an object bus, a client piece, and a server piece. The client and service pieces are based on definitions in an IDL file. The bus (ORB) provides a number of common services that are available to objects on the bus if they are needed. Such services include transactions, querying, naming, timing, properties, persistence, life cycle management, and concurrency. As a result, CORBA provides a complete solution to distributed object models. At the same time, the design is independent from implementation, language, and platform.

DCOM is the object model from Microsoft that is an extension of COM and OLE. Microsoft's ActiveX technology is based on DCOM. References to functions within objects are made through a table of function pointers.

Electronic Commerce

The Internet has been around for more than a decade. The commercialized Internet is much younger. In a business-driven society, it is important to make commerce activities simple and convenient. You will find a similar theme in the financial trends of the past few years, such as check cards and telephone banking. The Internet and the technology it brings have opened up a new spectrum of possibilities. The computer network can break geographical barriers and allow sellers and buyers to connect in unprecedented ways.

Electronic commerce is in its infancy, but its growth is almost unavoidable, and one of the main catalysts is the network computer and the network-centric model. There are successful examples of online shopping on the Web. Financial institutions are taking their business to the Web. Another new front is the network appliance market, which can be used to facilitate catalog shopping just as the telephone does today.

The missing element in electronic commerce is a standard financial framework. The Internet enables a merchant to reach millions of customers, but without a consistent framework, commercial transactions with all those customers are not possible. That would be like installing a national network for credit card usage, but then issuing a separate credit card for each state!

This chapter looks at some of the existing financial frameworks. In particular, the Java Commerce Application Programming Interface (API) and secure electronic transaction (SET) are discussed.

Simple Transaction Framework

Perhaps the simplest approach for Web commerce is the integration of existing technologies (mainly credit cards) with the Web (see Figure 9-1). Many shopping sites are successfully using this type of framework.

Rich, multimedia content is used to show the products, and HTML forms are used to capture order information from the visitor. That information is then put into ordinary verification channels for credit cards. To address security concerns about the transmission of credit card information over the Web, the Secure Socket Layer (SSL) protocol

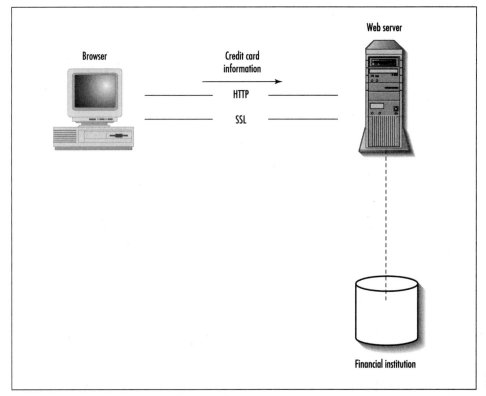

Figure 9-1 Simple transaction framework

usually is used. Through a combination of private and public keys and certificates, the authenticity of both the client and the server can be verified.

This simple framework fulfills the needs of many merchants and is the most common framework used today. Its drawback is that it is based on the integration of a new technology (the Web) and older technologies (credit cards). It has all the problems credit card transactions have and some of its own.

Third-Party Framework

To eliminate the transfer of credit card numbers over the Web and provide a complete commerce solution, several vendors have introduced a different framework, the *third-party framework*. The most notable is the one from CyberCash (`http://www.cybercash.com`). CyberCash offers a solution that has three different components:

- CyberCash Wallet

- Secure Merchant Payment System

- CyberCash Gateway Server

Figure 9-2 shows the interaction of these components. The CyberCash Wallet is a software component that resides on the client. During the installation process, the user binds his or her credit card information with the CyberCash Wallet and generates a CyberCash Wallet ID. This ID is all that is needed to identify the payment tool used. This payment tool is usually a credit card, but it may be electronic cash or other tools as they become available.

The secure merchant payment system (SMPS) is a server that works in conjunction with the Web server. It can communicate with the CyberCash Wallet using an encrypted channel and grab the wallet ID. The final piece is the CyberCash Gateway Server, which communicates to a banking system, validates the wallet ID, and checks for authorization. With an approval, the SMPS generates an electronic invoice that is sent back to the wallet. This completes the transaction.

Although the CyberCash method is more secure than simply transmitting credit card numbers, it does not address the real problem behind electronic commerce: universality. Not all merchants have or use the SMPS and not all consumers have the

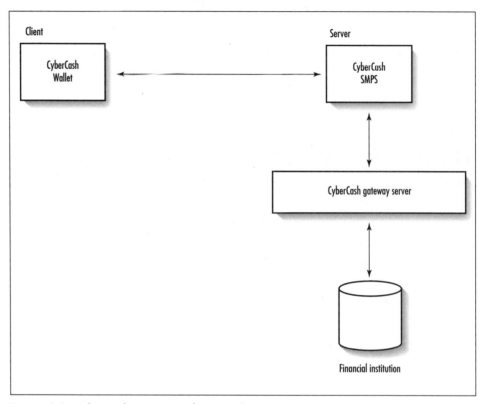

Figure 9-2 CyberCash commerce framework

CyberCash Wallet installed. The model warrants further discussion; a coalition of companies has taken a major step toward standardizing the third-party model by introducing the SET specification.

Secure Electronic Transaction

Secure electronic transaction (SET) is a standard created for secure transactions over the Internet. Its primary creators are Visa and MasterCard; the protocol is geared toward credit card payments. Many software and financial organizations were involved in the standard process, so SET has firm backing from the industry.

The model divides an electronic transaction into three parts:

Cardholder: The consumer who wants to purchase something

Merchant: The seller of the item or the service

Acquirer: The financial organization behind the transaction (for example, a bank or a credit card company)

As shown in Figure 9-3, SET not only covers the interaction among these three players, it also deals with a certification mechanism so each component of the model can trust the others.

A typical online shopping session may include browsing different catalogs and getting prices. At some point, the customer must initiate payment. This is where SET comes into play. It takes care of sending the virtual payment to the merchant. It also takes care of the validation step that occurs between the merchant and the financial institution. Finally, after shipping the product, the merchant uses SET to transfer money from the customer to the merchant's account.

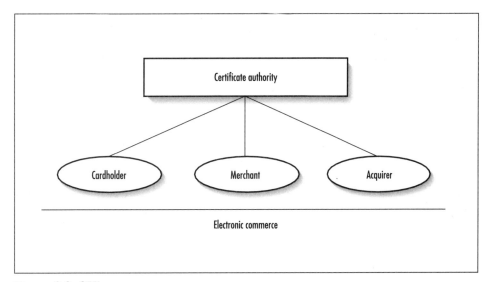

Figure 9-3 SET components

Use of Certificates

SET relies on a certificate system in addition to a public/private key encryption scheme. Each component of SET has a private and a public key associated with it. The security model depends on the fact that the private key stays private. In other words, it is assumed that access to private keys is restricted.

Based on the mathematical model behind public/private key encryption, a piece of data encrypted using the private key can be decrypted only with the associated public key. Private keys are assumed to stay exclusive to each entry. The public key, on the other hand, is in the open. By carrying a certificate, an entity can be sure that a given public key indeed belongs to its owner and is not fake. This is depicted in Figure 9-4.

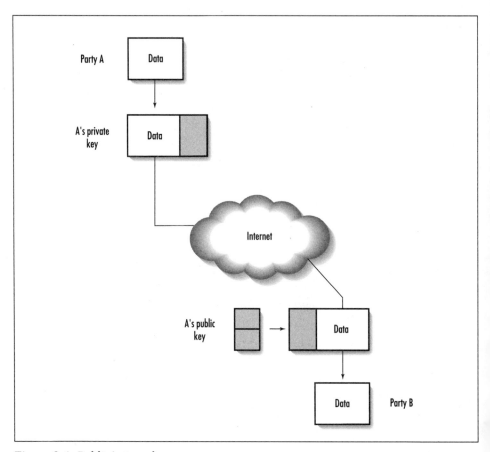

Figure 9-4 Public/private key

The card holder certificate contains the account information of the customer. Only the acquirer can decrypt the data and extract the account information. This reduces fraud because the merchant has no access to the account information.

The merchant requires a key pair for encryption purposes and another key pair for digital signatures. The digital signature authenticates the merchant to the acquirer. The encryption is used for secure transmission of data between the merchant and the acquirer. A merchant may have additional key pairs if it must interface with more than one acquirer.

Similarly, the acquirer also must possess two key pairs. One authenticates the acquirer to the card holder and to the merchant. The other is used for secure transmission of data.

SET relies on a chained certificate system. There is a "root" certificate authority and it has a number of certificate authorities branching out of it that act as its delegates.

Using the above scheme, SET provides a framework for electronic commerce that has the following properties:

- Confidentiality: Using public/private key pairs and the associated encryption algorithm, data transmission stays secure. Information such as card number and amount of purchase is available only to authorized components of the transaction. This is shown in Figure 9-4.

- Integrity: Using digital signatures, SET assures that the content of the data is not tampered with or changed during the transmission. This is shown in Figure 9-5.

- Authenticity: Using certificates, SET provides a mechanism by which each component can authenticate messages received from other components and act on them accordingly. This is shown in Figure 9-6.

Extensive documentation on SET is available at **http://www.visa.com**. The final version consists of three books. The first covers the business model of SET. The second is the programmer's guide to SET implementation. The third is the formal definition of the protocol. A reference implementation of the standard is also available at the Web site.

If your application requires electronic commerce, then you should seriously consider SET. It is an industry standard and it integrates nicely with Java's solution to electronic commerce, which is described in the next section.

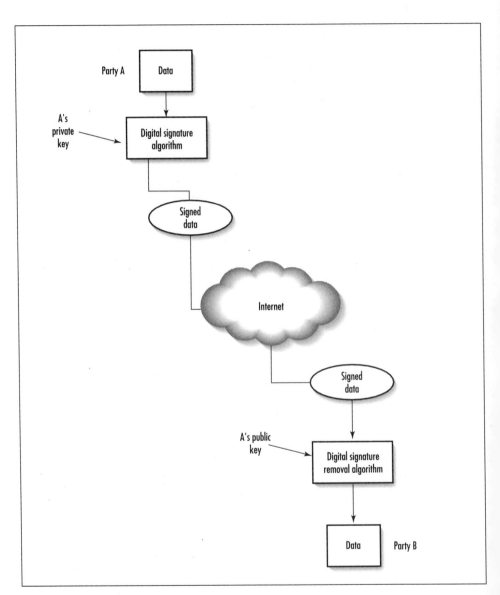

Figure 9-5 Digital signatures

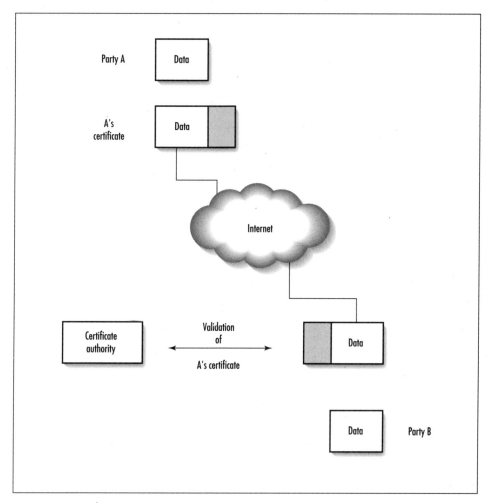

Figure 9-6 Authentication

The Java Solution

The frameworks discussed thus far work in any Web environment, and most network computers support a Web browser capable of SSL-based transactions. As the primary application language for NC, Java must also address electronic commerce. Although it can rely on other Web-based frameworks, to take advantage of its capabilities, it needs its own framework. JavaSoft's answer to this need is the Java Commerce API. This set of specifications and APIs gives the programmer the tools needed to create secure, interactive, and robust commerce applications using Java.

Based on this framework, a wide variety of applications are possible. Commerce API not only supports online catalog shopping, it can also be used for business-to-business financial transactions, service transactions, and internal billing applications. Because the framework is based on Java, such applications can be executed on any platform that supports Java, including the network device market.

The Java Commerce Toolkit consists of the following components:

- Java Wallet

- Java Cassettes

- Java Shopping Cart

The architecture is similar to that of CyberCash. The Java Wallet is an applet that acts as the user interface to the financial transaction. Because it is a Java program, it is fully customizable. It can integrate with Java Beans and use prebuilt components to create a rich user interface. Wallet implementations are a major part of the security architecture of the Java electronic commerce framework (JECF). The wallet includes monitoring and auditing tools so the owner of the wallet can control where the money is going and refer to logs for resolving any disputes.

The wallet's server counterpart is a Java Cassette. A cassette implements a particular online transaction protocol. Due to the cassette's open interface, vendors can create their own cassettes to be used with their existing transaction system. According to documentation from JavaSoft, the initial release of the Commerce Toolkit will include the following cassettes:

- Credit Card transaction (SET compliant)

- Mondex protocol

- CyberCash CyberCoin

The benefit of an open wallet-cassette architecture (see Figure 9-7) is that merchants can create an application suited for their own environment based on their existing systems. The Commerce Toolkit also includes a Java shopping cart for those types of applications that may require one. In principle, the shopping cart is almost identical to what is available at many catalog shopping sites today.

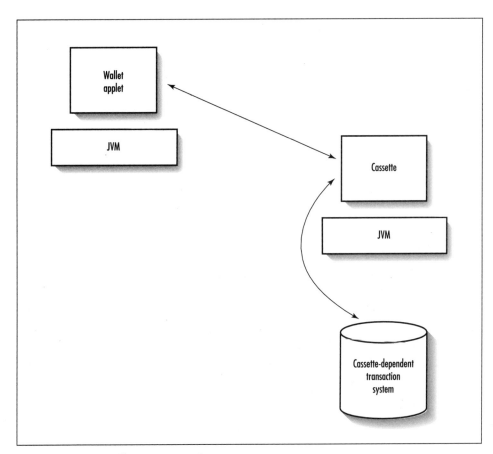

Figure 9-7 Java wallet-cassette architecture

JavaSoft has also introduced the Java Card API. This is a new set of APIs for writing applications that work with smartcards. Recall that Reference Profile 1 considers support for smartcards an optional feature. Smartcards promise to play a major role in network computing and the device market. Rather than using a Java Wallet applet, you can interface with the JECF using your smartcard. This means you don't have to be in front of your computer to engage in electronic commerce.

Security

JECF is based on the security model of Java itself. It also has an extra layer that deals with commerce-related security. Using the security scheme in JDK 1.1, wallet applets can be signed, and a signed applet can have access to local or network-based storage media. As a result, information about the user can be stored in encrypted files that the wallet can access. Note that such a scheme is not possible without the ability to distinguish between signed and unsigned applets.

Additionally, JECF uses a small database to store transaction-related information and user information. For example, the cassette needs to access this database to initiate and complete a transaction. The security model overseeing this type of transaction is the Java commerce gateway security model. A permission scheme is used to validate requested operations. The model defines three roles: user, owner, and maintainer. Depending on the operation and the information provided, a particular transaction with the database is allowed or disallowed.

One important point must be made regarding the database. Most online transactions are expected to have an interface to an existing non-Java transaction system (for example, a bank credit card validation system). It is imperative that the application synchronize the content of the database with other systems. In other words, if a transaction is not completed (for whatever reason), then this should be noted in the database logs. For example, if you use your Java Wallet to pay a bill, it is up to the application (the wallet) to make sure the transaction is recorded in the database correctly. This decision takes the burden off the non-Java transaction systems and places it in the hands of the Java-based applications. The design works well only when data consistency is maintained in a distributed network. The present infrastructure and technology are not at the level needed for full-blown Java-based commerce, but it is moving in the right direction.

The Commerce API

The pre-alpha release of the API includes the following packages:

- `java.commerce.base`

- `java.commerce.cassette`

- `java.commerce.database`

- `java.commerce.gui`

- `java.commerce.log`

- `java.commerce.merchant`

`java.commerce.set`

 `java.commerce.util`

Summary

Electronic commerce is a major component of network-based computing. Its feasibility relies on the assumption that computers and network devices will use the Internet to communicate with each other and to break the geographical barriers of traditional commerce activities.

The simplest model is an integration model in which the Web and traditional commerce channels such as credit card payments are linked together. This is the most common method deployed today. Its drawback is that it is integrating a new technology with an old technology. Security is another concern because many people are reluctant to enter their credit card number on a Web page.

CyberCash is an advocate of the third-party model. CyberCash provides software for the consumer, the merchant, and the financial institution. When all three use the same system, CyberCash guarantees a secure and reliable scheme for online commerce. The drawback is that not everyone has CyberCash software.

To remedy the problem, a committee consisting of Visa, MasterCard, and a number of other financial and software companies has defined secure electronic transaction (SET). SET deals with a card holder, a merchant, and an acquirer. It uses encryption, digital signatures, and certificates to maintain security and reliability throughout a transaction.

JavaSoft has introduced Java Electronic Commerce Framework (JECF), which provides Java applications with a consistent interface for performing online commerce. The Commerce Toolkit includes a wallet, a cassette, and a shopping cart. Consistent interfaces and classes are used to complete a transaction. Aside from its own security framework, JECF also relies on the security model inherent within Java.

Computer Telephony Integration

CHAPTER **10**

Computers and telephones are fundamentally different technologies. They do have one common element, however: the use of a network. Computer telephony integration (CTI) applications have really picked up in recent years. Anytime you call a customer-service center, chances are CTI is being used. This chapter provides an overview of CTI and some of its applications. The majority of the material is devoted to the Java telephony Application Programming Interface (API), which shows a lot of promise in network devices and call-center applications, both of which are a target market of network computers.

What Is CTI?

You have just received your credit card statement and you notice a charge you don't recognize. You pick up your telephone and call the customer-service center. After a few rings, you are connected to a representative. At the same time, the representative's computer monitor shows all the information about you. He or she may ask you for your name for verification purposes. You explain your problem and the representative finds the discrepancy in your records and credits your account accordingly.

The above scenario is so commonplace, you may not think about how the two components (telephone call and customer data) come together instantly. This is what CTI does. Actually, this is just one of the applications of CTI. There are many others.

Let's dissect the above scenario and see how it works. When you make a phone call, the call is routed through a gigantic network commonly called the *telephone network* or the *public switched telephone network*. This is a collection of switches scattered throughout the country operated by local and long distance companies. This giant network routes millions of telephone calls on a daily basis. When you pick up the phone to call a friend, your voice travels through this network and reaches your friend's telephone. Addressing on this network is done by the phone numbers you use. A phone number is unique in the network.

When the call reaches the customer-service center, a PBX (which is a switch) gets the call and routes it to the proper internal telephone inside the center. In the case of a call center, it is usually the next available telephone. Figure 10-1 shows this network and its main components. Please be aware that telecommunication networks are much more complex than what the figure shows.

So far, you have not seen a trace of a computer network in this picture. Do you remember caller ID hitting the market a few years ago? With caller ID, the PBX can determine the phone number from which the call is coming. Because phone numbers are unique, that information can be used to search a customer database. Your record can then be retrieved and sent to the same computer station the call is being sent to. A CTI server makes this integration possible, as shown in Figure 10-2.

A CTI server takes the caller ID information from the PBX. It can then perform a database search and retrieve the appropriate customer record. Note that this database can be a remote database and does not need to reside on the CTI server. It will then use a mapping table to figure out which agent station it should send the customer's record to. The representative gets a phone call from you, and your customer information appears on the representative's screen.

The CTI server is unique because it must communicate with two separate networks: the telephone network and the computer network. The connection to the computer network is usually based on TCP/IP. The connection to the PBX can be a proprietary protocol from the switch manufacturer or a TCP/IP connection if the switch supports it.

CTI applications are numerous. One example is the call-center application discussed above. Other popular applications are voice-response systems. These are the applications that take you through a menu (press 1 to do x, press 2 to do y, and so on)

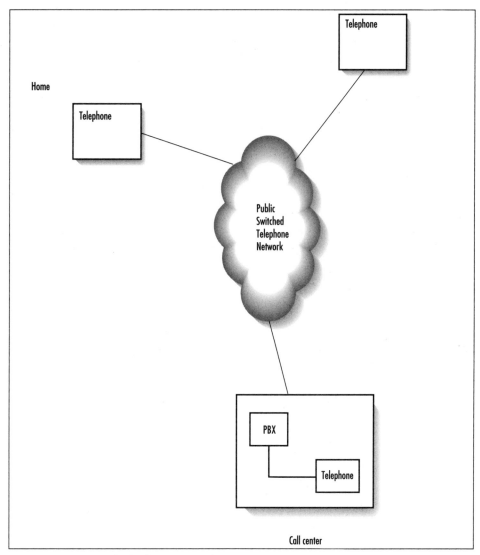

Figure 10-1 Typical telephone network

and even can ask you specific questions to which you reply using the number keys on your telephone. A good example is a banking application that allows you to get your balance and other banking information. You provide input through the phone system and the banking data is stored in a computer database. CTI acts as a bridge between the two.

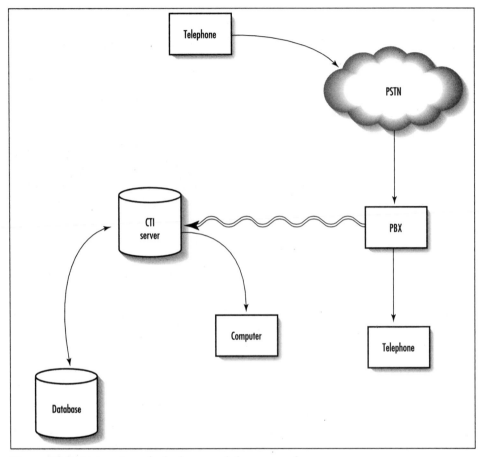

Figure 10-2 Integration of telephone and data networks

Faxbacks are another example of CTI applications. Whereas a banking application uses voice as output (recorded voice), faxback applications can send a facsimile as output. The information that is faxed to you is on a computer and CTI is your bridge to that computer.

As the Internet grows, we are seeing other types of CTI applications. These applications run on your telephone or a similar communication device. It is not unreasonable to expect a device that can provide email services, Web browsing, answering services, and telephone operations. A Java chip hosts the Java virtual machine (JVM), and Java applications can run on top of that. To create a consistent interface for Java applications to telephony devices (PBX, network devices, CTI servers, and so on), Sun has introduced the Java telephony Application Programming Interface (JTAPI). The remainder of this chapter explores this new API.

JTAPI Overview

CTI standards and APIs have been around for a while. The famous ones are

- TSAPI, developed by Novell and Lucent Technologies

- TAPI, developed by Microsoft and Intel

- CallPath, developed by IBM

- SunXLt, developed by Sun Microsystems

These standards have been used to create CTI applications under the specific environment for which the API was designed. For example, TAPI is commonly used under the Windows operating system. JTAPI has two goals:

1. Provide an interface for the integration of computers, telephones, and devices through the Internet

2. Provide a common set of APIs to enhance portability among the different hardware implementations

Suppose you have an NC that is running a Java telephony application. Figure 10-3 shows how the different layers stack up.

At the top level is the Java application. This is the application that you will design for your specific needs. The application code will contain references to the JTAPI methods and classes. JTAPI is at a lower level. It is not part of the core JDK, so it must be specifically installed. The entire application runs inside the JVM. Recall that JTAPI is not a low-level implementation: It is a common interface to the low-level implementation. As a result, calls to JTAPI will translate to specific APIs for which there is an interface to JTAPI. These lower-end APIs bind to the hardware device such as a fax card or a POTS card.

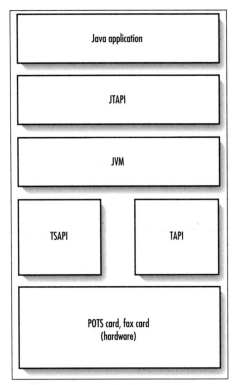

Figure 10-3 Java telephony application
on a single machine

The concept in Figure 10-3 can be expanded to include a network. This is shown in Figure 10-4. Rather than installing the telephony hardware on each computer, the telephony server will include the hardware or links to the hardware. The computer (client) simply must execute a Java application. Through remote method invocation (RMI) and telephony protocols, the Java application can interface with a server that will in turn act as the bridge to the physical hardware to make the call.

This type of configuration not only applies to call centers, it can also be used for a variety of other enterprise applications. Centralized telephone directories can integrate into the architecture, so you can make a phone call by simply clicking on the person's name. Another application is the integration of voicemail systems with a Java-based front end. Click on a message and hear it through your speakers.

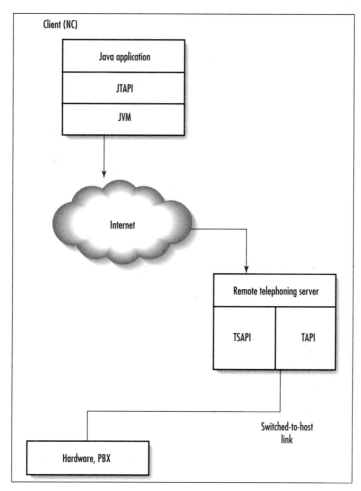

Figure 10-4 Java telephony application in a network

JTAPI Components

Like other Java APIs, the telephony API consists of several packages. The basic framework is provided by the core package. The functions performed by this package include

Placing a telephone call (`Call.connect()`)

Answering a telephone call (`TerminalConnection.answer()`)

 Dropping a telephone call (`Connection.disconnect()`)

This is all you need to add "phone" capabilities to your Java applications and your Java applets on the Web.

To understand the core telephony package, you need to learn about the JTAPI call model, shown in Figure 10-5.

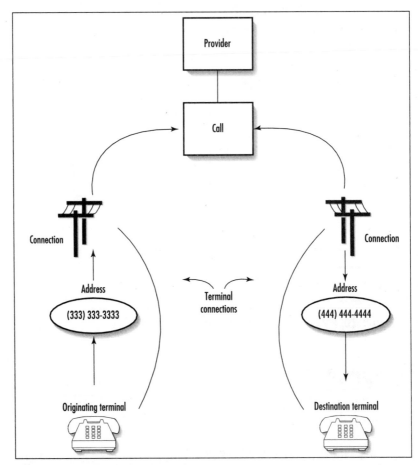

Figure 10-5 JTAPI call model

JTAPI classes are abstractions of the physical devices that make up a phone network and facilitate a phone conversation. The JTAPI model describes this framework. You can think of each component as an object. The collection of these objects makes up the communication framework. These objects are described below.

Provider Object

The software layer on top of the PBX or the POTS card in your computer is the *provider object*. As far as you are concerned, your application uses the provider object for its telephony needs. Your application will not make direct calls to device-specific APIs. The provider object provides a device-independent abstraction of the underlying hardware.

Call Object

When party A calls party B, a connection is established between the two and they can carry on a conversation. The *call object* is the representation of the telephone call itself. In the above example (a two-party phone conversation), there are one call object and two connections. A conference call includes one call object but more than two connections.

Address Object

Recall that the unique address identifier in a telephone network is the telephone number. The *address object* encompasses the telephone number. Because the abstraction is a logical one, one address object can point to several physical addresses. For example, the address object for Mr. Smith can point to three physical addresses: his office phone number, his home phone number, and his cellular phone number.

Connection Object

The communication link in a telephone network is represented by a *connection object*. The link is between a call object and an address object. A connection is usually described in terms of the state it is in. The state not only provides information about the connection, it also indicates what methods can be invoked on the connection. Following is a listing of the possible states:

 Idle: All new connection objects start in the idle state. The duration of the idle state is short compared to other states. No methods can be invoked when the connection is in the idle state.

In progress: The in-progress state indicates that a telephone call is currently being placed to a particular address. This is similar to the time period from when you press the last digit of the phone number until you hear the phone ringing.

Alerting: The alerting state indicates that the destination party of a telephone call is being alerted to an incoming telephone call.

Connected: When a phone connection is in place, this is the state the connection object goes into.

Disconnected: If for any reason the connection is terminated, the state changes to disconnected. No core methods can be invoked during this state.

Failed: Sometimes a connection cannot be established to the destination. This state is designated as the failed state. A busy signal is an example.

Unknown: If the provider cannot figure out the current state, it will label the state as unknown. Typically this occurs when a state transition is occurring. Subsequent inquiries should return a known state. Invocation of methods during this state lead to unpredictable results.

Figure 10-6 shows the state transition diagram, which shows the valid transitions from each state to another. This diagram is useful in understanding how the states work together to create the system.

Terminal Object

The *terminal object* is the abstraction of the physical communication device such as your pager or your home telephone. A terminal object must have an address object to be connected to the network. Just as pagers, cell phones, and office phones have different capabilities, terminal objects must correspond to the differences present in communication devices.

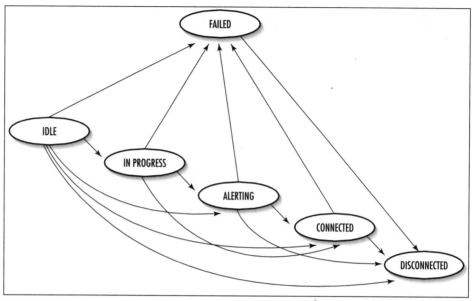

Figure 10-6 Connection object state transition

Terminal Connection Object

The *terminal object* is an abstraction of a physical device and the *terminal connection* object is an abstraction of a physical connection. The connection object is a logical view of the call. A terminal connection object describes the connection in terms of states. The following is a listing of the valid states:

Idle: The initial state of all terminal connection objects is the idle state (common beginning).

Active: When a terminal is sending and receiving communication, it is considered active. When you are carrying a conversation on your telephone, the state is active.

Ringing: This state is used to signal to the user that a call has been received. Typically, you can route the call to a different number or to an answering service based on the number of rings.

Dropped: After the telephone communication, the state changes to dropped. This is the state after you hang up.

Passive: In a two-way phone conversation, you don't see the passive state—unless one party is just talking to itself! This state applies to more advanced phones with conferencing features.

Unknown: This is similar to the unknown state of the connection object.

Figure 10-7 shows the state transition diagram for the states described above.

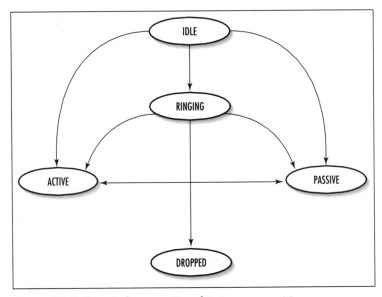

Figure 10-7 Terminal connection object state transition

Observer Model

The different parts of the call model must be able to communicate with each other. Because different parts can be in different states, communication can become a complex operation. Additionally, communication is of an asynchronous nature. Fortunately, the Java language has a solution for just this type of scenario. It is the observer/observable model.

The following objects have observers:

- Provider

- Call

- Terminal

- Address

The interfaces corresponding to these observers are

- **ProviderObserver**: Any state changes for the provider object are reported through this observer.

- **CallObserver**: Any state changes for connection objects, terminal connection objects, and the call object are reported by this observer.

- **TerminalObserver**: Reports state changes in the terminal. This is usually used to monitor for incoming calls.

- **AddressObserver**: Reports state changes in the address object. This is usually used to monitor for incoming calls.

A Simple Example

Some readers may find it helpful to look at sample code that uses JTAPI. The following code shows you how the core JTAPI can be used to place a phone call that is a routine operation in many CTI applications. To understand the code, please refer to the description of the call model above. The example code is modeled after code fragments in the JTAPI documentation from JavaSoft.

```
import java.telephony.*;
import java.telephony.events.*;

/* During a call several events can happen. An observer let's you capture these events
and act on them accordingly. Here the CallObserver interface is implemented.
*/

public class MyCallObserver implements CallObserver {
```

continued on next page

continued from previous page

```java
    public void callChangedEvent(CallEv[] evlist) {

       for (int i = 0; i < evlist.length; i++) {

          if (evlist[i] instanceof ConnEv) {

             String name = null;
             try {
                Connection connection = evlist[i].getConnection();
                Address addr = connection.getAddress();
                name = addr.getName();
             } catch (Exception excp) {
                // Handle Exceptions
             }
             String msg = "Connection to Address: " + name + " is ");

             if (evlist[i].getID() == ConnAlertingEv.ID) {
                System.out.println(msg + "ALERTING");
             }
             else if (evlist[i].getID() == ConnInProgressEv.ID) {
                System.out.println(msg + "INPROGRESS");
             }
             else if (evlist[i].getID() == ConnConnectedEv.ID) {
                System.out.println(msg + "CONNECTED");
             }
             else if (evlist[i].getID() == ConnDisconnectedEv.ID) {
                System.out.println(msg + "DISCONNECTED");
             }
          }
       }
    }
}


/*
This is a sample class that will actually make the call.
The call is coming from 1234567 to 7654321.
*/
public class MyOutcall {

   public static final void main(String args[]) {

      Provider myprovider = null;
      try {
         JtapiPeer peer = JtapiPeerFactory.getJtapiPeer(null);
         myprovider = peer.getProvider(null);
      } catch (Exception excp) {
         System.out.println("Can't get Provider: " + excp.toString());
         System.exit(0);
      }
```

```
/* The following code segment collects information about the Terminal originating the
call.
*/
    Address origaddr = null;
    Terminal origterm = null;
    try {
      origaddr = myprovider.getAddress("1234567");

      Terminal[] terminals = origaddr.getTerminals();
      if (terminals == null) {
        System.out.println("No Terminals on Address.");
        System.exit(0);
      }
      origterm = terminals[0];
    } catch (Exception excp) {
      // Handle exceptions;
    }


/* We can now create the Call object and add the observer to it.
*/
    Call mycall = null;
    try {
      mycall = myprovider.createCall();
      mycall.addObserver(new MyCallObserver());
    } catch (Exception excp) {
      // Handle exceptions
    }

/* Place the telephone call.
*/
    try {
      Connection c[] = mycall.connect(origterm, origaddr, "7654321");
    } catch (Exception excp) {
      // Handle all Exceptions
    }
  }
}
```

JTAPI Extensions

Aside from the core package, JTAPI consists of several extensions. It is beyond the scope of this book to go into the details of them. Plenty of information and examples are available on the JavaSoft Web site; some of these extensions are still being finalized. You are encouraged to take a look at these extensions before designing your next CTI application. Much of the functionality you may be looking for might already be implemented. Following is a brief description of these extensions.

Call Control

The java.telephony.callcontrol package extends the core package by providing more advanced call-control features such as placing calls on hold, transferring telephone calls, and conferencing telephone calls. Additional information about the states can be obtained using this package.

Call Center

Call center applications have their own unique requirements. The java.telephony.callcenter package addresses some of these needs. Examples are advanced call routing, automated call distribution (ACD), predictive calling, and associating application data with telephony objects.

Media

A CTI application often needs to get some information from the caller in the form of numbers punched on the telephone pad. The java.telephony.media package provides this capability by using media streams. Both touch-tone and non-touch-tone detection are supported. Other applications include answering services and faxback services.

Phone

The java.telephony.phone package permits applications to control the physical features of telephone hardware phone sets. Features of the telephone are encompassed in a set of components. You can take advantage of the special features of the hardware by communicating with these components. For example, a telephone that supports a variety of ring patterns would allow customization using a ring component.

Private Data

To take advantage of features of the switch (or any other telephony hardware) that are not supported by JTAPI, use the java.telephony.privatedata package. You must be cautious, however, because by doing so you are making your application hardware specific.

Capabilities

With the variety of telephony hardware available, an application may have to negotiate with the hardware as to what services are and are not available. The java.telephony.capabilities package provides a systematic mechanism for finding out about the capabilities of particular hardware. Static capabilities refer to features that are either supported or not. Dynamic capabilities refer to features whose supportability depends on the current state.

Summary

Data networks and telephone networks are inherently different, but their integration makes a lot of sense both economically and technologically. Computer telephony integration is a relatively new area that explores these possibilities.

Java's answer for this market is JTAPI. JTAPI is a series of APIs that allow a Java application to perform telephony functions such as receiving a call, placing a call, or routing a call.

A call model is used to encompass the different components of a typical call. Different objects correspond to these different components. They are provider, call, address, connection, terminal, and terminal connection.

A variety of other telephony functions is supported in Java using JTAPI extensions. These extensions provide advanced functionality, such as call center support, media support, and runtime capability queries.

CHAPTER 11

Inferno

When will your telephone handle your email or your television become your Internet browser? Believe it or not, we are not very far from such devices saturating the market and becoming as ordinary as a telephone is today. The NC promises to play an important role in the network device market. An important element of network-based devices is the operating system. Inferno, from Lucent Technologies, is an operating system specifically designed for operation under a network environment. Inferno is ideal for the device market due to its design and small size. It works on a variety of networks and systems. Applications have a consistent view of the network because the operating system takes care of the networking details. This chapter is a broad discussion of Inferno and its important elements. The discussion is based on the beta release of the software.

Design Principles

The design of Inferno is based on three simple but fundamental principles. All of them have to do with the network and the network-centric model. First, a consistent protocol called *Styx* is used for accessing all resources available to the application. These include local resources such as a local file or a disk drive and remote resources such as remote files or database servers.

The second principle is that all resources are represented as files in a hierarchical file system. This is similar to the manner in which the UNIX operating system handles resources. Operations such as open, read, write, and close are performed on resources such as printers, databases, network connections, and remote files. Presentation of all resources as files greatly simplifies the conceptual view of the network from an application perspective.

The third design principle of Inferno is that applications get a single view of the network. The elements of the file system can be a collection of local and remote resources, but that is not something the application should care about. The application should be able to access resources scattered throughout the network in the same manner as it accesses local resources. There is an inherent understanding that the performance will be different for accessing remote rather than local resources, but from an application design point of view, the two types should be treated equally.

These principles emphasize the importance of network and network resources, which is a fundamental part of the network-centric model on which NCs are based.

Elements of Inferno

Inferno is a complete system. It can be implemented directly on top of hardware, which most likely is the approach network device manufactures will take. This implementation is called the *native environment*. Another approach is implementation on top of an existing operating system such as UNIX or Windows NT; this is referred to as the *emulation environment*. Throughout this chapter, the latter approach is followed by using the Inferno system on top of Windows NT 4.0. You can download a copy of Inferno from `http://inferno.lucent.com`.

Inferno comprises four distinct parts:

- The Inferno operating system (kernel)

- The Limbo programming language

- The Dis virtual machine

- The Styx communications protocol

Figure 11-1 shows the above elements in the native environment. The Inferno kernel directly interacts with the underlying hardware through device drivers. Any kind of hardware can be used as long as it supports the functions needed by the kernel.

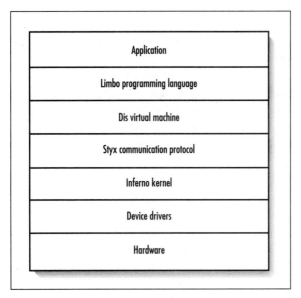

Figure 11-1 Inferno in the native environment

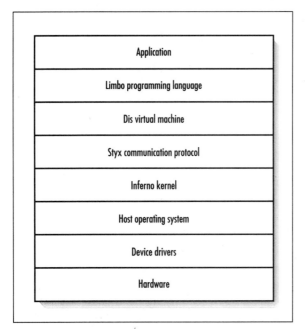

Figure 11-2 Inferno in the emulation environment

Figure 11-2 shows the same four elements in an emulation environment. In this case, the Inferno kernel relies on another operating system to provide the necessary interface to the hardware.

The Limbo programming language and the Dis virtual machine are very similar to Java and the Java virtual machine (JVM). Limbo is a C-like language used to develop applications for Inferno. It generates system-independent bytecode that can be executed by any Dis. As a result, Limbo applications run on any system that supports Inferno. As of the beta version, Limbo is the only language supported by Inferno; however, Java will also be supported in the future.

The Inferno kernel and Styx form the heart of the Inferno operating system. The kernel takes care of low-level tasks such as resource allocation, security, and interface to the hardware. The networking operations are supported by Styx, which itself depends on the kernel. Due to their nature, certain parts of the kernel are hardware specific. As a result, a different kernel must be used depending on the underlying hardware. Because the kernel is written in ANSI C, portability to different hardware environments is relatively easy as long as a C compiler exists for that environment. Currently, Inferno is ported to the following hardware architectures:

- MIPS

- SPARC

- Intel 386, 486, Pentium

- AMD 29000

- ARM

The following sections provide an overview of the four elements of Inferno.

Inferno Kernel

The kernel is the lowest layer of software in Inferno. It must support the networking and application layers above it. It does so by providing an interface or a link between the underlying hardware layer and the application layers. The kernel is responsible for process management, memory management, I/O operations, and name space management.

Memory management is one of the strongholds of Inferno. Memory is viewed at two different levels. The low-level view controls large blocks of contiguous memory. The high-level view deals with memory allocations per application. For example, memory must be allocated for network buffering, fonts, and program structures. Memory is stored in an unbalanced B-tree whose leaves are sorted by size. When a process requests memory, the B-tree is searched for a block that is large enough to handle the request. If the block is more than 25 percent larger than the requested size, that block is split. One piece is given to the process and the other piece is returned back to the B-tree. If the block is less than 25 percent larger, then the block is allocated and the remaining space is wasted. Figure 11-3 shows this process.

Scheduling processes is another task of the kernel. Inferno classifies processes into eight different categories based on their priority and keeps a separate queue for each class. Using a fixed time slice, the kernel services all eight queues in a round-robin manner.

Similar to UNIX, all devices are represented as part of the file system. **/** denotes the root file system. Other devices are identified with a pound sign followed by a letter. For example, **#V** is for television devices and **#D** is for secure socket layer. Communication to the devices is handled via the network. Each device should be able to respond to a set of system-level calls if applicable (see Table 11-1). You will see the counterpart to these calls in the discussion of the Styx communication protocol later in this chapter.

Table 11-1 Calls supported by Inferno devices

CALL	DESCRIPTION
init	Initialize the device driver
attach	Provide a channel to the root directory of the device
clone	Create a copy of an existing channel
walk	Traverse a node in the tree supplied by the device
stat	Provide the attributes of the device
open	Prepare a device for I/O operations
create	Create a file
close	Close a channel
read	Read data from a device
bread	Read a block of data from a device
write	Write data to a device
bwrite	Write a block of data to a device
remove	Remove a file
wstat	Output the attributes of a device

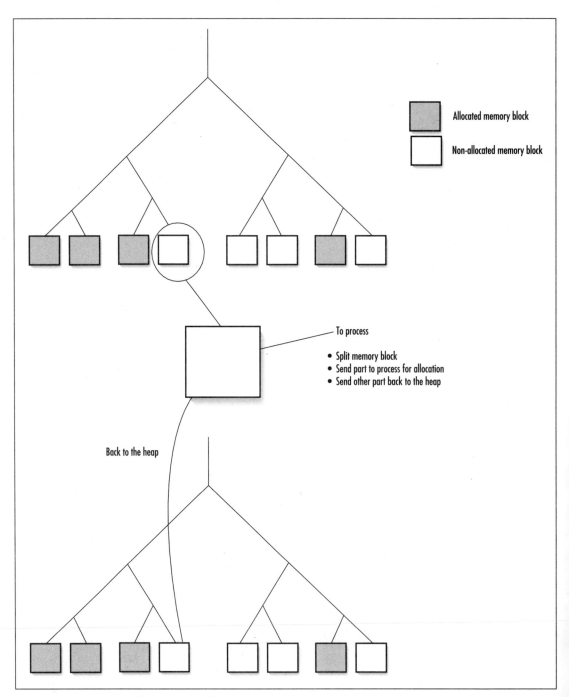

Figure 11-3 Memory allocation in Inferno

Another major responsibility of the kernel is the creation and maintenance of name spaces. A name space provides a view of the network resources to the process. Recall that these resources are organized as part of the file system. To create a name space, you first have to mount your resources and then you must bind them.

Local resources such as local files are usually premounted during system initialization. For example, once a camcorder is turned on, the local video device is automatically mounted. To access remote resources, resources must be explicitly mounted by the application; the Limbo programming language provides a syntax for doing that. To finish the process, you bind an already mounted resource to the desired name space. For example, you may mount a remote file system and then bind it to your local file system. The result is that the remote file system is viewed as part of the local file system. This is shown in Figure 11-4.

Prior to the establishment of a connection between two systems, the requests must pass the security verification of the kernel. This is important in a network environment to limit resources that can be accessed. For example, before you can view your favorite movie on your interactive television, the device must authenticate itself to the video server in your cable company. Public/private key encryption is used to authenticate the systems. The public key is composed of three parts:

- The public key algorithm

- The name of the owner

- The content of the key

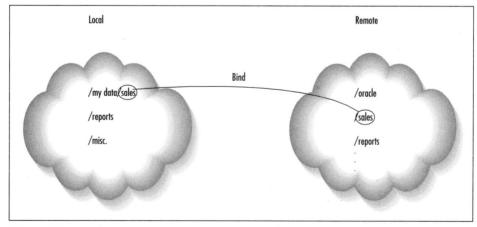

Figure 11-4 Binding a remote file system to a local one

Aside from this initial verification, the majority of the security burden is put back at the application layer. Depending on the application, you may or may not have to provide additional security.

As you can see, the Inferno kernel is not very sophisticated. The size of the kernel is reduced (making it suitable for network devices) and its portability is enhanced by cutting overhead and sticking to the necessary tasks.

Styx

Styx is a communication protocol used by Inferno devices to communicate and share resources on the network. As you might expect, all network connections and devices are represented as part of the file system. Several definitions are necessary to understand Styx.

- Server: Provides access to one or more file systems based on requests from authorized clients

- Client: Devices throughout the network that make requests to servers for access to network resources

- Connection: A bidirectional communication channel between the server and the client

The server usually has a representation of the services it offers or has access to in a file system. For a client to have access to those resources, the same representation must be created on the client. This is accomplished using the mount/bind sequence. It is up to the server to decide whether the mount request meets security standards. It is also up to the server to provide access to the same resource to different clients and to keep those mount points separate. With a hierarchical file system, this task is relatively straightforward because each client has its own space under the server.

To understand this better, consider a simple TCP communication. Information about TCP connections is stored on the server under the **/net/tcp/0** directory. Several files are stored there. The control file is used to return a descriptor to the client (via the **open** call), which is the handle for all subsequent communication. This communication remains open until a **close** call is received. The data file is the representation of the device in the file system. You write to the device by writing to the data file and you read from the device by reading from the data file.

The status file holds protocol-dependent information about the communication channel and its current state. The two files, local and remote, contain an IP number and a port number for each end of the connection. To respond to incoming calls from the network, a separate listen file is created. If a process opens the listen file, then the file will stay idle until an incoming call is received.

The Styx message structure is fully described in the Inferno documentation. It is briefly discussed here. There are two types of messages in the Styx protocol: initial transmission (T-message) and reply transmission (R-message). The first byte of the Styx structure indicates the type. The next two bytes hold a tag set by the client used to identify the message. Each outstanding message from the client must have a unique tag so that the message can be identified. The next two bytes hold a file identifier, which is used to denote the file on which the operation is to be performed. This value makes sense only when the Styx message operates on a file. The remaining portion of the message contains data specific to the operation being communicated.

Styx messages are divided into the following four categories:

- Messages to navigate through the file hierarchy

- Messages providing access to data inside the files

- Messages to control attributes of files

- Miscellaneous functions (synchronization, error messages)

The details of the Styx communication protocol are hidden from the application layer; this is a strong point in the design of Inferno. A **mount** call may translate into many Styx messages, but that extra detail happens behind the scenes. As an application programmer, you want to mount a certain network resource so you can use it in your application. Inferno and Styx make that happen!

Dis Virtual Machine

As you read the discussion about Dis and Limbo, you will see many similarities to JVM and Java. Limbo programs are interpreted within Dis. Dis must control memory allocation, execution schedules, and garbage collection.

There is only one instance of Dis running, and that instance has control of the heap. Memory required by the application is extracted from the heap by Dis and given to the application. To manage memory, Dis relies on type descriptors. Each object that occupies memory is associated with a type descriptor that contains its size and pointers to other objects on the heap. This information is generated by the Limbo compiler and is used by Dis to provide memory protection.

Limbo threads are categorized into several states, shown in Table 11-2.

Table 11-2 Thread states in Dis

STATE	DESCRIPTION
alt	Thread is communicating with other thread(s).
broken	Thread has crashed.
delete	Thread must be removed from the queue.
exiting	Thread has completed its instructions.
ready	Thread is ready to begin.
receive	Thread is prepared to receive communication from another thread.
release	Thread is to be removed from the queue due to a kernel call.
send	Thread is prepared to send communication to another thread.

Threads are placed in a queue and executed in a round-robin order. Once a thread finishes execution, it exits and releases its resources to Dis. A thread that cannot complete its tasks in the time frame given to it is removed and placed in a special queue that awaits CPU resources. Threads that communicate with other threads have an additional condition that may halt their execution. If a thread is placed in the send state, it will stay in that state until the receiving thread acknowledges the receipt of the message. The reverse is true for threads that have just gone to the receive state. By keeping threads in send and receive mode until the communication has completed, Dis enhances network communication and reduces the number of connections and threads due to premature disconnection. Finally, there are instances in which the kernel needs the resources and will block a thread to take care of critical system functions. Another instance of this is when the kernel cannot provide simultaneous access to the same resource (for example, a local drive) by multiple threads. By blocking one thread temporarily, it can handle multiple requests.

Two types of garbage collection mechanisms are used by Dis. The first mechanism is reference counting, which restores availability immediately after use. The second mechanism is that of mark and sweep. It applies only to cyclic structures and runs as a separate background process.

Limbo

Limbo is the programming language used by Inferno. As an application programmer, you will be writing code in Limbo; the details of Dis and Styx and the Inferno kernel will become secondary knowledge. Limbo is very much like C in its syntax. It supports basic data types, loops and decision-making structures, and a robust communication interface. The complete language specification is available from the Inferno home page http://inferno.lucent.com.

A Limbo application is divided into one or more units called *modules*. Each module has an interface declaration part and an implementation part. The declaration part lists the functions and data provided by the module, the data types, and any constants. The implementation part implements the functions and may also include implementations for internal functions.

To get a feel for the language, let's look at a very simple program.

```
implement FirstProgram

include "sys.m"
include "draw.m"

sys: Sys;

FirstProgram: module
{
    init: fn (ctxt: ref Draw->Context, argv: list of string);
};

init(ctxt: ref Draw->Context, argv: list of string)
{
    sys=load Sys Sys->PATH;
    sys->print ("This is my first Limbo program.\n");
}
```

The above program when executed prints the message **This is my first Limbo program.**. Its first line specifies that this program implements a module called **FirstProgram**. The next two lines are **include** statements, which are very similar to **#include** statements in C. The **print** statement is part of the **sys.m** module. In fact, you can look at its declaration by looking at the file **sys.m**.

The next line defines a variable called **sys** to be an instance of the module **Sys**. This variable is later used to access the **print** function.

The next section is the declaration part of the program. The module **FirstProgram**, along with its only function, is declared. The function name is **init** and its arguments are a drawing context (**ctxt**) and a list of strings (**argv**).

After the declaration comes the implementation. Note how the function name is repeated along with the parameters it expects, which should be the same as the declaration part. The **init** function (similar to the **main()** function in C), first associates the **sys** variable with the **Sys** module. This is done using the **load** function. **Sys->PATH** refers to a constant declaration within the **Sys** module that holds the path to where the module can be found on the system. This is a convention used by Inferno system modules.

Now that the **sys** variable is an instance of the **Sys** module, it can be used to call the **print** function using the notation

```
sys->print(string);
```

where **string** is the message to be printed.

In addition to the language specification, a paper by Brian Kernighan titled "A Descent into Limbo" is available at the Inferno home page.

Reference API

Just as Java comes with its own standard packages, classes, and Application Programming Interfaces (APIs), Limbo also has a reference API. This API is guaranteed to be available in any implementation of the Inferno system. As a result, a Limbo application that conforms to the reference API will run across multiple implementations of the Inferno system. Reference API files or modules generally have the **.m** extension and are in the **module** subdirectory. Figure 11-5 shows a partial listing of the files as they appear under the Windows NT 4.0 implementation.

The reference API is still under development. The discussion below gives you a general feel for what is currently available to application development.

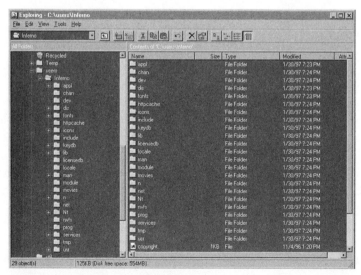

Figure 11-5 Reference API files

System Module (sys.m)

String manipulation: These functions support string conversion and tokenization (breaking a string into smaller parts based on a specified variable).

File manipulation: All files are referenced by a descriptor. The usual file operations such as **open**, **read**, **write**, **seek**, **mount**, **bind**, **remove**, and **create** are supported. Note that there is no **close** function because the garbage collection mechanism automatically releases the memory occupied by descriptors.

Printing: **print** and **fprint** write their output to **STDOUT** and to a file specified by a descriptor respectively.

Time: **millisec** returns the number of milliseconds since boot time and **sleep** halts a process for the specified time.

Network: Basic network communication functions are declared within this module. The important ones are

- **announce**: Establishes a network name to accept calls

- **listen**: When a call is received, returns a descriptor to a **ctl** file

- **dial**: Attempts to establish connection to a network service

Graphics Module

The graphics module comprises three distinct parts. The first part is the **draw** module, which provides basic drawing routines for Inferno applications. Examples include points, rectangles, images, fonts, and screens. These are implemented as abstract data types. As a result, you can access methods and properties specific to these types once you have created an instance. For example, the **dx** and **dy** methods return the width and length of a rectangle. The coordinate system used is identical to Java. The upper-left pixel in the grid has coordinates of (0,0). This module also provides the primitive types used by the other two modules described below.

The second component of the graphics module is the **prefab** module. This module is used primarily for creating a user interface to menu-driven applications controlled by infrared devices. Your television remote control falls into this category. Most televisions and VCRs display a menu on the screen that is controlled by the remote control. Through this menu, you can set up time and date, adjust volume and picture settings, and program your VCR. The **prefab** module is intended to be used for these types of user interfaces. Menu items are referred to as *elements*. Functions are provided to arrange the elements on the screen and traverse through them.

The last part of the graphics module is the **Tk** module, which is similar to the popular Tcl/Tk toolkit. This is a collection of widgets for creating graphical user interfaces (GUIs). All the usual widgets such as buttons, menus, lists, scroll bars, and radio buttons are supported. The Limbo/Tk implementation uses five standard functions to pass information from the Tk environment to the Inferno system; otherwise, the two environments are isolated from each other.

Security

Two modules are provided for applications that need advanced security features. The kernel provides security at a very low level by providing a registration (sign-on) process. After that, security is left to the discretion of the application. The application can sign all Styx messages using a digital signature to assure that the messages are not altered during the transmission. Both message digest function (MD5) and secure hash algorithm (SHA) are supported for this purpose. Note that a signed message does not mean that it is encrypted. The signature merely assures that the message's content has not changed.

To hide the content of the message from intruders, you must encrypt the message. Inferno uses a public/private key scheme to encrypt messages. The **keyring** module includes the abstract data types and functions necessary to access Inferno's security features. They are

- Type conversion and parsing

- Signature creation and validation

- Key and digest functions

- Authentication

External Device Module

The reference API can be extended to support specific hardware devices. Two such modules are included with Inferno to demonstrate this capability. They are the infrared remote control device module and the MPEG player module.

Miscellaneous Interfaces

Mathematical functions, regular expressions, and basic utilities functions dealing with time and strings fall under this category. There is also the **Shell** module, which provides a template for applications than run under the Inferno shell.

Inferno Environment

The Inferno system can run under the following environments:

- Inferno shell

- Electronic devices (for example, TV), as demonstrated by the **mux** application

- Network and desktop computers, as demonstrated by the **wm** application

As an explanation and example of the above environment, let's use the Inferno emulator for the Windows NT operating system, available from Inferno's home page. After installing the application, you should have a directory with the following subdirectories:

- **appl**: Contains Limbo source code for demonstration applications

- **chan**: Location for writing channel control files

- **dev**: Location for writing device control files

- **dis**: Location of Dis programs (the virtual machine)

- **fonts**: Location of font files

- **httpcache**: Location of Web browser cache

- **icons**: Location of graphic icons

- **keydb**: Location of digital signature keys

- **lib**: Location of nonprogram data

- **locale**: Location of time zone localization files

man: Location of documentation

module: Location of modules for Limbo programs

movies: Location of files used by the sample mux application

n: Location of network-related files

net: Location of network-related files for all available network devices

<os>/bin: Platform-specific files

prog: Location of thread-related control files

services: Location of service-related files

usr: Location of user home directories

Inferno Shell

You can start the shell from the Start menu (Start - Programs - Lucent Inferno - Emulator). This should start the shell similar to Figure 11-6.

From the shell, you can execute a number of UNIX-like commands. A subset of these commands follows.

Figure 11-6 The Inferno shell

- **Cat filename**: Display the contents of a file

- **cd directory**: Change to a different directory

- **cmp filename1 filename2**: Compare two files

- **cp filename1 filename2**: Copy **filename1** to **filename2**

- **date**: Print the date

- **ls**: Print a directory listing

- **mkdir**: Create a new directory

- **netstat**: Print status of network connections

- **os command**: Execute command in the host operating system

- **ps**: List running processes

- **pwd**: Print the path to the current directory

- **rm filename**: Delete **filename**

- **sleep milliseconds**: Halt execution for the specified number of milliseconds

- **wish**: Open up a Tcl-like command shell

Network Devices

Inferno's primary market is that of network devices. These devices generally use a different user interface than traditional applications. The interface is similar to what you see when you program your VCR or store phone numbers in your cellular phone. The **mux** application is a demonstration program that shows this environment. You can invoke the **mux** environment by typing **mux/mux** in the shell. You will get a window similar to that shown in Figure 11-7.

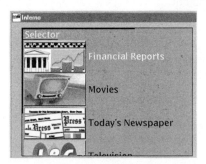

Figure 11-7 The **mux** application

Your basic navigation tools are the following:

▶ Ⓜ or down arrow: Move down the menu

▶ Ⓛ or up arrow: Move up the menu

▶ (ENTER): Select the highlighted menu item

▶ Ⓧ: Bring the menu to the front

▶ Space bar: Kill the current menu selection

Using the above keys, you can see the different services available and appreciate how such devices might look.

Inferno Window Manager

Inferno can also be used for traditional computer applications. You can see some of these applications and get a feel for the window manager environment by typing the following at the shell:

`wm/logon`

You should get something similar to Figure 11-8.

Type **inferno** to log on to the system. You will then enter the Inferno window manager, shown in Figure 11-9.

On the lower-left side, you will find a menu similar to the Start menu of Windows 95 and NT. Figure 11-10 shows the Notepad application, the date/clock application, and a listing of running processes (similar to task manager under Windows).

Figure 11-8 The Inferno window manager logon

Figure 11-9 The Inferno window manager

You can maximize, minimize, and close windows by clicking on the boxes in the upper-right side of the window.

Another useful application is launched from the Local menu item. It is similar to Explorer (Windows 95) and lets you see the files and other resources on the local system (see Figure 11-11). You should explore the Inferno directories at this time and become familiar with their structure.

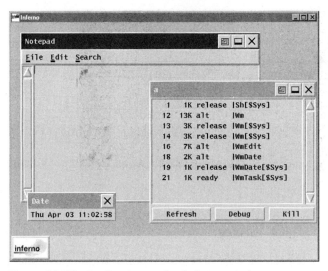

Figure 11-10 Application under Inferno window manager

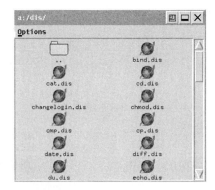

Figure 11-11 Graphical view of local resources

Application Development under Inferno

You are now familiar with the different components of the Inferno system. The process of developing applications for Inferno using the Limbo language is very straightforward.

The Limbo compiler is called **limbo** and is located in the **<root>/NT/386/bin** directory. It is an executable that compiles Limbo source code (files with **.b** extension) and generates binary files to be run under the Dis environment. The generated files have the extension **.dis** and are similar to the bytecode files generated by the Java compiler.

Figure 11-12 shows the commands to compile and execute the sample program **MyFirstProgram**.

```
Emulator                                              _ □ ✕
Inferno BETA.2 Build 16 main (pid=114) interp
Initialize Dis: /dis/sh.dis
crc3$ cd usr/inferno
crc3$
crc3$ limbo FirstProgram.b
crc3$
crc3$
crc3$ FirstProgram
hello, world
crc3$
```

Figure 11-12 Compiling and executing the MyFirstProgram
application

There is also a graphical debugger. To use the debugger, compile your programs
using the **−g** option. The debugging information is stored in a file with the **.sbl** extension. At this time, the debugger is somewhat unstable, but the Inferno documentation
provides a good discussion of its features and how it can be used.

Summary

Inferno is an operating system from Lucent Technologies. Its design principles emphasize
the importance of the network and the ability of applications to access network resources
in a transparent and seamless way. At the very low level is the Inferno kernel, which is
responsible for interfacing with the underlying hardware or the host operating system in
an emulation environment. The kernel schedules tasks and does memory allocation. On
top of the kernel is the Styx communication protocol. Almost all messages among network
clients, servers, and devices are communicated through Styx. The underlying supported
protocols are TCP, IP, and UDP.

The Dis virtual machine is responsible for execution of bytecodes generated by the
Limbo compiler. The Limbo language is similar to C in syntax. A typical Limbo application is composed of one or more modules. Each module has a declaration section and
an implementation section.

A reference API assures portability of Limbo programs across different platforms. All
implementations of Inferno regardless of the underlying hardware must support the reference API. As a result, your Limbo application will run everywhere Inferno is supported.

The Inferno environment exists in three different contexts. The simplest one is the Inferno shell, which is a UNIX-like command-line interface to the Inferno system. The second environment is similar to the desktop environment on Windows 95 and is called the Inferno window manager. The third environment is designed for network devices. The interface is similar to the ones offered by VCRs and cellular phones.

For development, typically the Limbo compiler is used to generate bytecode for the Dis virtual machine. The **−g** option can be used to generate bytecode with debugging information. A graphical debugger is also provided as part of the Inferno window environment.

Java Management API

This chapter talks about the Java management API (JMAPI)—an Application Programming Interface (API) for the development of system, network, and service management solutions for heterogeneous networks. The chapter starts off by explaining what is meant by system, network, and service management. It then deals with the different types of management tools available today. Designing management tools with a Web interface has many advantages; this is the next topic covered in the chapter, followed by a discussion of the JMAPI demonstration application developed by JavaSoft, and concluding with the relevance of JMAPI technology to network computers.

Background

In today's computing environment, where different platforms, operating systems, networks, and network protocols exist side by side in an enterprise, it is difficult to maintain the systems. In fact, maintenance is a complex and costly affair, and the heterogeneity of the environment adds to the problem. Tools exist for managing the systems and the networks, but these tools manage only pieces of the whole system, forcing system and network administrators to use several tools. Most of the time, these tools are based on proprietary technology and are complex to use and install.

Network management standards such as Simple Network Management Protocol (SNMP) and Common Management Information Protocol (CMIP) hide differences between network resources and provide a way of handling these resources uniformly, but the problem again is that the tools available are complex. JMAPI provides a way of managing system and network resources in a heterogeneous environment, allowing administrators and custom application developers to build what they need when they need it and integrate it with other Web and Java applications and applets. But before discussing JMAPI, let's look at what is meant by network and system management and the issues involved.

System Management

System management or system administration involves maintaining user accounts, taking care of the hardware and software installed on the system, fixing problems when something goes wrong with the hardware or software, and installing new hardware and software. Other issues related to managing a system are the ways in which users can make requests to system administrators and report troubles and how system administrators can access the requests/trouble tickets and address them. A mechanism must exist for the system administrators and end users to communicate with each other. Also, mechanisms must exist for the administrators to be notified when something goes wrong with the hardware or software, to diagnose problems, and to correct these problems.

Suppose several different systems exist in the enterprise; for example, Solaris, Windows NT, and HP-UX. Management tools exist to manage these systems, but each tool manages a particular platform; different tools must be bought to manage all the systems. It is difficult to find people with skills to manage all the different systems. Plus, it is difficult to build a system for trouble tracking/reporting that works on all these systems uniformly. Without a systematic approach, system management becomes a complex and costly affair. Figure 12-1 depicts the elements of system management.

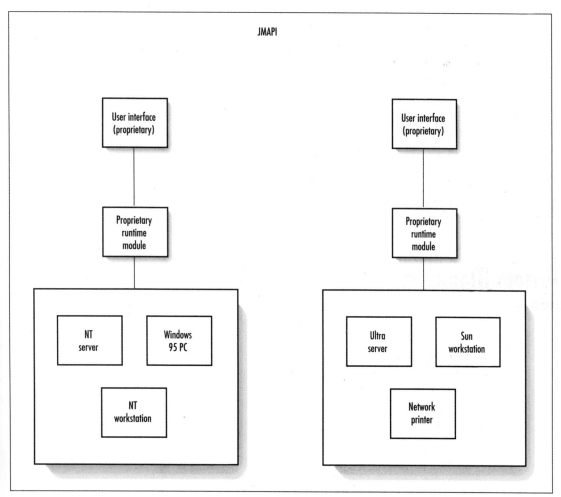

Figure 12-1 System management

Network Management

Today's networks comprise several heterogeneous systems. Different types of devices are connected using bridges, routers, and the like. Network management involves not only monitoring these pieces of hardware, but also maintaining the software used to monitor the hardware, taking into account the different protocols used by the various pieces of equipment for communication and the fact that the equipment can be several thousand miles apart.

Management tools such as HP-OpenView and NetView assist in network management. But these tools may be complex to learn and install and may be based on proprietary technology. In many cases, too much data is available to mean anything to the network managers. It may be difficult to cull data that makes sense because most of the tools are not able to access the data in the first place. An example is data provided by systems accessible only by RS-232 ports, which is not gathered by tools like NetView or SNMP.

Web-Based Management Paradigm

To overcome the problems mentioned above in dealing with system and network management, several companies are working to provide a Web interface to management tools. There are several advantages of Web-based management tools.

- They provide a common interface across all the platforms. This greatly reduces training costs.

- Almost all the platforms support browsers. This reduces the amount of software porting that would have been necessary otherwise.

- Many people are using the Web as a tool for accessing several services. So the Web is becoming a de facto interface for information.

- Only the server piece of the software needs to be upgraded when there is a change, because the client software is a Web browser. This greatly reduces the amount of work for system administrators.

JMAPI provides developers a set of APIs to build system and network management tools based on the management-through-the-Web paradigm.

JMAPI

To overcome the above problems, JavaSoft has come up with a set of APIs to build tools for network, system, and service management solutions for heterogeneous networks. Tools built using these APIs can be used across a variety of platforms, architectures, operating systems, and network protocols. Moreover, because the APIs are written in Java, the tools will run on any platform for which the Java virtual machine (JVM) exists.

JMAPI provides the user with interface guidelines, Java classes, and specifications for developing integrated system, network, and service management applications.

JMAPI Architecture

For any new technology to succeed, it not only must provide new and innovative solutions, it must also take care of the existing customer base. Not every customer can upgrade to new technology immediately—either because of the costs involved or because of a wait-and-see attitude. Also, customers do not like to throw away their existing infrastructure. Technology developers should use as much of the available technology as possible instead of developing everything on their own. For example, when upgrading from Windows 3.x to Windows 95, Microsoft had to ensure that data stored in Windows 3.x could be read by Windows 95.

JavaSoft took a similar approach in developing JMAPI. Instead of starting from scratch by providing all the functionality, JavaSoft used existing technology like SNMP and built upon it to provide an integrated solution for network and system management. In addition, instead of requiring users to install new infrastructure, JMAPI leverages the existing infrastructure by using technologies that are widely available and adopted, scaleable, and provide the necessary functionality. The resulting architecture thus has the following dependencies:

Java-Enabled Web Browser: A Web-based approach toward system and network management has several advantages. Because JMAPI is written in Java, the browser must support Java. The two leading browsers—Netscape Navigator (2.x and later) and Microsoft Internet Explorer (3.x and later)—provide support for Java and account for more than 95 percent of the market share. Thus, by providing a Web interface, JMAPI tries to give a common interface to all management tools.

HTTP Server: To process the requests made by the browser, a server is essential. A Hypertext Transfer Protocol (HTTP) server processes the requests made by browsers. Thus, an HTTP server is needed.

Java 1.1: In addition to the classes provided by Java 1.0, JMAPI uses the remote method invocation (RMI) and security classes provided by Java 1.1. Thus, Java 1.1 is needed.

Database with a JDBC Driver: Any database that has a Java database connectivity (JDBC) driver is also needed.

Components of the JMAPI Architecture

The following make up the JMAPI architecture.

User Interface: The JMAPI architecture provides a browser interface for the applications. The browser is used as the front end of the management application. All operations performed by the system manager will be done using this interface.

Operation-Performing Module: Whenever a system manager performs some operation on the user interface, the request has to be carried out by something. That something in this case is the operation-performing module of the admin runtime module.

This module processes the request from the system manager on the appliances.

Appliance: An appliance is any device or element that is being managed. It could be a personal computer, a printer, or a file server. Operations on these appliances are performed by the admin runtime module based on the commands issued by the system manager using the browser user interface.

Figure 12-2 shows an outlay of the JMAPI architecture. In this example, there are two admin runtime modules: one performing systems management and the other performing network management. Note that the user interface for both these modules is the same. Also, in this example, the appliances are the workstations in one case and the file server in another.

A Sample Application Based on JMAPI

JavaSoft provides a sample application built using JMAPI. This application provides an integrated platform for system and network management. Let's look at the demo so that the key concepts behind this chapter can be better understood.

This demo application can either be downloaded or run using a browser. If you are behind a firewall or using a slow network connection, it is better if you download the application and run it locally.

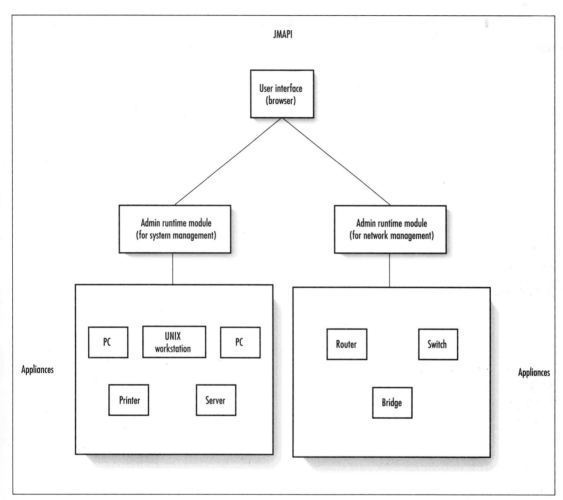

Figure 12-2 JMAPI architecture layout

Running the Application on the Network

To run the application over the network, go to `http://www.javasoft.com/products/JavaManagement/` and click on the link that says `Run a Demo`. This should start the demo running.

Downloading and Installing the Demo Application

For Windows 95 or Windows NT, follow the instructions below:

Go to `http://www.javasoft.com/products/JavaManagement/` and click on the link that says `download the Demo either as a ZIP file or a compressed tar file`. Download the ZIP file.

This will bring up the Save As pop-up box. Select the folder where you want to download the software.

Click the Save button on the pop-up box. The file will be downloaded to that location.

Bring up the MS-DOS command prompt by selecting Start, Programs, and Command Prompt.

Go to the directory where you downloaded the software.

Unzip the file `jmapiDemo.zip` by using the following command: `pkunzip jmapiDemo.zip`. This will extract all the files.

Exit from the command prompt

For the Solaris platform, follow these instructions:

Go to `http://www.javasoft.com/products/JavaManagement/` and click on the link that says `download the Demo either as a ZIP file or a compressed tar file`. Download the compressed tar file.

This will bring up the Save As pop-up box. Select the directory where you want to download the software.

Then click the Save button on the pop-up box. The file will be downloaded to that location.

Go to the directory where you downloaded the software.

Uncompress the file **jmapiDemo.tar.gz** by using the following command: **uncompress jmapiDemo.tar.gz.**

Extract the files using the following command: **tar xfv jmapiDemo.tar.** This will extract all the files.

Running the demo application:

Start your browser.

In the File menu, select Open File.

This brings up the selection box. Go to the folder where you have extracted the files.

Select the file called **demo.html.**

This starts the demo application running. It should bring up the page shown in Figure 12-3.

As you can see, the administrator can maintain both the system and the network using this application. Let's look at one example of each.

System Administration

The following procedure is an example of *system administration*: dealing with the creation of a new user ID.

Click on the Create pull-down box and select User. This will bring up a window as shown in Figure 12-4.

Figure 12-3 A screen shot of the demo application

You should see a list of properties that can be set for a user, such as home server, mail server, and groups that the user can belong to.

Fill in all the information for a hypothetical user.

At the bottom of the list, you can select whether to enable a Solaris account and/or a Windows NT account. (Thus, using the same application, you can administer different platforms.)

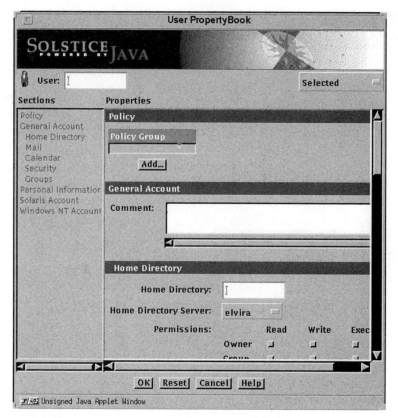

Figure 12-4 Creating a new user

 After filling in all the information, click OK.

 Though clicking on OK does not do anything at this stage, this example demonstrates how easily system administration tools can be built to maintain different platforms using the same user interface.

Several other system administration tasks can be performed on the demo application—for example, maintaining the user's list, troubleshooting a user's problem, and maintaining different devices like the printers.

Network Administration

The following procedure is an example of *network administration*: alarm handling on a network problem.

On the main demo page, in the Alarms section, double-click on the alarm that says `Saturn : Threshold on ipOutNoRoutes exceeded 09:19`. This should bring up the Alarm Property book shown in Figure 12-5.

The Alarm Property book displays information such as the name of the device, its type, the probable cause of the problem, and alarm number.

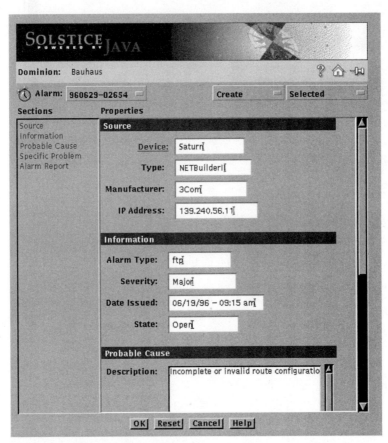

Figure 12-5 Alarm Property book

Click on the **Backup Logs** hyperlink. This should bring up the Transcend Backup Log page.

Select the last item in the list: **Before device is upgraded to V8.3**.

From the Selected menu, select Restore. A pop-up box that shows the status of the restoration is displayed.

Other network administration tasks such as creating a router and adding network services can also be viewed in this demo.

Advantages of JMAPI

There are several advantages to building management tools based on JMAPI:

Uniform Interface Across All the Platforms: Because the application will have a Web front end, the applications will have a uniform interface, no matter which platform is used. This greatly reduces the learning curve.

Written in Java: Because JMAPI classes are written in Java, applications that take advantage of JMAPI need to be written only once and they will run on any platform that supports the JVM.

Security: Only trusted Java code runs on the client machines. All requests for Java classes are authorized and authenticated by a secure remote method invocation.

Easy Migration: JMAPI is protocol independent; native libraries can be used to access data provided by the standard network management protocols like SNMP.

Summary

The Java management API is an API for the development of system, network, and service management solutions for heterogeneous networks. Even the best-designed networks must be maintained and managed, because networks are dynamic by nature. JMAPI provides a consistent interface for this task through Java. In a network-centric model, management of networks is and will continue to be a complex task. JMAPI is one step in the right direction toward the future of network management. NCs can be used to access the management applications designed using JMAPI. Because these applications will run on any platform, NCs provide a convenient tool for administrators to access the management applications. JMAPI combined with NCs should make the task of system and network administration simpler while at the same time reducing costs.

CHAPTER 13

Java Development Tools

An important step in moving to a network-centric environment and the NC is application development. Java has emerged as the premiere language for network-centric applications. Java is merely a language, however, and development tools are needed to facilitate large application development efforts. A common element in all advanced development tools is the graphical user interface (GUI). As component models such as JavaBeans become more common, the GUI will help developers visually design sophisticated applications. It should come as no surprise that most Java development tools on the market take this visual approach.

The network-computing model affects development efforts and software design. An ideal environment would allow a team of developers to work on a project together. It would use the network itself to eliminate geographical barriers. Developers could work on traditional workstations or network computers. The key point is that the network plays an important role not only in the utilization of the application, but also in the design and development of the application. This behavior is consistent with a true paradigm shift as discussed in earlier chapters.

Another important attribute of NC development tools is the capability to interface with databases. Almost all business applications use a database. The client/server era pushed us to use tools for creating database applications, and the network-centric era will build upon that. New applications must be capable of using any database situated anywhere as long as network connectivity exists. Standards such as Java database connectivity (JDBC) and common object request broker architecture (CORBA) are a step in the right direction; now development tools must incorporate such standards in the applications they build.

This chapter talks about some of the Java development tools available in the market today. All the tools discussed in this chapter provide a visual environment for developing Java applications. Some products provide support for building JavaBean components. This chapter is not intended to be a review of the available Java development tools. Rather, it is intended to provide brief notes about some of the available products and their features. As such, product blurbs taken from companies' Web sites are included liberally. Depending on your environment and application goals, some tools may suit you better than others.

Ten tools are included in this chapter; they have been arranged in alphabetical order. The main features of each product, along with the download site and the requirements to run each of the tools, are included.

Jamba by Aimtech

Although officially described as "Java authoring software," Jamba is more of a multimedia presentation tool that uses Java as the delivery vehicle. It lets users create animation using a variety of techniques, special effects, and presentations without the need for programming. This is useful for adding multimedia effects to Web pages. Jamba does not compile any source code, which is one of the main reasons for its speed. It lets users download compressed applets using Microsoft's CAB format or the Zip format (used by Netscape). These applets are then installed locally.

Some important features of Jamba are listed below.

Jamba provides support for adding objects created by users.

It supports ActiveX objects that install into Jamba and behave just like those that ship with Jamba.

Jamba can also access common gateway interface (CGI) applications on the Web server.

Support is provided for calling public methods of classes designed in Java, as well as calling JavaScript functions.

Download Site

An evaluation copy of Jamba is available for download at `http://www.jamba.com/`
`experience/download.html`. This trial version expires after 30 days or 100 uses. But
the applets created using the trial version will not expire. A full version can be purchased
online or at local retail stores. See `http://www.jamba.com` for details.

Availability/System Requirements

Table 13-1 shows the system requirements for Jamba.

Table 13-1 System requirements for Jamba

	CPU	RAM	HARD DRIVE	SOFTWARE
Win32 Systems	486 or above	At least 8 MB	The full download of the evaluation version of Jamba requires 8.7 MB disk space	Windows 95 or Windows NT 4.0 Any Java-enabled Web browser

Java Workshop 2.0 by Sun Microsystems

Java Workshop 1.0 was the first application development tool written in Java for designing Java applications visually. It has several advantages:

- Web browser interface

- Web publishing tools for organizing and publishing Java projects on the Net

- Integrated toolset for fast and efficient development

    Java Workshop 2.0 extends these features by including the following enhancements:

- A fast javac compiler to generate bytecode quickly

- Built-in just-in-time (JIT) compiler to increase the performance of Java code

Wizards to help create projects rapidly

Support for JDK 1.1 and JavaBeans

Support of JavaBeans may be the biggest enhancement as far as the advancement of Java is concerned. Whereas other enhancements make the life of the developer easier and the code run faster, support for JDK 1.1 and JavaBeans is essential for the industry to deploy and use JavaBeans. (For more details on why JavaBeans should be used, refer to Chapter 7, "Distributed Applications on the NC.")

Figure 13-1 shows many of the above-mentioned features.

Download Site

At the time of writing this chapter, Java Workshop 2.0 was still in the pre-beta stage. A pre-beta version can be downloaded for evaluation from `http://www.sun.com/workshop/java/jws20_dev/download/index.html`.

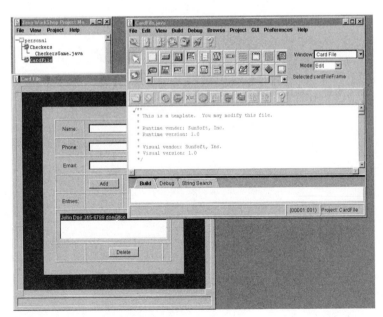

Figure 13-1 Java Workshop 2.0

Version 1.0, which is a full-release version, can be downloaded for evaluation from `http://www.sun.com/developer-products/java/tnb/index.html`.

Availability/System Requirements

Table 13-2 shows the system requirements for Java Workshop 1.0.

Table 13-2 System requirements for Java Workshop 1.0

	CPU	RAM	HARD DRIVE	SOFTWARE
Win32 Systems	486 (100 MHz or faster) or above	At least 24 MB	At least 15 MB	Windows 95 or Windows NT 3.51 or later
Solaris	SPARC systems or Intel 486 (100 MHz or faster) or Pentium systems	At least 32 MB	At least 15 MB	Solaris 2.4 or later

Table 13-3 shows the system requirements for the pre-beta release of Java Workshop 2.0.

Table 13-3 System requirements for pre-beta release of Java Workshop 2.0

	CPU	RAM	HARD DRIVE	SOFTWARE
Win32 Systems	486 (100 MHz or faster) or above	16 MB minimum, 32 MB recommended	40+ MB	Windows 95 or Windows NT 3.51 or later
Solaris	SPARC systems — SS2 minimum, SS10 recommended	At least 32 MB	43+ MB	Solaris 2.5 or later OSF/Motif 1.2.3 or later

JBuilder by Borland

JBuilder is a visual Java application development tool that combines Borland's award-winning Delphi environment with a Java-optimized tool for building cross-platform, Web-delivered applications.

Important features include (but are not limited to) the following:

 JBuilder provides a visual, component-based, development environment. These components are based on JavaBeans, which allows faster creation of Java-based applets and applications. For more information on JavaBeans, please refer to Chapter 7, "Distributed Applications on the NC."

 JBuilder is a Two-Way Tool, meaning programmers can switch back and forth between visual design and the corresponding pure Java code. See also Visual Café, later in this chapter.

 JBuilder includes DataDirector, which offers a combination of database components and tools to help build database applications. DataDirector supports any JDBC- or ODBC-compliant data source.

Download Site

JBuilder is still in the development stage, with a selected number of candidates being accepted for Borland's preview release. To participate in the JBuilder Preview program, or to get more information on JBuilder, go to **http://www.borland.com/jbuilder**.

Availability/System Requirements

Information is not available at the time of writing this chapter about the minimum system requirements needed to run JBuilder.

JFactory by Roguewave

JFactory is a visual application builder that lets programmers drag and drop elements to create applications without writing source code for the interactions, connections, and properties of the interface.

A big plus for this tool is its availability for several platforms (Windows 95, Windows NT, Solaris, HP-UX, and OS/2). This tool is mostly useful for rapid prototyping because it allows programmers to make changes and view them immediately.

Several important features of this product are listed below.

 Project templates: JFactory provides three predefined project templates—**Applet**, **App**, and **Menu App**. With these templates, you can design an application project with a main window or an application project with basic application menus.

Menus: Design of menus is automated using JFactory.

Visual components: A set of visual components is provided that extends the standard components provided by the Abstract Window Toolkit (AWT).

Object library: An object library is provided in which programmers can store objects so that they can be reused in any other project.

Code generation: The necessary source code is generated by JFactory automatically. It generates two types of source code files—HTML and Java. Also, an option is provided for users to add their own code.

Figure 13-2 shows many of the above-mentioned features.

Download Site

A demonstration copy of JFactory for Windows 95 and Windows NT is available for download at `http://www.roguewave.com/cgi-bin/jfdldemo.cgi`. The demo version is limited to generating code for a total of five windows or dialogs. A full version can be purchased online; see `http://www.roguewave.com/sales/sps.html` for more details.

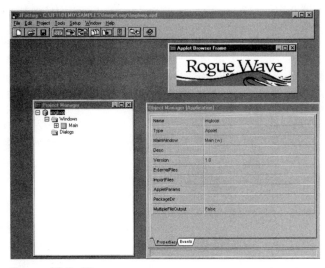

Figure 13-2 JFactory

Availability/System Requirements

Table 13-4 shows the system requirements for JFactory.

Table 13-4 System requirements for JFactory

	CPU	RAM	HARD DRIVE	SOFTWARE
Win32 Systems	486 or above	At least 16 MB	At least 25 MB free	Windows NT or Windows 95 JDK 1.0.2 Java-enabled browser, such as Netscape 2.0 or appletviewer A graphics design tool for editing GIF-format bitmaps (optional)
Solaris	UNIX workstation capable of running Solaris 2.4 or 2.5	Enough RAM to run X11R5	At least 25–30 MB	Solaris 2.4 or 2.5 bX11R5 JDK 1.02 Java-enabled browser, such as Netscape 2.0 or appletviewer A graphics design tool for editing GIF-format bitmaps (optional)
HP-UX	UNIX workstation capable of running HP-UX 10.01	Enough RAM to run X11R5	At least 25–30MB	Solaris 2.4 or 2.5 X11R5 JDK 1.02 Java-enabled browser, such as Netscape 2.0 or appletviewer A graphics design tool for editing GIF-format bitmaps (optional)
OS/2	486 or above A two-button mouse is preferred	16 MB RAM	At least 25 MB	IBM Operating System/2 (OS/2) Warp 3.0 JDK 1.0 IBM build OS/2-19960412 or later (both the run-time and the toolkit)

IntelliCraft by SourceCraft

IntelliCraft is loaded with several features that provide an integrated Web solution for building intranets. Several important features include (but are not limited to) the following:

In addition to generating applets, IntelliCraft can generate server-side Java classes.

IntelliCraft provides drag-and-drop integration of SQL databases using standard ODBC interfaces. Connectivity to the databases is available through applets or through HTML documents.

An extensible Java HTTP server can be deployed free of charge.

Download Site

An evaluation copy can be downloaded from **http://eval.sourcecraft.com/**. The evaluation period expires after 30 days. For more information on purchasing this software, go to **http://www.sourcecraft.com**.

Availability/System Requirements

Table 13-5 shows the system requirements for IntelliCraft.

Table 13-5 System requirements for IntelliCraft

	CPU	RAM	HARD DRIVE	SOFTWARE
Win32 Systems	Pentium processor	At least 16 MB (32 MB for Windows NT)	15 MB free hard drive space	Windows 95 or Windows NT 4.0 Netscape Navigator 3.0 (or later) or Microsoft Internet Explorer 3.0 (or later) Web browser

Mojo 2.0 by Penumbra Software

Mojo combines the ease of a high-level GUI designer with the power of a low-level coder. Mojo consists of two parts: a designer and a coder.

The designer (the terms *Mojo designer* and *designer* are used interchangeably in this chapter) uses a GUI that provides a visual means for building Java applets. The Mojo designer provides several built-in components that users can drag and drop into the designer. These components have properties associated with them on which actions can be performed. Actions can be added to a component by simply pointing and clicking on an available action list.

The coder (the terms *coder* and *Mojo coder* are used interchangeably in this chapter) organizes Java objects and gives the user direct access to all aspects of code. These objects are organized into a visible hierarchy for ease of use. The Mojo coder includes a class finder to search for components and existing classes easily and a way to create menus and dialogs easily.

Some important features of Mojo 2.0 are listed below:

- Third-party component incorporation allows third-party components to be added easily.

- Extensible component-based architecture allows users to add components easily.

- Class hierarchy search allows users to find components and their method calls easily.

Figures 13-3 and 13-4 show the designer and the coder.

Download Site

An evaluation copy of Mojo 2.0 can be downloaded from `http://www.penumbrasoftware.com/fresh.htm`. The trial version expires after 30 days and limits the build to eight components. For more information on purchasing this software, go to `http://www.penumbrasoftware.com`.

Availability/System Requirements

Table 13-6 shows the system requirements for Mojo 2.0.

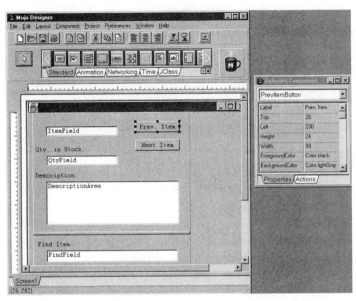

Figure 13-3 Mojo designer

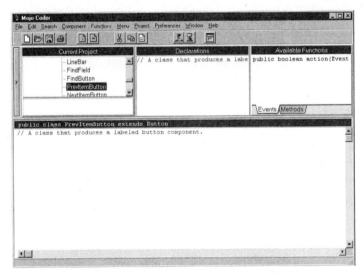

Figure 13-4 Mojo coder

Table 13-6 System requirements for Mojo 2.0

	CPU	RAM	HARD DRIVE	SOFTWARE
Win32 Systems	Pentium 75 MHz or faster	At least 32 MB	60 MB free hard drive space	Windows 95, Windows NT 3.51, Windows NT 4.0

NetDynamics by Spider Technologies

NetDynamics provides a very powerful client/server application development environment using the Web paradigm. NetDynamics consists of NetDynamics Studio and NetDynamics application server. NetDynamics Studio is a visual development environment that incorporates wizards and drag-and-drop facilities for rapid application development. The NetDynamics application server is a high-performance, scalable server for processing application logic, performing transactions against data sources, and creating and submitting dynamic Web pages to a Web server for distribution to a Web browser. The NetDynamics application server can be distributed across multiple CPUs and operating systems for greater performance.

The greatest strength of this product is the integrated approach it takes toward connecting databases to the Web. Instead of using several pieces to connect the browser to the database, NetDynamics provides a single environment with which Web-database connectivity can easily be achieved. It provides connectivity to several databases, including Oracle, Sybase, and Microsoft Access.

The NetDynamics application server works in conjunction with the Web server to provide a powerful environment to connect Web-based applications to databases. Applications developed using the NetDynamics Studio are deployed to the NetDynamics application server. When a user submits a URL, it is interpreted by the Web server, which passes the request on to the NetDynamics application server. The application server processes the Java logic for that application and makes the relevant connections to data sources to retrieve data. The resulting data is then formatted according to the settings defined in the page template and returned to the Web server as an HTML page.

Download Site

An evaluation copy of NetDynamics can be downloaded from `http://www.netdynamics.com/download/`. The trial version is a fully functional copy and can be evaluated for 30 days. At the end of 30 days, contact NetDynamics to make purchase arrangements. See `http://www.netdynamics.com` for more details.

Availability/System Requirements

Table 13-7 shows the system requirements for NetDynamics.

Table 13-7 System requirements for NetDynamics

	CPU	RAM	HARD DRIVE	SOFTWARE
Win32 Systems	Pentium processor	For Windows NT, at least 20 MB is needed; 32 MB RAM is recommended for development For Windows 95, 16 MB is required	20 MB free hard drive space	Windows 95 or Windows NT 4.0 A Web server A Web browser A database
UNIX	A UNIX box capable of running Solaris	64 MB required	50 MB of disk space required	Solaris (the application server runs on HP-UX and SGI-IRIX) A Web server A Web browser A database

VisualAge for Java by IBM

VisualAge for Java is an application development environment designed to connect Java clients to existing enterprise server data, transactions, and applications. It makes this task easier by generating JavaBean components and middleware components that connect the Java client to existing transaction, data, and application servers. It also provides an environment to create Java applets and applications or JavaBean components. VisualAge for Java has several components that provide an integrated environment.

> Integrated development environment: This allows programmers to develop Java programs rapidly.

> Visual composition editor: Applets, applications, and beans can be assembled using this editor.

> Enterprise access builder: This allows for connection to transaction servers, databases using JDBC, and applications written in C++ (using remote method invocation—RMI).

Download Site

At the time of writing this chapter, VisualAge for Java is still in beta. A beta version can be downloaded for evaluation from **http://www.software.ibm.com/ad/vajava/**. VisualAge for Java is scheduled to be made available in the second half of 1997.

Availability/System Requirements

Table 13-8 shows the system requirements for VisualAge.

Table 13-8 System requirements for VisualAge

	CPU	RAM	HARD DRIVE	SOFTWARE
Win32 Systems	Pentium processor	At least 32 MB	100 MB free hard drive space	Windows 95 or Windows NT 4.0 JDK 1.1 Java-enabled Web browser
OS/2	Pentium processor	At least 32 MB	100 MB free hard drive space	OS/2 Warp Version 4.0 JDK 1.1 Java-enabled Web browser

Visual Café 1.0 by Symantec

Visual Café by Symantec is perhaps the most widely used rapid application development (RAD) tool for developing Java applications. Several important features of Visual Café 1.0 are listed below.

With Visual Café, complete Java applets and applications can be assembled from a library of standard and third-party objects without having to write source code.

Like JBuilder, Visual Café provides two-way programming, meaning programmers can build components visually as Visual Café generates the corresponding code, or programmers can build applications by writing code.

Visual Café provides a full-featured project management system to help manage complex Java applications. The project window lists all forms, components, and classes in a project.

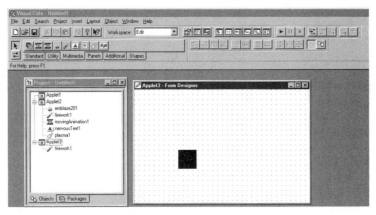

Visual Café provides a form-centric development environment.

An interaction wizard provides the ability to build relationships between objects that specify the action to take when an event is triggered on an object graphically. Visual Café automatically generates the necessary Java code for the specified relationship.

Visual Café provides a faster JIT compiler.

Many other features such as an integrated visual debugger, a breakpoints window, a threads window, and a watch window are also available.

Figure 13-5 shows many of the above-mentioned features of Visual Café.

Download Site

A preview version of Visual Café is not available for download. Visual Café can be purchased online at `http://cafe2.symantec.com/vcafewin/`.

More information on Visual Café can be obtained at `http://www.symantec.com/vcafe/`.

Availability/System Requirements

Table 13-9 shows the system requirements for Visual Café.

Figure 13-5 Visual Café

Table 13-9 System requirements for Visual Café

	CPU	RAM	HARD DRIVE	SOFTWARE
Win32 Systems	386 or above	12 MB required (16 MB recommended)	20–30 MB depending on configuration	Windows 95 or Windows NT (3.51 and 4.0)

Visual J++ 1.1 by Microsoft

Visual J++ is an environment for writing Java applets and applications whose compiler and type library wizard allow Java programs to access COM libraries and controls. In addition to supporting Java components, Visual J++ supports ActiveX components so that components written in other languages can be reused. It also allows programmers to create code that can be reused not only in browsers but also in other tools such as Visual Basic, VC++, PowerBuilder, Delphi, and Excel. Like the other products described in this chapter, Visual J++ contains a visual environment along with a debugger to create Java applications.

Download Site

A free trial version of Visual J++ 1.1 can be downloaded from `http://www.microsoft.com/visualj/`.

Availability/System Requirements

Table 13-10 shows the system requirements for Visual J++.

Table 13-10 System requirements for Visual J++

	CPU	RAM	HARD DRIVE	SOFTWARE
Win32 Systems	486 required (Pentium processor recommended)	If running Windows 95, 8 MB required (12 MB recommended) If running Windows NT, 16 MB required (20 MB recommended)	43 MB for typical installation 33 MB for minimum installation 50 MB for complete installation	Windows 95 or Windows NT 4.0

CHAPTER 14

What's Next?

Although you have come to the end of a book about NCs, the paradigm shift to the network-centric model of computing is just beginning. In the next few years, the boundaries between the network and the computer will become smaller and smaller and you will wonder how you ever lived without a network. In this chapter, let's take a look at what lies ahead, discuss some of the typical questions IT managers must answer with regard to the deployment of NCs, and make some opinionated forecasts about what computing may be like in the near future.

Will the NC Stay?

As a technology that makes sense, the NC is here to stay in some shape or form. Many companies that ridiculed the concept at first are gradually shifting their strategy. The NC exploits a narrow but growing market niche and fits that niche perfectly because its advancement is so heavily associated with the network infrastructure currently in place. Fortunately, networks such as the Internet and intranets are still growing. A number of vendors have quickly manufactured their versions of the NC. Most were in the terminal and X-terminal business, so the switch was relatively easy. A second wave of NCs with a bottom-up design is now hitting the market. These NCs are designed from scratch. This evolution will continue as the NC matures and gradually encompasses the network device market. A large number of companies are rallying behind the NC and making concrete commitments to support it.

From the software side, more and more traditional software packages are coming up with new releases that incorporate Internet capabilities, such as Office 97. We are also seeing a slow emergence of applications designed and written with the network and an NC environment in mind, including Corel Office. Java has emerged as the primary language for NC applications due to its portability and its network awareness. JDK 1.1 has fixed many of the early shortcomings of Java and has poised the language as a reliable and robust environment for enterprise applications. Java security still needs some work, and a tighter integration between Java and CORBA is required for a robust distributed object model based on Java. These enhancements will arrive soon. We will see a greater number of application development tools for Java, which should address one of the main cries of the programming community.

The infrastructure (both hardware and software) for supporting the NC is gradually taking shape. Wide deployment of the NC depends on how fast the infrastructure shapes up. Most large organizations have the networking muscle to support NCs, and there are numerous reports of successful deployment. Other organizations must concentrate on growing their network and making it more reliable before a switch to an NC environment makes sense for them. The important thing is that the direction toward a global network-centric model is set and the industry is following it. The Internet is seeing tremendous growth on a global basis, and more and more organizations are adopting intranet and extranet topologies to perform their daily tasks.

An important market for the NC is the device market. Originally, the NC was targeted at corporate IT environments. Large corporations were the only entities with the networking infrastructure for supporting NCs in place. The NC market will expand to include smaller organizations and households. A device that can act as a telephone, an email reader, and a Web browser is not science fiction. There is a legitimate need for such a device, and that need will be exploited.

What the device market is lacking right now (and will probably continue to lack in the near future) is a reliable infrastructure. The telephone is a common communication device—so common, that it is almost taken for granted, yet the infrastructure for telephone communication is still changing. We don't have a similar infrastructure on a large scale for supporting the network. Most homes still use a modem to "dial" into the network. For the device market to truly make sense, the networking infrastructure must be more complete than it is today. Connections to the network must be fast and continuous. From a global point of view, we have a long way to go.

Technologies such as ATM and cable modems promise to bulk up the infrastructure, but there are other barriers. The addressing scheme used in the Internet today is reaching its peak utilization. We are running out of numbers to identify network entities. At some point, the switch to a new Internet Protocol (IP) scheme must occur to provide support for a larger number of nodes on the global network.

The Decision

The NC has had an important side effect: It has caused a sharper focus on the network and network implementations and infrastructures. This shift has been supported partially by the argument that network environments (including the NC) will reduce costs in the long run. This is why we have seen tremendous efforts across IT departments for intranet deployments, platform integration, and an emphasis on cross-platform application development.

Early on, the NC was presented as a cost-saving alternative to existing desktop systems. There is certainly a different cost associated with the NC, and that is the network infrastructure. If you ignore this (and you really can't), then the maintenance cost of the NC is lower than that of a typical desktop or workstation. The cost issue is still up for debate, and different studies come to different conclusions. What is clear is that IT executives have more options about their desktop deployment, and that is a giant step forward.

At one end of the spectrum are power-packed PCs and workstations. These include UNIX- and NT-based machines for users who depend on their power and flexibility to get their job done. Application development falls under this category. Reading email once a day does not. Generally, these systems are expensive to own and maintain. Numerous upgrades are associated with them and the owner must be able to have control over system resources for testing and development purposes. Network access is also crucial.

On the other end are low-cost PCs and Net PCs. One can argue that these systems were introduced in a defensive move against the NC, and they are fighting to compete against the NC. They use some flavor of the Windows operating system and have access to the network. From a cost perspective, these machines are cheaper initially, but the maintenance costs are similar to other machines (considered high by NC standards). Typically, these systems are used for very specific tasks on a daily basis. Users are application users and not developers or system administrators. The NC competes directly with these systems. The NC thrives on an open environment for enterprise-side application deployment. Figure 14-1 shows the relative placement of the NC in the enterprise.

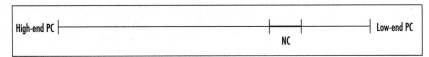

Figure 14-1 The NC in the enterprise

NC Technology

People have made cases for and against the NC from a business point of view. Debates and discussions about costs of ownership and maintenance have filled much of the media coverage of the NC evolution. This is the marketing and business approach and will continue. This book provides a technical perspective of the NC and presents the case that evolution of the NC represents a "paradigm shift in computing." From a technical point of view, the NC opens up an array of opportunities in the computing world.

The NC is a device. The Net PC and NC Reference Profile are specifications. Java is a programming language. Paradigm shifts are not dependent on one technology or one product. They are caused by shifting perspective on how something can be done. In this case, that "thing" is computing.

The network-centric model of computing has broken the barriers between the network and the computer. It has redefined clients and servers. Technologies such as applets and servlets distribute computing over the network. It is no longer a dumb client versus a powerful server; it is a smart client versus a smart server. Both pieces are capable of performing computation. The application specifies what types of computations occur on which network entities. Switching among servers is seamless to the client. The network-centric model encompasses servers, clients, applications, and networks.

The NC advocates smaller and modular applications that can be downloaded and maintained over the network. It encourages the use of component models and object models that allow the client to use only the part of the application it needs without worrying about the entire application. The NC pushes deployment of distributed applications. A single client may execute an application whose pieces reside on several servers. The NC encourages these designs and provides the infrastructure to deploy such applications successfully.

In short, the network-centric model offers a simpler and more effective way to do computing. We got ourselves in trouble with the old mainframe mentality, and client/server bailed us out. After a while, we got ourselves in trouble again, and NC is bailing us out! Technologies that offer a better way of doing something are not ignored. They will eventually become the norm, and the NC holds a similar future. The bottom line is that the NC makes technological sense; along with that comes business, marketing, and other kinds of "senses" that collectively make up a paradigm shift.

NC Devices

The NC revolution has put the spotlight on an emerging market of network-based devices and embedded systems. Although these devices can be computers or computer-like devices, they don't have to be. Telephones, television sets, stereos, radios, and heaters are all examples of devices. Do these devices have a concept of a global data network such as the Internet? Today the answer is no, although technologies such as Internet telephony and push technologies are changing this. Should these devices have a concept of a global data network? The NC revolution insists on an affirmative answer. Computers perform data processing and manage information and they can certainly benefit from a networked environment. Devices, too, can benefit from networks not only from a management point of view, but also because networks can add to devices' functionality and allow them to do more than what they can do today in a standalone mode. Many of the devices mentioned here have been working for years doing the same thing and perhaps improving slightly. The network is not necessary for these devices to survive, but if you stretch your imagination and think of what the devices could do in a network environment, the point should become clear.

Other than technological barriers, there is no reason why a telephone cannot be used for voice communication or a computer cannot be used for email communication. As far as the network-centric model is concerned, these are both forms of communication supported by a device. The supporting device in the first case is a telephone and in the second case is a computer. Could these two types of communication be performed by a single device? Of course they could, as long as the device is network aware.

The telephone is the most common example used when it comes to NC devices because it relies on a network for its functions, except the telephone network is different than the data network NCs rely on. We use a number of other devices today; more could be invented to take advantage of the possibilities network computing provides. For years television has been a one-way communication device. With network connectivity, it can become a two-way channel where you can participate in surveys and discussions or request your favorite show. This is possible with a network. How exactly network integration will be utilized in a device like a television depends on the market and the innovative force behind it. Products such as WebTV are a step in the right direction, but they are just the beginning. Accessing Web sites and ordering a product through your TV on a regular basis are not very far away.

The device market extends beyond communication devices. Consistent management and control of devices has been a sought-after function for a long time. Factories are a good example of how a large amount of machinery (related and unrelated) must work to produce a product. Coordination and management have always been problems, especially because many of the devices are unrelated in the task they perform. A system that manages electric power is different than one that controls hydraulic pressure in robots. To account for such differences, a different control system has been designed for each operation and the result is a maze of control systems that collectively control the entire factory operation. In the near future, embedded systems running under operating systems such as JavaOS and Inferno will flood the market. These embedded systems are network aware and can communicate with other systems. A single application can control a number of different operations because a common interface (network and operating system) exists among these systems.

The network offers a better solution. It provides a consistent interface to all devices regardless of their functions. It allows each device to participate on the network according to an application standard that it provides and supports. Similar devices can find each other on the network and be managed collectively. Dissimilar devices enjoy the common layer of network interface and work on building application layer interfaces to each other. Although it doesn't make sense to connect just any two devices together via a network, for related devices—such as computers, telephones, and fax machines—such a connection can be very beneficial. Once again, the network-centric model provides a better way of doing something.

Once the infrastructure for execution of this premise is in place, you can expect to be able to change the room temperature of your living room from a network device at the airport before you head home! The network is your interface to the heating system. The heating system serves the application you need to adjust it. All you need is a network-based device to act as your client. A simple Web browser will do.

We are not there yet. Government regulations, security concerns, and a reliable infrastructure are some of the issues that must be resolved. The technology for such networks is not unreachable. Implementation of these technologies based on social, moral, economical, legal, and political arenas is another story.

The Network

I have made numerous references to the "network" and the "network-centric model of computing." Think a moment about what, exactly, the network is. A telephone network carries voice communication. This network has been around for a long time and is very advanced. Another type of network deals with wireless voice communication, also referred to as the *cellular network*. This is an emerging and fast-growing network and is responsible for making cell phones function. Another network carries television signals. Cable companies and satellite companies are involved with this network. Another network is responsible for carrying data packets for Internet communication.

These networks seem very different from a technical point of view, but conceptually the networks are very much alike. Data networks can and do carry both voice and video communication, once the data is digitized. Data networks may not be as fast and effective as radio and TV signals, but we have seen great improvements in the past couple of years. Conceptually, all networks carry some form of data. The device at the end decides how the data is presented.

Network infrastructures are expensive to put in place and maintain. We will continue having different networks for different types of communication, but the next few years will also witness a massive integration effort. The ultimate goal will be to carry digital data because it encompasses all the other data types, such as voice and video. Convenience and cost are probably going to be the major forces behind this integration effort. Cellular phones do the same thing that regular phones do. Why did we make such huge investments to come up with cellular networks? Convenience: The public paid and continues to pay for convenience. Could cellular phones have become so popular without a cellular network? In a similar fashion, the convenience of a global data network will not be realized until the network and the devices to connect to it are in place.

In a global economy, many large companies must do business in multiple countries and across continents. For these companies, network-based enterprise is not only a convenience, but a necessity. The ability to disseminate information at lightning speed across all divisions and locations of a company and the ability to distribute up-to-date databases have become essential parts of modern business.

Enterprise Applications

So where is the enterprise going with all of this? Certainly IT shops are not rushing to rewrite every line of code of their applications in Java and embrace network-centric computing at once. For new projects, Java should be given serious consideration. Java has successfully been used in a number of different projects across industries such as banking, telecommunication, military, and entertainment. It has passed its infancy stage, and JavaSoft has positioned Java as a complete programming environment for serious applications.

Security continues to be an important consideration as corporations move toward a network-based environment. Accessibility is a desired feature only when it is appropriate and authorized. At one extreme is the position that no sensitive data should be placed on the network; at the other extreme is the argument that any type of data can be placed on the network as long as access to it is controlled. The industry will probably settle at some middle ground and will continue to advance security schemes.

Implementation will occur at several levels, including applications, servers, and physical networks. One thing that network computing will bring is a push toward standardization of security schemes so that different computers can communicate with each other in a secure manner. Standards such as Secure Socket Layer (SSL) are a step in the right direction.

How do we move the existing infrastructure to the new paradigm? Although it may seem simple, the answer is "Very slowly." The NC can be used right now to access applications running on the Web, on a mainframe, and under Windows NT (using emulation software). This is fine, but it barely shows the potential of the NC and the changes it will bring about. That potential can be exploited only once applications written specifically for the network-centric environment are deployed across the enterprise. At that time, the NC not only will make sense, it will become an essential component of the enterprise.

Growth in Internet and intranets will continue for the foreseeable future. Corporations will struggle to achieve common application standards across business units, and programmers will struggle to consolidate duplicate efforts in application development and support. It is safe to state that most IT organizations understand the implications behind network computing and are making an effort to move toward such an environment. This move may not be in the form of immediate deployment of network computers; what is important is that companies continue to move toward a network environment by investing in Web-based applications and corporate intranets. It is already happening today at a very rapid pace.

Summary

The NC is a rapidly changing technology. The stage is set for moving to a global network-centric environment, but how we get there, how long it will take, and, in the eyes of some skeptics, whether we will ever get there remain to be seen. The benefits of the network and its integration with our computing model are overwhelming. Based on this reason, the NC and the technologies it advocates are here to stay.

With the proper infrastructure in place, the network device market should see an explosive growth in the near future. A wide variety of networks is in place for carrying different data types. The industry will go through an integration phase in which new technologies attempt to make these networks work together. This effort requires new infrastructure as well as building on top of the existing framework.

A Guide to ActiveX

To understand ActiveX technology, you should understand the trend of other technologies. A few hundred years ago, before the industrial revolution, all products were custom made. If you needed a jacket, for example, you would go to a tailor and describe the specifics of what you wanted. The tailor would take your measurements and make a jacket according to your measurements and specifications. The same was true if you needed a table, a gun, or a shoe. At this stage of evolution, parts were manufactured for products as needed (see Figure A-1).

In the very early stages of the industrial revolution, small workshops were created with several waged workers and one owner who also was a worker. To keep the workers busy during slow times, the owner anticipated market need and manufactured goods for future markets. This led to an important advancement in industry: Owners discovered the profitability of manufacturing only the more difficult parts of the products during slow times, which led to the build-up of an inventory of certain parts. The next advancement was when owners discovered that they could design their product around the parts available in their inventory.

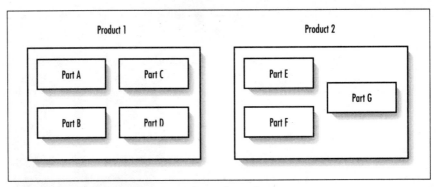

Figure A-1 Products before the industrial revolution

The industrial revolution occurred when manufacturing the parts became a completely separate task from manufacturing the products. Shops began to manufacture parts for purchase by manufacturers of products. Today, a product may have several thousand parts; few are built by the manufacturer of the product itself. Parts specialists manufacture parts based on available technology and potential products (see Figure A-2). The manufacturer designs the product based on the available parts and assembles them in a container. The efficiency of manufacturing products in this way stimulated the economy to such a degree that thousands of products were made available to the public at costs that were affordable to more people than ever before. This also caused manufacturers and designers to come up with new products that were previously unthinkable. We live comfortably today using products such as cars, phones, and computers. All came after a brilliant idea: reusable parts.

The trend in computer software technology is somewhat similar to the trend in the industrial revolution. Ever since digital computers were born, programmers have been busy programming them to solve problems. It took the programmers a few decades instead of 10,000 years to figure out that solutions to different problems have similar components (aren't programmers smart?). Wouldn't it be nice to be able to reuse a component from a previous program, or—better than that—wouldn't it be nice to select components from a pool of available components and just build a container?

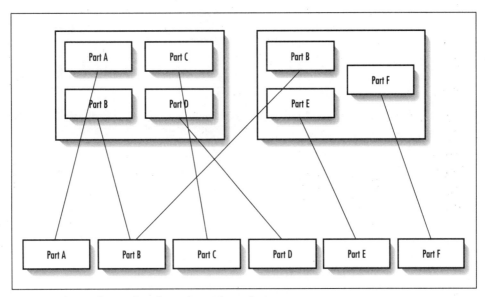

Figure A-2 Products after the industrial revolution

Reusable Software Libraries

In the past few decades, computer scientists have spent a great deal of time figuring out methodologies that address the issue of software reusability. Prior to the popularity of object-oriented technology, many methodologies were invented based on modular design and structured programming to create reusable software libraries. Reusable software libraries are packaged in files, usually with the LIB extension, and consisting of a collection of different routines that have some common functionality. Examples of software libraries are a communication library, a graphics library, a user interface library, and a database library. Usually an application (such as a word processor or a database) uses the library to perform some common tasks. The software library is linked to the main application, which means it becomes an integrated part of it, just like other codes that were written for that particular application. In the past, no standard dictated how to use the libraries, so each software library had its own proprietary interface. If the programmers wanted to replace their library with a similar one, they had to revisit the codes that use the library, make the modifications, and compile, link, and generate a new executable file that contained the new library. Even if the library was a small part of the entire application, the whole application had to be regenerated to include the new library. Furthermore, in most cases, libraries were not only language dependent but also language-version dependent. Figure A-3 represents the relation between applications and traditional libraries.

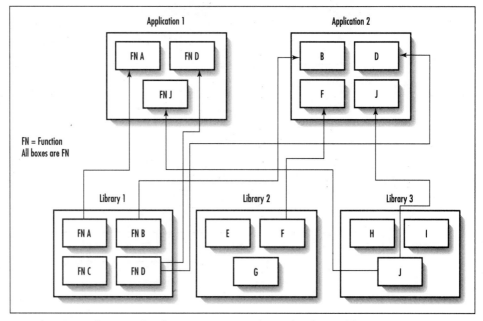

Figure A-3 Application development using traditional software libraries

Let's have a look at a typical software library, a communication library package, for example. Many different applications need to communicate with another computer and can use a communication library. A simple communication library could consist of the following routines:

Set up the modem: Select a modem type, set modem parameters, set up user parameters.

Initialize modem: Check for dial tone, establish communication to modem.

Dial a number: Send a command to the modem to dial a number, verify if the other modem answered, and establish communication.

Send data: Send a number of bytes, check for errors.

Receive data: Receive a number of bytes, check for errors.

Send a file: Select a file transfer protocol, activate the protocol.

Receive a file: Detect the protocol, activate the file receiving the protocol.

A communication library can get more involved than just the routines outlined above; for example, it may contain fax transmission routines and transmission scheduling. For the sake of this discussion, however, let's stick to the above model.

There are a number of problems with the sample communication library. Let's take a look at the first library routine listed above: Set up the modem. One of the tasks of this routine is to select a modem from a list of modems preprogrammed in the library. The end user has to identify the specific modem type because each modem might be different. At the time the software library was written, the programmers included all available modems. Maybe they went even further by including some modems that were going to be manufactured in the near future. But a software library by itself is not complete and functional. To save development time, the programmers who write an application (a word processor, for example) use the library. Well, the computer industry targets are dynamic targets (not just moving targets). The targets move and change while the bullets are still in the air. By the time the final application is in the market and actually installed in users' computers, chances are that new modems have come to market that are not supported by that application. Because the software library is an integrated part of the main application, the only way to update your system is to update your application. That means that even if a new version of the communication software library is available, you have to rely on the people who provided your application to generate an update for you. The result, as you have probably experienced at one time or other, is that many users experience periods during which their modems are not supported by an application. In summary, traditional software libraries addressed the issue of software reusability to some extent, but revealed many drawbacks, including:

- They are not directly reusable by the end user.

- They are language and version dependent.

- They do not have a well-defined interface.

- Several applications that use the same libraries have to duplicate the library codes.

Object-Oriented Technology and Reusable Software Libraries

Traditional software libraries were difficult to use and were prone to bugs. However, until recently, they were the most common way to achieve software reusability. Most problems with such libraries are inherent in traditional methods of programming, or *procedural programming*.

Object-oriented technology addresses the problems that exist with software reusability inherent in the traditional software libraries. Software codes are encapsulated in objects, providing a cleaner interface and hiding many of the internal complexities from other objects. The buzzword for reusable software libraries in the object-oriented world is *object libraries*. Because the new generation of software libraries had a better-defined interface, the need for a mechanism to replace them at runtime became more apparent. This need led to the dynamic link libraries (DLLs). Each DLL file may contain one or more objects that can be used by several applications. The end user can update a DLL without relying on the vendor of the applications. Furthermore, if a DLL is updated, all the applications using that DLL are updated (see Figure A-4).

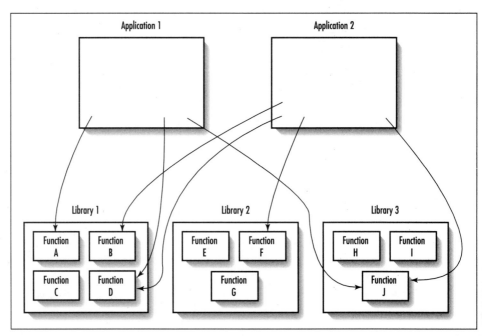

Figure A-4 Dynamic link libraries

Shrink-Wrapped Software Products and End User Development Tools

Software object libraries and dynamic link libraries resolved many of the problems that existed with traditional software libraries. Using these technologies, the end users can update their systems when an update to a library becomes available. In fact, not only can users modify their existing libraries; they can also add new functionality to their existing applications by installing new components that were not part of their original application.

Add-in technology is a step beyond software reusability. It gives end users the capability to purchase an application and then choose the optional features they would like to have at a later time.

Suppose you buy a word processor application for simple word processing tasks. After a few months you realize a need to scan pictures into your word processor documents. You may then buy a scanner that connects to your word processor program as an add-in component. You install your scanner and now your word processor has scanning capability. At a later time, you may decide that you need to convert and import text documents from a tape recorder or microphone. You can then purchase another add-in to import voice to your document. There are thousands of possibilities for add-in components for a word processor application: language translation, communication, database links, Internet links, sound capability, and drawing capability, to name a few. End users can pick the components that best suit their specific needs and taste.

On the other hand, you may find many features already installed on your word processor that you never use. You can eliminate those features to simplify your word processor while keeping the functionality you need. An application with add-in features is called a *shrink-wrapped product*. A shrink-wrapped product is not a rigid application that is created to perform certain tasks; it is a flexible container that can be used as an end user development tool to build a custom application.

Using end user development tools to create custom applications has many advantages over the traditional methods of application development:

- The development process is faster. With these tools, you do not have to start from scratch to develop a new application. You use an existing product and enhance it by adding new features to it and simplify it by removing the features that are not needed.

- The final products are easier to use.

- It is less costly to develop applications using end user development tools.

In the traditional development process, you have to come up with a specification for the whole project in advance. Often, needs are overlooked or completely skipped at this stage. This results in an application that is less than what the user needs. With end user development tools, users do not have to limit their needs because they overlooked them in the beginning. These tools also encourage need-driven development.

Business changes continuously. New needs arise as business changes. End user development tools can address these changes as well.

What Is OLE?

To understand ActiveX technology, you must understand OLE. OLE stands for object linking and embedding (pronounced like the Spanish bull-fighting term *olé*, but the meanings are not exactly the same!) and is based on the component object model (COM). In our language, it means a software model that is composed of multiple components with a specific well-defined interface; each component is an object. The following example will make this concept simpler to understand.

Suppose you have a Microsoft Word document and you want to include a picture in it. One way is to prepare your figure using a program such as Microsoft Paint. Then select the Insert Picture menu item in Microsoft Word to insert your Paint file into your document. There is only one drawback in using the above technique. Every time you want to edit that figure, you have to open another application, edit and save the picture, open your Word document, delete the old picture, and insert the new version of it.

Another way is insert your figure as an object rather than a picture. Select the Insert Object menu item in Microsoft Word. Then select an application such as Paint Brush. Microsoft Word will create a Paint Brush object for you inside your Word document. Anytime you are editing your document, you can also edit your figure without leaving Word. By inserting a Paint Brush object into your Word document, you add not only a figure but also paint functionality to your document. This is the key to understanding objects and OLE. A picture is a picture, whereas an object picture in this case is the picture with functionality to edit the picture.

By inserting an object into your Microsoft Word document, you used OLE. The Microsoft Paint program became an OLE object for your Word document.

VBX Controls

The above is an example of OLE for an end user using Microsoft Word. Programmers use the same concept to program with OLE objects. Microsoft introduced VBX files with Visual Basic (VB). Although they are not true OLE controls, VBX files have a defined functionality ranging from a simple command button to a rather complicated database browser. Each VBX file is associated with a control object in Visual Basic and can be customized using its specific properties. The concept of VBX for programmers as OLE objects is similar to the way a picture object is inserted into a Word document in the above example. The difference is that when using VBXs, you can do everything programmatically. Once an instance of a VBX object is created inside a Visual Basic program, its functionality is available to the programmer by using the object's methods. An application can create several instances of the VBX control. In fact, several applications running in multiple processes can generate multiple instances of the same VBX control object. Examples of methods for a database browser object are next record, previous record, and find a record.

VBXs provide a feasible way of incorporating complex functionality into a reusable package. Although they are a breakthrough in desktop applications, VBX controls do not fit well in the world of the Internet and its distributed model because of their large size and the fact that the basis of their design is not for a distributed environment.

OCX Controls

VBX controls were definitely a success in breaking the ground for reusable OLE controls. OLE custom controls (OCX) were introduced as the next generation of VBX controls with Visual Basic 4.00. OCX controls are superior to their predecessors because of their simplicity and more powerful functionality. OCX controls support both 16- and 32-bit architecture, whereas VBX controls support only 16-bit architecture.

Both VBX and OCX controls have some deviation from the original OLE standard specification. However, many of the OCX controls are designed based on the distributed component object model (DCOM), which makes them suitable ActiveX controls.

What Is COM?

Before continuing the discussion of ActiveX controls, let's look at the fundamental technology behind all these types of controls. The technology behind shrink-wrapped software applications is based on object-oriented design and programming. COM is the underlying framework of the Windows operating systems, which makes shrink-wrapped products, OLE, VBX, OCX, and ActiveX modules possible or at least practical. Microsoft Corporation has incorporated this technology in the Windows family of operating systems for several years.

COM is an object-based standard that allows the development of software components by different developers using a variety of languages and platforms. In-house developers and end users can obtain new components or develop their own and integrate them with an existing application.

The key to understanding COM is to look at the different ways software modules can communicate with each other. Following is a list of the different ways that communication can take place (see Figure A-5):

An application calls a function and talks to it by passing parameters. This is the more traditional way of communication between software modules. The called function is an integrated part of the main application and runs in the same process.

An application uses the functionality of another application that runs in a completely separate process. In this case, the calling application must send its request via some sort of messaging protocol to the called application and expect to receive a response via the same protocol.

An application uses the services provided by the operating system. In this case, the application makes system calls served by the operating system. From the programmer's point of view, the interface is similar to normal library calls.

An application may use the services provided by another application running on a different process that runs on a different computer. The computers are connected via some sort of network. Several methods have been used for such communication, including sending and receiving messages or invoking a remote procedure call (client/server model).

All the above methods address one fundamental relation: the relation between a calling module and a called module, or in more modern terminology, the relation between one component accessing the services provided by a second component. The question is why do we need so many different approaches to one fundamental need? The answer is chaos theory. If we want to have reusable components, it would be nice to have one standard approach that software components can use to communicate with each other. This is exactly what COM attempts to achieve. COM provides a standard so that all types of components, including applications, system software, and libraries can communicate via a common architecture.

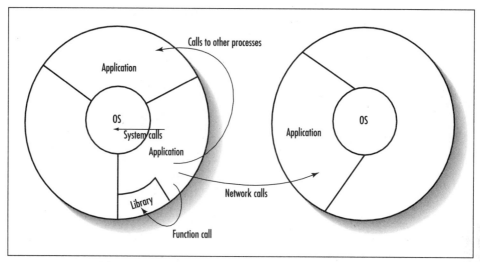

Figure A-5 Possible ways of communication between software components

How COM Works

To understand COM, it is important to understand its key features, interfaces, classes, servers, object life cycle, binary interoperability, and location transparency.

Interface is the most important element in understanding COM objects. An interface is a set of one or more properties and methods through which other components can access the functionality of a COM object. Communication of a COM object to the outside world is limited to its interface (see Figure A-6). Each COM object must support at least one interface called **IUnknown**. **IUnknown** provides methods that other components can invoke to find out about the specific characteristics of the COM object. One of the methods of **IUnknown** interface is **QueryInterface**. Using this method, an external component can determine whether or not the COM object supports a specific interface. Suppose you have a database browser COM object. Examples of possible interfaces are **IOpenDatabase**, **ICloseDatabase**, **IAddRecord**, and **IQueryDatabase**. Just like any other software component, a COM object is expected to evolve over time. As a result of this process, it may support a new interface or a revised version of an existing interface. Each interface, including the newer versions of an existing interface, is assigned a unique interface ID. Therefore, other components can continue to use the COM object exactly the way they used it before it was revised.

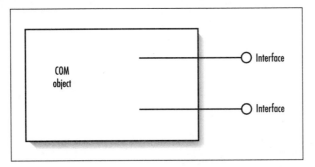

Figure A-6 Interfaces are the gateways to a COM object

Another key feature of a COM object is its classes. A COM class is the body of the code embedded in the COM object that supports the internal functionality of the COM object. In addition to internal functionality, each COM class supports one or more interfaces. Just like interfaces, each class is identified with a unique ID called *CLASID* (class ID). For any client to be able to use a COM object, it has to know about at least one of its CLASIDs and one of the interface identifiers (IIDs) supported by that class. The client can then request the COM object to create an object based on the above information. If everything goes well, the COM object creates an object and returns an interface pointer to the client. The interface pointer is the specific interface of that client to the instance of the object that was just created. It is via this interface pointer that that the client can use the functionality of the COM object by invoking its methods and properties.

COM servers are collections of one or more COM classes. In its simplest form, a COM server can be implemented in several different ways. It can be implemented as a DLL. In this case, as soon as any class within the server is accessed, the COM server is loaded into the client process as if it was originally part of the same process. This type of COM server is called an *in-process server* (see Figure A-7).

Another implementation of a COM server is a separate EXE file. This type of COM server runs on a separate process than the client process. The process can be on the same machine as the client or at a remote machine, which talks to the client via networks. An EXE COM server is called an *out-of-process server* (see Figure A-8).

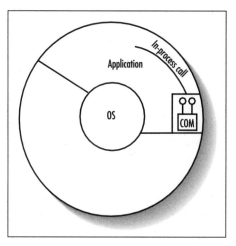

Figure A-7 An in-process call

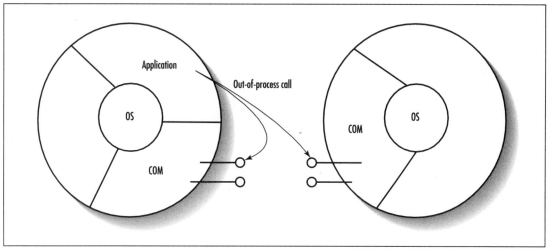

Figure A-8 Out-of-process calls

Whether the server is an in-process server or an out-of-process server, the interface remains the same and the client code to communicate with the server is exactly the same. The internal mechanism of communicating with an in-process server is different from communicating with an out-of-process server, however. In the case of an in-process server, the calls go directly to the server in the same process (that is, DLLs). In the case of an out-of-process server, however, the calls go to a middleman called a *proxy object*. A proxy server is an in-process COM server. The proxy server in turn translates the client's request to procedure calls and sends them to the appropriate server. Similar to the middleman on the client side, the middleman on the server side is responsible for receiving requests from clients, translating them back to COM class requests, and dispatching them to the appropriate server for response. The server's response takes the same route in the opposite direction to reach the client. The mechanism of communicating to a local out-of-process server (an EXE COM server running on the local machine) is the same as communicating to a remote out-of-process server (an EXE COM server running on a remote machine). The only difference is that there are separate proxy objects for local communications and remote communications (see Figure A-9).

COM has a binary standard for the layout of the communication messages between components. Interoperability resulting from this binary standard allows developers to create COM objects independent of the environment they run. It also allows COM components to be created and distributed without worrying about distributing the source code.

Another important feature of COM is packaging transparency. As mentioned before, COM components can be implemented by DLL or EXE files. In addition, EXE files can run locally or remotely. Developers using COM components do not need to worry about how the components are packaged or whether they are local or remote. In fact, they do not even need to know where a particular DLL or EXE file is located. Prior to invocation of a COM server by a client, the COM server has to be registered in the registry of the

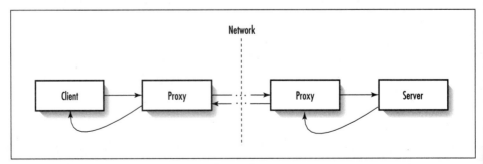

Figure A-9 The internal mechanism of out-of-process communication

machine that it runs, along with information about its type and location. As the server's machine receives a request for a COM server, its COM service control manager (SCM) looks in the local registry, finds the location, and performs the proper tasks to activate the server. All this is done behind the scenes by the COM library. The developers of the client application only have to worry about using the proper CLASID to invoke a COM object.

Now that you have an overall understanding of COM technology, let's look at how COM objects are created at runtime and their life cycle.

Each COM server has one or more COM classes. A COM object is an instance of a COM class. Creating instances of a COM class is done by the COM class factory, which is another COM class that is associated with the original class. The class factory supports a standard interface called **IClassFactory**. COM class instances are created and an interface pointer to the resulting object is returned to the calling application via this standard interface. A client application simply passes the CLASID of the desired COM class and the rest is done behind the scenes. COM architecture defines a standard way of keeping track of the number of reference pointers generated for a given object. It is the responsibility of each COM class to keep track of the number of instances created by the class factory. Therefore, any internal methods that create and return a reference pointer must call the standard method **AddRef()** to increment the number of instances. A COM object can be destroyed when its total number of references reaches zero.

Distributed Software Components

The discussion so far has centered on reusable software components. This is the area that researchers have been focusing on since the early stages of software technology. Let's pause the discussion about software reusability and look at another growing aspect of this technology: distributed software components.

In the early stages of PC networks, the networks usually consisted of one or more computers acting as file servers, with several computers attached to them as workstations. The main server's job was to act as a central location for programs and data to be shared by workstations. A typical scenario was to activate a program from the server's hard drive to perform some tasks on a collection of local and remote data and save the result on the server. In this type of architecture, the programs are stored at the server but run on the local machine. As the program requires data from the server, the data is sent from the server to the workstation. The workstation then performs some manipulation of the data. The resulting data, if any, is sent back to the server in the same manner. This architecture works nicely for small amounts of data but tends to be impractical with large data collections. Imagine searching the U.S. Social Security database using this architecture. You would have to transfer the entire population's data to a workstation to be able to select one person. This is impractical because it not only takes a long time for the search, it saturates the network capacity, locking out other users.

How do you perform the search without that huge data transfer over the network? The answer is easy and natural. You let the search take place at the server's side instead of the client side. This is where client/server architecture comes into the show. In this case, a query is sent from the client to the server. The server performs the query on its local data and sends a response back to the client. In client/server architecture, procedures can be saved along with data on the server side. Both servers and clients are capable of running codes that are logically interrelated. Client/server architecture is the first step toward distributed computing.

In the past few years, computer technology has been thrusting forward on another front: the Internet. The advances in data communication technologies and the advent of the World Wide Web have brought tremendous growth to the Internet. Today, the Internet is emerging as the main vehicle for information exchange among computers.

In the early stages of the World Wide Web, simple documents were transferred from servers to clients at the client's request. The browsers on the client side would merely display the documents based on the local hardware. The browsers also had the capability to request another document based on the user input.

Well, if we can send documents, we should also be able to send code to execute tasks at the client side to enhance the documents. This is why the next generation of browsers was script-enabled. *Script* refers to the codes embedded inside the document that may get executed upon certain events after the document is downloaded. Every time a document with embedded scripts is downloaded, its associated code is also downloaded. In addition, the downloaded code cannot be easily reused in another program or document. That is why scripts meet the criteria for being distributed software components but not reusable ones.

Reusable software and distributed software components are finally getting married. Sun Microsystems, a leader in innovative distributed software components, has made them reusable (JavaBeans); Microsoft, a leader in software reusability, has made them distributable (ActiveX).

What Is DCOM?

Although the original COM standard was designed with distribution in mind, it was never completely implemented. COM objects could be packaged as a DLL and run in the same process as the client, or they could be packaged in EXE files and run in a separate process on the same machine as the client. The implementation lacked access to services provided by a COM server in a separate machine connected by networks.

DCOM is the extension of COM to include extra features. DCOM implementation extends location transparency to anywhere in a network. COM clients may have access to any server that is registered on any machine in a network configuration without knowing where the EXE file is located. When a client makes a request for a remote object, the local SCM sends the request to the remote request. The remote request locates the desired server and launches it. The remote SCM then sends a remote procedure call (RPC) pointing the new object back to the local SCM. The local SCM then creates a proxy object for the client. From this point, everything continues as if the objects were on the same machine.

DCOM also includes the free-threading model, in which a multithreaded server object can leverage the multiprocessing power of a server machine and achieve increased throughput. COM limits each COM object to be accessed only by the thread that created it. In DCOM, multiple requests to the same object can be dispatched to the same object in different threads.

DCOM addresses the issue of security by providing an access control list (ACL). The ACL contains a list of users and groups that have access to this particular COM object. The system administrators can edit the ACL.

DCOM has a better way of reference counting for servers. Servers keep track of the number of clients accessing the server. If the number of clients is zero, then the server can be destroyed. If a client connection dies before releasing the server, however, the number of references never will reach zero. DCOM resolves this issue by sending keep-alive messages from client machines. If a client connection dies, DCOM detects the situation and releases the server if it is no longer needed.

ActiveX Controls

Both reusability and the ability to distribute software components converge in ActiveX technology. ActiveX controls are true OLE controls based on DCOM; they address the problems that exist with the way computers interact with each other over the Internet. ActiveX technology is not limited to the Internet and network applications and can be applied to regular desktop programming. It is an attempt to bring regular desktop programming and Internet programming together. Most ActiveX controls can be used in HyperText Markup Language (HTML) documents as well as regular programming languages such as Visual Basic or C++ to create active Web pages. In short, ActiveX controls are OLE controls that can be used on the Internet. Most OCX controls can be used as ActiveX controls.

If you have an application that requires the cooperation of multiple components running on different Windows machines, consider ActiveX technology. Also, if your requirements dictate that your application be movable from the desktop to the Internet or an intranet or vice versa, ActiveX is a good candidate.

ActiveX-Supported Platforms

ActiveX is currently supported by the Windows family of operating systems. Microsoft Corporation is working with Metrowerks (a leading provider of Macintosh development tools) and Macromedia to support ActiveX on Macintosh operating systems. Microsoft is also working with UNIX development companies such as Bristol and Mainsoft to develop ActiveX support on UNIX systems. Many experts are skeptical about the outcome of Microsoftís efforts to adapt ActiveX to other platforms in the near future, however.

In the PC world, Microsoft Internet Explorer and Mosaic browsers support ActiveX. In addition, ActiveX-enabling plug-ins are available for the Netscape browser from NCompass Labs. For more information on Netscape ActiveX plug-ins, refer to `http://www.ncompasslabs.com/products/scripactive.htm`.

ActiveX System Requirements

DCOM was developed with the requirement that it must be suitable for various types of platforms. Any platform that supports DCOM can also support ActiveX. DCOM is part of Windows NT Version 4.0; it is available free for downloading from `http://www.microsoft.com/oledev/olemkt/oledcom/dcom95.htm`.

You will be able to redistribute DCOM for Windows 95 with your applications royalty free. In addition to the platform, each ActiveX control may require the presence of certain system files. For example all the controls in Internet Control Pack (ICP) need `NMSCKN.DLL` in addition to their OCX control. Most of the ICP controls also require `NMORENU.DLL` and `NMOCOD.DLL`.

Because of the diversity inherent in the ActiveX design, no one set of files can make your system completely ActiveX-enabled. Each new ActiveX control may have a new file requirement.

ActiveX Versus Java

Both ActiveX and Java aim at solving some problems inherent to large networks in general and the Internet in specific. Both Java programs and ActiveX controls can be downloaded over the Internet and run on a local machine.

Is ActiveX technology competing with Java? It is difficult to answer this question. Microsoft does not believe so. It reasons that ActiveX is an integration technology, whereas Java is a programming language. In addition to being a programming language, Java is also a way of doing distributed computing. The two technologies are in competition with each other in their ability to transfer code that runs on multiple platforms over the Internet. Sun Microsystem's JavaBeans is a new product of the Java family that is in more direct competition with ActiveX technology.

The approaches taken by the two technologies are, however, completely different. Java transfers bytecode, which runs on Java virtual machines (JVMs) locally. The virtual machine software is similar to an interpreter. There is a major advantage to this approach: The bytecode is developed once for multiple platforms. Once a program is available, it can run on any local machine that has JVM software running. On the disadvantage side, some people argue that the bytecode runs slower because it has to go through another layer of interpretation by the JVM software (JavaSoft is addressing this issue by introducing just-in-time compilers). Another argument is that, depending on a particular JVM, bytecode can be less powerful than the native code of each local computer. Many functionalities of the local processor may not be available in bytecodes. This will impose a drawback in design and development of certain bytecode applications.

Let's have a look at ActiveX technology in regard to the above issues. ActiveX components are in native machine code (currently available only on Intel processors). This might give the illusion that the ActiveX code runs as fast as any other code on the local machine and can take full advantage of the local processor capabilities. The truth is that, just like Java, ActiveX code has to go through another layer on the system to reach system resources. That both slows down performance and restricts resources. Currently, the only layer available for ActiveX controls is Windows operating systems.

Here is how ActiveX gets activated. The combination of the local machine ActiveX manager and a properly designed application or HTML page requests the proper ActiveX control from the server and installs it on the local machine. For that reason, the server has to have as many different versions of the ActiveX controls as the number of the platforms it supports. Each control is written for its native platform. This feature makes it substantially more difficult to develop true multiple platform applications using ActiveX controls. The ActiveX technology will likely be mainly centered on the Windows world in the near future.

Available ActiveX Controls

Several controls were shipped with Microsoft Internet Explorer 3.0 and ActiveX Control Pad. The following controls are not licensed. That means that you can download them for free and reuse them in your Web pages and programs and redistribute them without paying royalties to Microsoft.

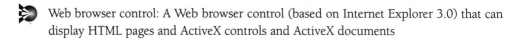

Web browser control: A Web browser control (based on Internet Explorer 3.0) that can display HTML pages and ActiveX controls and ActiveX documents

Timer: Can be programmed to execute actions/scripts at set time intervals

Marquee control: Scrolls any HTML files in either a horizontal or a vertical direction and can be configured to change the amount and delay of scrolling; this control is built-in to Internet Explorer

ActiveMovie control: Displays streaming and nonstreaming media, such as video, sound, and synchronized images with sound

The HTML layout control: Displays two-dimensional HTML regions inside Internet Explorer 3.0 using new World Wide Web Consortium (W3C) extensions to HTML

Microsoft Forms 2.0 label: Used for creating basic text labels

Microsoft Forms 2.0 text box: A multiline text-entry and text-display window

Microsoft Forms 2.0 combo box: Allows users to choose from a drop-down list of options

Microsoft Forms 2.0 list box: Allows users to choose from a scrollable list of options

Microsoft Forms 2.0 check box: Allows users to check an option

Microsoft Forms 2.0 option button: Allows users to choose between multiple options

Microsoft Forms 2.0 toggle button: A button that has a toggle state (for example, on/off)

Microsoft Forms 2.0 command button: A basic push-button control

Microsoft Forms 2.0 tabstrip: Provides multiple pages that can be selected via tabs

Microsoft Forms 2.0 scroll bar: Basic horizontal and vertical scroll bars

Microsoft Forms 2.0 spin button: A button that can be pushed up or down

 The Microsoft ActiveX image control: Displays progressively rendered images in metafile, **.JPG**, **.GIF**, **.BMP**, or wavelet formats

The Microsoft ActiveX hot spot control: Used to add a transparent hot spot within the HTML layout control

For more information on available ActiveX controls, see the Internet Explorer page at **http://www.microsoft.com/ie/default.asp**.

In addition, an evergrowing list of ActiveX controls is available from third-party software development houses. At this time, well over 1,000 ActiveX controls are available from dozens of third parties.

Where You Can Get ActiveX Controls

Probably the best place to look for third-party ActiveX controls is the ActiveX Component Gallery at **http://www.microsoft.com/activex/gallery/**.

In addition, any time you browse an ActiveX-enabled HTML page, you may encounter a control. If you do not have that particular control installed in your system, your Web browser automatically downloads and installs the control in your system. If that control is not a licensed type, you can reuse it in your Web pages and programs.

Like any other software, ActiveX controls are available from software distributors as well, and there will soon be an abundance of ActiveX control manager tools. Using these tools, you will be able to keep track of the history of the ActiveX components on your system and you will benefit from enhanced capabilities to use them in your Web pages.

Using ActiveX in a Web Page Programmatically

ActiveX controls must be inserted to a Web page using the **<OBJECT>** tag of the HTML layout control. This can be done in two ways: using an ActiveX tool or directly editing the HTML file. If you are not a programmer, you may want to skip the following section.

The following shows how the ActiveX control label can be used in an HTML file:

```
<OBJECT
      id= Iepop1
      clasid="clsid:0482B100-739C-11CF-A3A9-00A0C9034920"
      width=1
      height=1
      align=left
      hspace=0
      vspace=0
>
```

continued on next page

continued from previous page

```
    <PARAM NAME="Menuitem[0]" value="This is the first item">
    <PARAM NAME="Menuitem[1]" value="This is the second item">
    <PARAM NAME="Menuitem[2]" value="This is the third item">
    <PARAM NAME="Menuitem[3]" value="No way this is the fifth item">
    <PARAM NAME="Menuitem[4]" value="This is the fifth item">
    </object>

<script language="VBScript">
sub Iepop1_Click(ByVal x)
    Alert "Menu click on item:   "&x
    call Iepop1.RemoveItem(x)
    call Iepop1.AddItem("Added Me", x)
end sub

Sub ShowMenu_onClick
    call Iepop1.PopUp()
End Sub
</script>
```

ActiveX Control Pad

If you are not a programmer, you still can apply an ActiveX control to your Web page by using a tool such as ActiveX Control Pad. ActiveX Control Pad is available for free download from Microsoft at **http://www.microsoft.com/workshop/author/cpad/**.

Using Control Pad is very simple. You start the control pad and then open the HTML page that you would like to edit. The page is displayed in a normal edit window. From the Edit menu, select Insert ActiveX Control. The program will display a list box with available controls. You then select the desired control and click on the OK button. The control and its property box appear on two forms on the screen. Figure A-10 shows a calendar ActiveX control inserted in the HTML document by Control Pad.

At this point, you can visually edit the control and modify its properties. Once you close the control form, the program modifies your HTML code with the proper **<OBJECT>** tag, **CLASID**, and the like (see Figure A-11). At this point, you can use the script wizard to add VB scripts to your page to make use of the controls you inserted.

The wizard presents two windows with all available objects in both windows. One window is titled "events" and the other one is titled "actions." By selecting an event, you actually start writing an **event** subroutine. You then can select multiple actions, which will transform into code lines inside your subroutine. If an action needs a value, the program prompts you for the value. You can select to view your script in code view or list view modes. When you are done, you can click on the OK button to return to edit view of your HTML page.

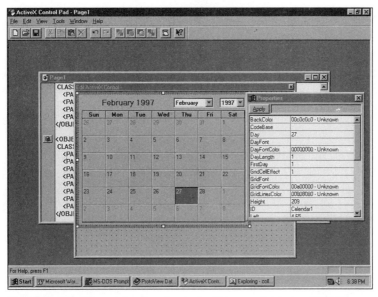

Figure A-10 Microsoft calendar ActiveX inserted into an HTML page using Microsoft Control Pad

```
<PARAM NAME="_ExtentX" VALUE="847">
<PARAM NAME="_ExtentY" VALUE="847">
<PARAM NAME="_StockProps" VALUE="0">
</OBJECT>

<OBJECT ID="Calendar1" WIDTH=372 HEIGHT=279
CLASSID="CLSID:8E27C92B-1264-101C-8A2F-040224009C02">
<PARAM NAME="_Version" VALUE="458752">
<PARAM NAME="_ExtentX" VALUE="9843">
<PARAM NAME="_ExtentY" VALUE="7373">
<PARAM NAME="_StockProps" VALUE="1">
<PARAM NAME="BackColor" VALUE="12632256">
<PARAM NAME="Year" VALUE="1997">
<PARAM NAME="Month" VALUE="2">
<PARAM NAME="Day" VALUE="27">
</OBJECT>

</BODY>
</HTML>
```

Figure A-11 HTML code as shown in Microsoft Control Pad

JavaScript, VBScript, and ActiveX Script

Scripting refers to a method that makes a Web page smarter by placing some code within the HTML page. Placing code inside your HTML page enables your computer to perform certain tasks locally instead of relying on the server for even simple operations. This avoids some network traffic, lowers the server's execution burden, and results in much faster response time for tasks that can be accomplished by scripting.

For example, suppose you are designing a Web page in which you would like to have two input boxes. After the user inputs the two numbers and clicks on a button, the sum of the numbers must be displayed in a third box. Without scripting, the page containing the two numbers must send the values to the server. The server then adds up the numbers and sends back the result. A simple Java script or VB script can accomplish this task. The following example uses JavaScript:

```
<HTML>
<HEAD>
<Title> A Sample Java Script </Title>
<SCRIPT Language = "JavaScript">
<!--
function SumThem(aForm)
{
    aForm.sum.value = (aForm.numb1.value)* 1 + (aForm.numb2.value)* 1;
}
-->
</SCRIPT>
</HEAD>
<BODY BGCOLOR = "FFFFFF">
<H1> Sum Sample Script </H1>
<H3> Enter Two Numbers Then Press the Sum Button </H3>
<FORM>
<P> First Number:
<INPUT TYPE="TEXT" NAME="numb1" SIZE = "10" MAXLENGTH="10">
</P>
<P> Second Number:
<INPUT TYPE="TEXT" NAME="numb2" SIZE = "10" MAXLENGTH="10">
</P>
<P> Result:
<INPUT TYPE="TEXT" NAME="Sum" SIZE = "11" MAXLENGTH="11">
</P>
<P>
<INPUT TYPE="BUTTON" NAME="Sum" VALUE = "Sum"
onClick = "SumThem(this.form)">
</P>

</FORM>
</BODY>
</HTML>
```

This example can be written using VBScript with some modifications. JavaScript is the language that Sun Microsystems introduced. VBScript is the native Visual Basic language by Microsoft Corporation. Microsoft also supports JavaScript, but Sun's JavaScript and Microsoft's JScript are not completely compatible.

The terminology *ActiveX scripting* is somewhat confusing. No scripting language is assigned as ActiveX scripting, as there is for VBScript and JavaScript. ActiveX scripting refers to the use of other scripting languages to use the ActiveX object inside a Web page. The menu example above uses VBScript for ActiveX scripting.

ActiveX also supports customized script languages (that is, languages other than VBScript and JavaScript). It is expected that ActiveX script engines will be developed for a number of other languages such as Perl. The ActiveX scripting engine specification is so versatile and open-ended that you can even design your own language and create your own scripting engine. If you decide to create your own scripting engine, be ready to design and implement something as complicated as a whole programming language compiler.

How Does an ActiveX Web Page Work?

You are surfing the Net and you come across a page that contains an ActiveX control. If you are using a Web browser that supports ActiveX and you do not have the latest version of that control on your system, a series of actions takes place on your system. First, the control code is downloaded to your system. Second, the control is checked for security. Next, the control is registered in your system.

Once that control is installed on your local machine, you will browse a similar page faster the next time because your system does not have to download the control again. Once the control is registered in your system, its code is executed according to the scripts in the Web pages that contain the control, adding desktop power and speed to the Web pages.

How About Security?

It seems pretty scary that, as you are surfing the Net, codes are downloaded to your system and become activated. What if the people who created thousands of vicious viruses such as Joshi, Stoned, and Jerusalem write malicious ActiveX controls and distribute them in Web pages? After all, they have more power using ActiveX technology than using those sneaky virus-programming techniques. How can you trust a Web page? The ActiveX standard addresses the issue of security through a technology called *authenticode*.

The authenticode technology lets users identify the publisher of a software component before downloading it from the Internet. We all trust the authenticity of software sold in retail stores by examining the name of the publisher and ensuring that nobody has tampered with the software. Retail software is shrink-wrapped and uses holograms to verify that it hasn't been tampered with. Microsoft authenticode provides an even higher level of security.

When you are about to download a piece of software over the Internet, Microsoft Internet Explorer 3.0 shows you a certificate. This certificate identifies the publisher and informs end users about any possible tampering with the original code. At this point, end users can make a decision as to whether or not they want to continue to download the software. Internet Explorer can be customized as to how it should treat unsafe code—that is, code that does not have a valid software publisher certificate or code that has been tampered with.

Authenticode is not an ActiveX technology. It is a general approach to resolving the issue of software security over the Internet. However, Internet ActiveX technology would be almost useless without such a security solution.

For more information about authenticode, refer to the following Web sites:

http://www.microsoft.com/workshop/prog/security/misf8.htm

http://www.microsoft.com/workshop/prog/security/authcode/codesign.htm

http://microsoft.ease.lsoft.com/archives/authenticode.html

ActiveX Licensing

To promote the development of ActiveX controls, Microsoft has provided a licensing mechanism. Developers can create two different types of controls: licensed and nonlicensed. Nonlicensed controls can be freely distributed and will work on every system. The current controls provided by Microsoft in Internet Explorer, ActiveX SDK (Software Development Kit), and ActiveX Control Pad are not licensed and can be freely distributed. Licensed controls, however, will not work on a computer that is not licensed to use that control.

To understand ActiveX licensing, you first must understand the existing mechanism for licensing OLE controls for use in Visual Basic. In the existing scheme, a VB programmer buys a design-time license for a control. When the programmer creates a VB form, Visual Basic embeds a free runtime license for the control inside the form, allowing anybody to use the form without paying for the control.

A similar mechanism is implemented in licensing for ActiveX controls. For a nonlicensed computer to be able to view an ActiveX HTML page, a license package (LPK) file must be downloaded for that ActiveX control. In addition, the HTML page must have an **<OBJECT>** tag for local licensed manager software. The license manager is another ActiveX control that is part of the browser. The license manager checks the validity of the license of any ActiveX component before that component can be installed on the local system.

Creating Your Own ActiveX Controls

ActiveX controls can be created using a variety of programming languages such as C, C++, Visual Basic 5.0, and Microsoft Visual J++, the Microsoft Visual Java development environment. Unless you are a programmer or plan to be one, you are better off using the existing library of ActiveX controls.

In addition, the Microsoft ActiveX Software Development Kit (SDK) contains a variety of technologies that Microsoft is introducing to help develop ActiveX Internet applications. To use the SDK, you will need to install the latest version of Internet Explorer. You also will need the latest Win32 SDK. For more information on the SDK, refer to **http://www.microsoft.com/workshop/prog/sdk/**.

How to Use ActiveX in Your Web Page

The key to using an ActiveX object in a Web page is the new HTML **<OBJECT>** tag. The **<OBJECT>** tag is a container tag. This means that you insert an object into a HTML document by enclosing it between **<OBJECT>** and **</OBJECT>**.

The space between the tags is used to define the object's parameters. The object itself is identified by its name, its **CLASID**, and its properties following the word **OBJECT** at the top of the definition. The **<OBJECT>** tag was added to HTML 3.2 specification for hypertext documents. (For more information on HTML specification, refer to **http://www.w3.org**.)

Following is an example of the usage of the **<OBJECT>** tag in an HTML page:

```
<OBJECT ID="Calendar1" WIDTH=372 HEIGHT=279
  CLASID="CLSID:8E27C92B-1264-101C-8A2F-040224009C02"
  CODEBASE="http://www.activexplanet.com/sample.htm">
    <PARAM NAME="_Version" VALUE="458752">
    <PARAM NAME="_ExtentX" VALUE="9843">
    <PARAM NAME="_ExtentY" VALUE="7373">
    <PARAM NAME="_StockProps" VALUE="1">
    <PARAM NAME="BackColor" VALUE="12632256">
    <PARAM NAME="Year" VALUE="1997">
    <PARAM NAME="Month" VALUE="4">
    <PARAM NAME="Day" VALUE="23">
</OBJECT>
```

Every object that is inserted into a page must be identified to the Web page by its ID. This ID can be used by scripts in the page to refer to the object's properties and methods. **WIDTH** and **HEIGHT** define the visual size of the object on the screen. **CLASID** is the attribute that identifies the object within the target computer system. The CLASID is a unique ID used for each software that is registered in the local machine. One way to find CLASIDs on your system is to look at your registry by running the program **regedit** from the Start menu of your Windows 95 or NT.

Another property is **CODEBASE**. This property defines a URL address on the Web where a copy of the control can be found. The browser uses this property to download ActiveX controls automatically.

There are two ways to insert a picture into a word document. A picture can be inserted as either a picture or as a OLE document. If it is inserted as a picture, it is a dead picture in the document. If it is inserted as a OLE object, however, it has all the functionality that comes with the OLE object, for example, the ability to edit, move, and rotate the picture.

Similarly, a picture can be inserted into a Web page in two different ways. One way is as a picture, in which case the HTML **<IMG>** tag is used. An example follows:

```
<IMG SRC="/somedir/apicture.gif" WIDTH="30" HEIGHT="30"  BORDER=0 >
```

The above statement causes the browser to download the picture **apicture.gif** file from the specified directory on the server and display it at the current browser location on the screen.

Another way to insert an image in a Web page is to insert it as an ActiveX object. In this way, you have access to functionality that the ActiveX object provides. For example, a picture ActiveX object may have the functionality to rotate the picture in three dimensions. The functionality is imported to the Web page by inserting the object in the HTML file using the **<OBJECT>** tag. The means of using the available functionality is by using the script language. For example, some push buttons may be added to rotate the picture in different directions. In the **click** events of the push buttons, the proper methods are used to rotate the picture.

```
<OBJECT
        id=3DPicture
        clasid="clsid:xxxxxxxx-xxxx-xxxx-xxxx-xxxxxxxxxxxx
        width=100
        height=100
        align=left
>
</OBJECT>

<BODY>
<FORM>
<P>
<INPUT TYPE="BUTTON" NAME="Left" VALUE = "Left" onClick="3Dpicture.Left() >
</P>
<P>
<INPUT TYPE="BUTTON" NAME="Right" VALUE = "Right" onClick="3Dpicture.Right() >
</P>
<P>
<INPUT TYPE="BUTTON" NAME="Up" VALUE = "Up" onClick="3Dpicture.Up() >
</P>
<P>
```

```
<INPUT TYPE="BUTTON" NAME="Down" VALUE = "Down" onClick="3Dpicture.Down() >
</P>
</FORM>
```

ActiveX File Types

Several different file types are used for storing ActiveX objects.

Executables files: These are the files with EXE extensions and contain ActiveX objects that can be used as out-of-process servers.

Dynamic link libraries: These are the DLL files and provide ActiveX controls that are always used as in-process controls at runtime. In the development environment, they can be linked to an application to generate an EXE or DLL file.

OCX files: These are standard VB version 4.00 control files. These files are used mainly in the development environment.

CAB files: These are new Microsoft compressed files. These files are general compression-type files similar to the more traditional ZIP files. They carry ActiveX controls. Once a CAB file is downloaded into the user's system from the Internet, it automatically extracts. The ActiveX browser then installs the components in the system. If the CAB file contains an INF file, the necessary specific information to install the controls is present in this file. INF files are similar to Windows INI files.

ActiveX technology is a Microsoft proprietary technology. The file types described above are all Windows types. There is no limitation, however, on the types of files used to store ActiveX controls.

Summary

Based on Microsoft's DCOM, ActiveX controls are true distributed OLE objects that can serve as reusable and distributed software components. ActiveX controls can be used in regular programming languages and HTML documents for both desktop applications and active World Wide Web documents. Currently, ActiveX controls are functional only on Windows NT version 4.0 and Windows 95. For ActiveX objects to gain momentum on the Internet as multiplatform objects, other platform operating systems must support ActiveX as well. Microsoft Corporation is currently working with Metrowerks and Macromedia to support ActiveX on Macintosh operating systems. Microsoft is also working with UNIX development companies such as Bristol and Mainsoft to develop ActiveX support on UNIX systems. Software AG and Digital Equipment Corporation are also listed as Microsoft partners in this endeavor. A beta implementation of DCOM for Solaris is available from Software AG; it is expected to be released this year.

An area in which ActiveX technology may pick up some momentum is accessing information in databases. ActiveX objects based on Microsoft OLE can isolate the detail of data implementation from applications while providing flexible user interface and efficient client/server procedure calls across the networks.

Today well over 1,000 ActiveX components are available from various resources. You will find most of the controls that you need off the shelf in the near future. You can also create your own control using one of several development tools.

APPENDIX B

Push Technologies

Push technologies can be categorized as an evolution within a revolution. Their success depends on the network and the network infrastructure under which they are deployed. They also open up a new and exciting set of application development frameworks. This appendix provides an overview of push technology and discusses the details of some of the specific implementations, such as Marimba's Castanet.

What Is Push Technology?

The phrase *push technology* has been used to describe many things. It is generally used to label a framework that is somewhat different from the World Wide Web model. The existing Web model is considered a *pull* model. The user indicates what URL he or she wants to visit and the client then retrieves that URL. Perhaps the pull model became prevalent because of the role a client plays in the traditional client/server environment. It was always the client who had to find the appropriate server and connect to it.

Although this is the predominant model, there is nothing to stop the reverse. That is, just as you can expect a client to pull data from servers, you can also have the server push data to the clients. It is like thinking of a glass of water as half full or half empty. Either the client is pulling the data or the server is pushing the data.

To appreciate the new framework, try to forget what you are used to and think in a different way. This will help you appreciate push technology and come up with ways it might be used in your organization for your applications.

One of the simplest applications using push technology is an email list. By subscribing to a particular email list, you are expressing interest in the information the mailing list provides. After you subscribe, the new information is pushed to your machine via email on a regular basis. Many email readers now support Hypertext Markup Language (HTML) directly inside the email reader. This allows a mailing list to send rich HTML pages via email. The same page that you are so used to going to every morning can be pushed to you via email. This is similar to the way a television works. You select a channel, which is similar to subscribing to an email list, and the content of the channel is then pushed to your TV set continuously. Many advocates of push technology see the future of the Web as a hybrid of interactive television, with different Web sites serving as different channels. Before this happens, however, the network-centric model of computing must become prevalent and the network itself must become reliable and transparent.

Pushing content is only one possible application of push technology. There are many others. For example, a server could push application patches to machines that have subscribed to an upgrade agreement. This way, the machines will always have the latest version of a program.

By now, you should have a feel for what push technology is all about. Let's turn to a popular implementation of push technology by Marimba Corporation.

Castanet by Marimba

Java has become a popular programming language suitable for the network-centric model because of its portability across platforms and because you can download the code and execute a Java applet seamlessly through a browser. There are, of course, other reasons for the popularity of Java. Castanet by Marimba (which, by the way, was founded by four of the original members of the Java team) takes the principle behind Java a step further.

In a plain Java environment, the server serves out a `.class` file (bytecode for the Java program) just like it serves out any other file. The client (usually a browser) receives the file, and its Java virtual machine (JVM) then interprets the bytecode and runs the application. There are clear boundaries for the beginning and ending of this process. Castanet puts a wrapper around this process.

The applet is wrapped in a channel. The server uses a transmitter to serve out the channel and the client is now a tuner. The tuner and the transmitter work together to ensure that the latest version of the channel is always sent to the tuner. This automatic update is perhaps Castanet's most important contribution to the "usual" Java model. If the channel contains stock quotes, then it is probably updated every 15–20 minutes. If the channel is a database application, then it may be updated every month or so. The update frequency is adjustable. Figure B-1 shows the architecture of Castanet.

Tuner

You can think of the tuner as the client for Castanet. Not surprisingly, the tuner itself is a channel and therefore can be updated on a regular basis. Through the tuner, you can subscribe to different channels. The tuner is responsible for downloading the subscribed channels and keeping them updated. You also can start and stop a channel application through the tuner. Figure B-2 shows the tuner under the Windows NT environment.

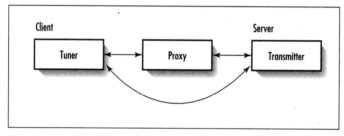

Figure B-1 Castanet architecture

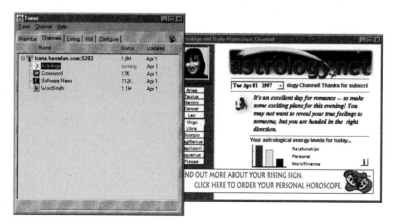

Figure B-2 The tuner

You can download the tuner from **http://www.marimba.com**. You must specify a directory that will be used as the channel repository. All the data for the subscribed channels will be placed in this directory. This is a bit more relaxed than the security policy for an untrusted applet. Recall that an untrusted applet has no disk access at all. The next wave of channels are "secure" channels that probably will have wider access to the local resources. At the early stage of the game, the above security policy is sufficient. Additionally, the underlying engine behind the tuner and its channel is the JVM, so channels are guarded by the Java security manager as well.

Once you have the tuner up and running, subscribe to a few channels to get a feel for how everything works. Here are possible places to find new channels:

The tuner's Hot page is a list of channels chosen by Marimba; the list is updated with the tuner each week

The Marimba button on the tuner's Marimba page (**http://trans.marimba.com**)

The Marimba Channels Web page (**http://www.marimba.com/channels/**)

The Gamelan Java directory
(**http://www.gamelan.com/pages/Gamelan.channel.html**)

The Excite Channel guide
(**http://trans.excite.com:80/ExciteChannelGuide?start**)

Before you can subscribe to a channel, you must select a transmitter from the Listing tab. You can type in the name of the transmitter if you know it. A listing of the channels available from the selected transmitter can be seen by clicking on the Channels tab. To subscribe to a channel, simply double-click on the channel's name. The status column will change to "Running." You can stop a channel by double-clicking on it again. You can configure when a channel is updated through the Configure tab.

Transmitter

The transmitter is the server part of the Castanet architecture. It is responsible for serving files requested by the tuners. The service is differential. That is, only the files that must be updated are served to the tuner. This greatly enhances the efficiency of the system as compared to a "blind" HTTP server that serves any file requests regardless of whether a copy of the file exists on the client or not.

The publisher tool is used to place a new version of a channel on a transmitter. Immediately after placement of a new version, the transmitter will serve the update to any tuner that has made a request for that channel.

Each channel can have a plug-in on the transmitter. A plug-in adds to the functionality of the channel and to the transmitter. A tuner requests a channel. The plug-in for that channel is invoked by the transmitter. Usually, the plug-in receives some instructions or data from the tuner. For example, the channel may collect some data from the user (such as name and hobby). That data is passed on to the tuner and the tuner sends that back to the transmitter. The transmitter uses the plug-in to take action on the received data. This path is shown in Figure B-3.

When you install the transmitter, directories are created. Each channel served by the transmitter has a directory under the **channels** directory. If the channel uses a plug-in, it is placed under this directory.

The **files** directory stores all the files served by the transmitter. An internal naming convention is used for these files. Generally, the transmitter will take care of all the details such as what to do with duplicate files and what to do when a file is replaced by a newer version.

Sometimes changes to a file are very minor. Castanet uses a mechanism by which the difference between the older and newer version of the file is sent to the tuner and the tuner will apply this difference to the channel. This eliminates the need to serve an entire new file. The details of these "difference" files are kept in the **diffs** directory.

If a channel uses a plug-in, then it needs a place to write any data it receives from the tuner. This would allow the plug-in to be able to reference the data in the future. The **data** subdirectory is where this information is stored.

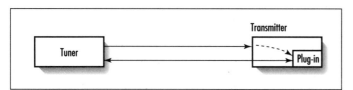

Figure B-3 Data to the plug-in

Finally, the transmitter generates two log files. The access log records actions initiated by the tuner. The publish log records actions initiated by the transmitter (publisher).

The access log contains the following fields:

- IP address of tuner

- Date and time

- Tuner ID string

- Tuner protocol version

- Bytes transferred/request duration in milliseconds

- Request type: This is **UPD** for update or **UPD/OPT/T** or **UPD/OPT/F** for an optimized update request that either succeeds (**T**) or fails (**F**)

- Channel name

- Optional comment

The publish log contains these fields:

- IP address of host doing the publish

- Date and time

- The name and port number of the host that the user is publishing from

- Channel being updated

The last file, and perhaps one of the more important ones, is the **properties.txt** file, which stores all the properties of each channel when it was created. If you are familiar with the Windows operating system, think of the properties file as the place where registry information is kept about a particular channel. The following list shows the elements in the **properties.txt** file.

- **type**: Indicates the channel's type; possible values are **applet**, **application**, **presentation**, and **html**.

- **main**: The name of the main application class that must be run by the tuner.

- **codebase**: You can change the **CLASSPATH** environmental variable by specifying a value here.

- **name**: This is the name of the channel as it appears in the channel listings.

- **update**: This parameter specifies the frequency of updates; possible values are **inactive**, **frequently**, **hourly**, **daily**, and **weekly**.

- **http.access**: By setting the value of this parameter to **TRUE**, you indicate to the transmitter that the channel contains HTML files that can be accessed through a regular HTTP proxy; the default value for this parameter is **FALSE**.

- **copyright**: Copyright notice.

- **author**: This is an optional parameter that contains the name of the author of the channel.

- **admin**: This is an optional parameter that contains the name of the administrator of the channel.

- **description**: This parameter contains a brief description of the channel.

icon: A small 64x64 GIF file can be associated with the channel—its name is specified here; this is not used on the Windows platform.

windows.icon: Same as icon, except for the Windows platform; the image format is BMP.

Castanet Proxy

The Castanet proxy is very similar to the Hypertext Transfer Protocol (HTTP) proxy used for Web traffic. A proxy server can increase efficiency and response time by using a cache to store the most recently requested files. The proxy is stationed between a collection of tuners and transmitters. It controls the communication between the two collections. If a tuner sends some data for a plug-in on transmitter A, the proxy intercepts that request and then forwards it to transmitter A as if it came directly from the tuner.

When a tuner requests a new file (because it must update an existing file), the proxy intercepts that request and looks in its own cache to see if it finds a file matching the request. Another tuner may have requested the same file and the request could still be in the cache. If the proxy finds the file, it sends it to the tuner as if it came from the transmitter. This saves a trip back to the transmitter. If the file is not found, then the request is sent to the transmitter like other requests. Figure B-4 shows how a proxy works.

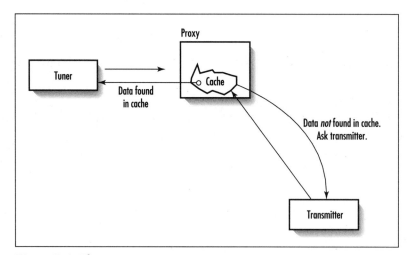

Figure B-4 The proxy

Bongo

Channels are basically Java applets that use the channel classes and Application Programming Interface (API) to conform to the Castanet environment. To facilitate the development of channels, Marimba introduced another tool called Bongo. Bongo is a graphical user interface (GUI) for creating interactive channels. It allows you to create basic GUI; you can add interactively by associating scripts with GUI elements.

For example, to create a channel that displays animated text, follow these steps:

From the Bongo menu, select File/New presentation. This will create an empty presentation screen on which you can place your own widgets.

Select New/AnimatedText and this will place the AnimatedText widget on the screen. You can then set the properties for this widget and add scripts to it.

You can preview your channel using the File/Browse menu item. Figure B-5 shows Bongo under Windows NT.

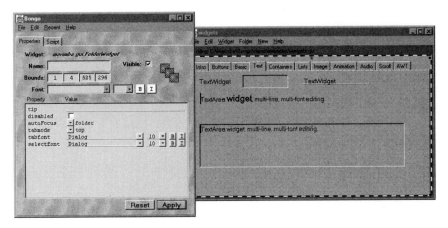

Figure B-5 Bongo

Channel Definition Format

The channel definition format (CDF) has recently been submitted by Microsoft. It is a specification for push technology involving a Web server and a client. Before you continue, please note that this specification has nothing to do with Marimba's Castanet. The two may use similar terminology, but the meaning is different under each context. The specification defines the following elements, which are used in a manner similar to HTML tags within a page:

Channel: The definition of a channel

Item: A unit of information available from a channel

User schedule: Schedule specified by the client

Schedule: Definition of a schedule

Logo: An image associated with a channel

Tracking: Specifies properties on how usage of a channel is tracked

CategoryDef: The definition of a category

CDF is the core push technology in Internet Explorer 4.0.

Netscape Netcaster

Netscape Netcaster is a component of Netscape Communicator that is responsible for implementing push technology. It uses the concept of a channel to define a set of Web pages, which form the content that must be pushed. This is netcasting in its simplest form. The same approach can be expanded to offer offline browsing. Netcaster supports Castanet channels, which means that supported content is not limited to Web pages but includes Web applications as well.

Summary

Push technology is still in its infancy stage, but it shows a lot of promise in a networked environment. The push model deviates from the standard client/server model in that a subscription-type arrangement is made between the client and the server. After that, the data is automatically pushed by the server to the client. Marimba's Castanet provides a framework for pushing applications (Java applets) to subscribing clients. Such technology in conjunction with a component model such as JavaBeans and a distributed object model such as CORBA can create exciting opportunities in the way network computing works.

Online Resources

 Acer (`http://www.acer.com`). Acer is a manufacturer of desktop and workstation computers. It also promises to be a major player in mobile computing and network computing.

 Advanced Configuration and Power Interface Specification, Version 1.0 (`http://www.teleport.com/~acpi`). ACPI is an open industry specification proposed by Intel, Microsoft, and Toshiba. The Web site is dedicated to this proposed standard. ACPI defines a flexible and extensible interface that allows system designers to select appropriate cost/feature trade-offs for power management. The interface enables and supports reliable power management through improved hardware and operating system coordination. The specification enables new power management technology to evolve independently in operating systems and hardware while ensuring that they continue to work together.

 Agave Software Design (`http://www.agave.com`). Agave offers a Java database connectivity (JDBC) NetServer that enables database access via applets written in Java to the JDBC API. By using the SQml Client applet and other Java applets with the JDBC server, legacy SQL database applications can be extended to run on the Internet and on

intranets in any Java-enabled browser with minor modifications. Agave's JDBC NetServer, written in Java, is provided in two components, a JDBC server and a JDBC client. The JDBC client, a set of Java classes, runs on the client's Web browser and supports requests for database access through the JDBC server residing on the server side.

Borland International Inc. (`http://www.borland.com`). Borland has been known for its suite of development tools. In the Java arena, Borland's product is called JBuilder. JBuilder is a visual and integrated development environment for Java. In addition to supporting database access through JDBC, JBuilder delivers some of the exciting aspects of the Java language, such as JavaBeans. JBuilder also promises to integrate with other Borland development tools easily.

Boundless Technologies (`http://www.boundless.com`). Boundless Technologies is a major manufacturer of network computers. The Boundless family of hardware products consists of the Network Computer TC, XL, and XLC. The company also offers two software suites, one geared toward Windows and the other toward Java.

Bulletproof (`http://bulletproof.com/jagg/`). JAGG is a JDBC/ODBC tool that allows Java applets and applications to connect to databases. All ODBC-compliant databases are supported. The company also has a product called JDesignerPro that is a database application development and deployment tool. Both Windows and UNIX versions are available.

Caribou Lake Software (`http://www.cariboulake.com`). This company has built a reputation around its expertise in Ingres and OpenIngres. JSQL/Ingres is a JDBC-compliant driver for connecting Java applications to Ingres. SQLRunner allows you to execute SQL commands from Java to run against JDBC-compliant databases.

Common Information Model (CIM) (`http://www.dmtf.org/work/cim.html`). This is part of the Web site for the Desktop Management Task Force. It contains information about the common information model. Members of the task force include Computer Associates, Hewlett-Packard, IBM/Tivoli (Steering Committee sponsor), Intel, Microsoft, Novell, and SunSoft.

Connect, Inc. (`http://www.connectsw.com`). This company's main product is FastForward, which is a database connectivity product based on JDBC. FastForward Release 2.8 supports Sybase and Microsoft SQL Server running on all platforms. Oracle and Informix products are under development. The product also includes a proxy component for dealing with Internet versus intranet deployment issues.

Cyber SQL Corporation (`http://www.cybersql.com`). Cyber SQL's ActiveWeb is a Java class library for database connectivity. The library is based on JDBC, but because it is at a higher level, much of the nitty-gritty of database application is taken care of by the library. Demonstrations are available from the site.

CyberCash (`http://www.cybercash.com`). CyberCash has been a pioneer in the world of Internet commerce. CyberCash provides a mechanism by which participating merchants and consumers can perform commerce over the Internet, using CyberCash as the middle layer.

DataRamp (`http://dataramp.com`). DataRamp has a suite of products for connecting ODBC-compliant databases to the Web. Its products also support ODBC-JDBC translation. More details and examples are available at the Web site.

Desktop Management Interface Specification, Version 2.00 (`http://www.dmtf.org/tech/specs.html`). The latest about DMI specification can be found at this Web site.

Device Bay Interface Specification, Version 1.0 (`http://www.device-bay.org`). This Web site is the home for the Device Bay Interface specification developed by Intel, Microsoft, and Compaq.

Dharma Systems Inc. (`http://www.dharmas.com`). Dharma is another developer of database connectivity tools based on ODBC and JDBC.

Esker (`http://www.esker.fr`). This company has a product called Tun SQL, which is a database connectivity tool for use over a TCP/IP network. The product is based on ODBC and JDBC for Web connectivity. The company also has some JDBC drivers.

Gupta Corporation (`http://www.gupta.com`). This is the home page for Gupta Corporation, a major database vendor. In addition to finding information about a variety of Gupta products, you can also download evaluation copies.

HDS (`http://www.hds.com`). HDS is a manufacturer of network computers. Its main NC is the @workstation, which was one of the first network computers on the market. HDS also has netOS, which is an operating system developed specifically for HDS's network computers. HDS WebRef is a reference platform for Internet appliances. There are details about all these products at the Web site.

IBM (`http://www.ibm.com`). IBM plays an important role in both the hardware and the software side of network computing. On the hardware side, IBM has its own network computer. On the software side, IBM has a suite of Java development tools and database connectivity drivers based on JDBC.

IBM's Database 2 (DB2) (`http://www.software.ibm.com/data/db2/index.html`). This is where you go for information related to the DB2 database from IBM. You can also find JDBC drivers for this database.

IDEA (`http://www.idea.com`). IDEA Internet Client Station is a network computer based on the NC Reference Profile 1.

IDS Software (`http://www.idssoftware.com`). IDS Server is a tool intended to bring database connectivity to both HTML pages and Java applets. Access to all ODBC-compliant database systems is supported. Native support of Oracle, SQL Server, and other major database systems is expected soon. IDS Server has a small set of HTML tags specific to the server that instruct the server on how to integrate results of database queries onto an HTML document. In addition, IDS Server supports JDBC, which means Java clients (applets and applications) can connect to IDS Server and access the database through that server. No client-side code or runtime component is needed on the applet side, which leads to easy deployment.

Imaginary (mSQL) (`http://www.imaginary.com/~borg/Java/`). mSQL is a light database server and works well for simple Web applications. JDBC driver is also available for this database. Aside from its practicality, it is a great learning tool for JDBC newbies.

Inferno (`http://inferno.lucent.com`). Lucent Technologies is a major communications equipment manufacturer. Bell Laboratories, Lucent's R&D arm, has developed a new operating system called Inferno that is suitable for network applications and network devices. The above site is the home page for Inferno and all related product information.

Information on Net PC, Zero Administration Windows (`http://www.microsoft.com/windows`). This page contains a number of useful links for Windows-related issues and events. It is updated regularly and is a great start for finding the latest about Windows-based specifications.

Informix Software Inc. (`http://www.informix.com`). Informix's main product is a database server by the same name. JDBC drivers for Informix can be found at the above Web site.

Informix Universal Server (`http://www.informix.com`). Informix's latest database release is called the Universal Server, which is an object-based server. This type of database is a more natural match for the multimedia world of the Web.

Intel developer information (`http://developer.intel.com`). This is an excellent site for hardware and software developers who need information about Intel technologies. The site includes links to many specifications put out by Intel.

Intel/Duracell Smart Battery System Specification (`http://developer.intel.com/ial/powermgm/specs.htm`). Several specifications related to power management can be found at this Web site.

International Color Consortium Profile Format Specification (`http://www.color.org`). The International Color Consortium was established in 1993 by eight industry vendors for the purpose of creating, promoting, and encouraging the standardization and evolution of an open, vendor-neutral, cross-platform color management system architecture and components. This is their Web site. In addition to information about the members and links to members' Web sites, you can also find white papers and specifications from this page.

Interoperability Specification for ICCs and Personal Computer Systems (`http://www.smartcardsys.com`). This site is devoted to interoperability between PC and ICCs (integrated circuit cards, or smartcards).

InterSoft Argentina, S.A. (`http://www.inter-soft.com`). This fast-growing company has a suite of products related to Java, JDBC connectivity, and the Web in general.

Intersolv (`http://www.intersolv.com`). Intersolv has been a leader in the database drivers market. It has continued this leadership by providing a number of JDBC drivers for a variety of databases. New drivers are added on a regular basis, so check the Web site for the latest.

Jamba from Aimtech (`http://www.jamba.com`). Jamba is a Java development tool for adding animation, sounds, and other "lively" items to your Web pages. It is particularly useful for Web page designers who want to use Java's capabilities without learning the details of the programming language.

Java Development Kit 1.1 (`http://www.javasoft.com/products/jdk/1.1/index.html`). This site is a must if you plan on developing Java applications. JDK 1.1 contains all the libraries and tools you need to begin development. Many development tools incorporate the Java Development Kit (JDK) into their environment or provide their own version. The JDK also comes with documentation (organized in a hierarchy of HTML pages). At the Web site, you will find the latest on Java and Java technologies from JavaSoft.

Java Management API (`http://www.javasoft.com/products/JavaManagement/`). This site contains information about the Java management API from JavaSoft.

Java Workshop from Sun Microsystems (`http://www.sun.com/workshop/java/jws20_dev/download/index.html`). Java Workshop is a visual Java development tool. It is written in Java; version 2.0 brings some major improvements, including support for JavaBeans.

JavaBeans Development Kit (`http://splash.javasoft.com/beans/bdk_download.html`). JavaBeans is a component-based model for developing Java applications. By writing your programs based on the Bean specification, you can increase reusability of your application components and at the same time take advantage of many of the flexibilities provided by the Bean API. The Bean Development Kit (BDK) is a very good example of using Beans in an application.

JBuilder from Borland International (`http://www.borland.com/jbuilder`). JBuilder is a visual Java development tool from Borland International. It supports JavaBeans and JDBC under an integrated development environment.

JFactory by Roguewave (`http://www.roguewave.com/cgi-bin/jfdldemo.cgi`). JFactory is another visual Java development environment. It is available for a variety of platforms. A demo version can be downloaded from the Web site.

Microsoft (`http://www.microsoft.com`). Microsoft has placed the Internet at the forefront of its future strategy. It has transformed almost all its products to become network aware and has produced a number of new products specifically designed for the Net, such as Explorer and its suite of Web servers. Microsoft is also the main driving force behind the NetPC specification.

Mojo from Penumbra Software (`http://www.penumbrasoftware.com/fresh.htm`). SuperMojo is a Java development tool that is written in Java. As a result, the tool runs on multiple platforms. It is also one of the first tools to create Beans, which means your application is composed of a number of components that you can reuse in other applications. A demo version can be downloaded from the site.

Motorola (`http://www.motorola.com`). Motorola is an industry leader in communication equipment. It is also behind a series of network-based technologies and is positioned for a share in the network device market.

NC Reference Profile 1 (`http://www.nc.ihost.com`). The complete text of the Reference Profile 1 can be found here.

NCD (`http://www.ncd.com`). Network Computing Devices is a manufacturer of network computers. It has a number of product lines. Its NCs are geared toward corporate users, and it offers a variety of other enterprise tools for application deployment and usage.

NCWorld Magazine (`http://www.ncworldmag.com`). An IDG publication, this online magazine discusses the latest in NC technology every month. It includes a comprehensive news section and links to a variety of NC vendors.

NetDynamics (`http://www.netdynamics.com/download`). NetDynamics is a tool for integration of the Web and databases. It offers a multilayer solution suitable for almost any database server. The product is very complete and offers a level of sophistication and robustness that makes it suitable for enterprise applications. A demo version is available at the site.

O2 Technology (`http://www.o2tech.com`). This company offers a complete set of solutions for object-based databases. In addition to the server, it also has a suite of development products. If you are looking for database development using object technology, then this site is worth a visit.

Object Design Inc. (`http://www.odi.com`). Object Design offers a suite of products related to Java, object databases (ObjectStore), and Web connectivity.

ODIN specification (`http://www.national.com/appinfo/ns486/odin.html`). National Semiconductor has taken the network-computing era to the next level and produced an embedded processor suitable for a variety of network devices, thin clients, and network computers. The ODIN specification can be found here.

Open Horizon (**http://www.openhorizon.com**). This company offers a number of products and services in the area of distributed computing, especially in an enterprise environment involving distributed databases.

OpenLink Software (**http://www.openlinksw.com**). OpenLink is a major vendor of ODBC and JDBC drivers and solutions.

Oracle (**http://www.oracle.com**). Oracle is a major vendor of database servers and development tools. The company is also a major proponent of network computers and has restructured its product line around the network computing architecture (NCA). Oracle is rapidly moving toward a network-centric enterprise solution. Its site offers a variety of information about its products and network computing trends.

PC 97 Hardware Design Guide (**http://www.microsoft.com/hwdev/pc97.htm**). The design guide for PC 97 from Microsoft is available from this Web site. This guide is referenced extensively by the Net PC specification.

PCI Bus Power Management Interface Specification (**http://www.pcisig.com**). This Web site is put up by an independent association that supports the PCI architecture.

Persistence Software (**http://www.persistence.com**). If you are looking for solutions to bridge the gap between your object-oriented systems and your relational databases, then visit the Persistence Software Web site. It offers a number of good solutions for complex enterprise applications using CORBA and other network-based technologies.

Presence Information Design (**http://cloud9.presence.com/pbj/**). JDBC driver for Oracle databases can be found at this Web site.

PRO-C Inc. (**http://www.pro-c.com**). The WinGEN for Java product from PRO-C is a nice Java development tool that also supports database access through JDBC. It is a Java code generator in addition to a visual development tool.

Recital Corporation (**http://www.recital.com**). This company has a number of database connectivity tools for both Web-based and non-Web-based deployment. Its newer tools use JDBC and Java.

RogueWave Software Inc. (**http://www.roguewave.com**). RogueWave Software is the creator of JFactory.

Sanga (`http://www.sangacorp.com/products.html`). This company offers pure-Java solutions for enterprise database and application design, development, and deployment.

SCO (`http://www.vision.sco.com/brochure/sqlretriever.html`). This company produces SCO SQL-Retriever, which can be used by Windows developers to access data on UNIX SQL database systems. A new release also supports JDBC.

Secure First Network Bank (`http://www.sfnb.com`). SFNB was the first bank doing all its business on the Web. It became a classic example of Web-database integration and proved that Internet commerce and banking are indeed possible. To appreciate some of the things network computing can do, visit SFNB's site.

StormCloud Development (`http://www.stormcloud.com`). One of StormCloud's main products is WebDBC, which is a tool for connecting the Web and databases. The tool accesses databases through a variety of means, including JDBC, ODBC, ISAPI, and NSAPI.

Sun Microsystems (`http://www.sun.com`). As one of the leading proponents of network computing, Sun Microsystems offers a variety of hardware and software solutions. The company sells Java development tools and Java OS (a Java operating system). Sun also sells JavaStation, which is its version of a network computer.

Sybase (`http://www.sybase.com`). Sybase is a major database vendor. Aside from information and product demos, you can also find JDBC drivers for Sybase's database systems at this site.

Symantec (`http://cafe.symantec.com/cafe/`). Symantec is the creator of Visual Cafe, which is a Windows- and Mac-based Java development tool. Its just-in-time (JIT) compiler makes development and execution of Java applications faster, and its visual interface has won industry praise.

Thought Inc. (`http://www.thoughtinc.com`). One of this company's products is CocoBase. It is a centrally managed middleware product for secure and fast object-to-database connectivity over the Web. It uses JDBC for database access and connectivity. It also uses technologies such as common object request broker architecture (CORBA) and remote method invocation (RMI) to access multiple data sources. The product itself is written in Java.

Thunderstone (`http://www.thunderstone.com/`). As an independent R&D company, Thunderstone has developed expertise in the area of natural language query and text search and retrieval. It provides a variety of tools that allow you to perform sophisticated text searches on multiple data sources over the Web. A demonstration of its technology is available at its Web site.

Universal Serial Bus, Version 1.0 (`http://www.usb.org`). This is a Web site devoted to the universal serial bus specification and its adoption across the industry. This site offers an FAQ, technical documentation, and press releases.

VISA (`http://www.visa.com`). VISA is a major backer of the SET standard, which provides a consistent framework for doing Internet commerce.

Visigenic Software Inc. (`http://www.visigenic.com`). This company is a leader in CORBA/IIOP and distributed object solutions. A variety of demonstrations, downloads, and documentation related to these technologies is available at this Web site. The company also has a variety of database connectivity products based on JDBC.

Visual Café from Symantec (`http://www.symantec.com/vcafe`). Visual Café was one of the first visual Java development tools. It is available for the Windows and Macintosh platforms. Its user interface is very intuitive, and database connectivity through JDBC is provided in the professional version.

Visual J++ 1.1 (`http://www.microsoft.com/visualj`). Visual J++ is an integrated Java development environment. The Java compiler is very fast, but the environment lacks the visual interface that some of the other tools provide.

Visual Java from IBM (`http://www.software.ibm.com/ad/vajava`). Visual Java is IBM's attempt at a visual development tool for Java. At press time, the product is still in beta development. Visual Java is geared toward enterprise application development: It allows a team of developers to work on a project. It also has extensive database application development support.

WBEM Specifications (`http://wbem.freerange.com`). Web-based Enterprise Management is the focus of this Web site. This site is fairly technical with a lot of online documentation available.

WebLogic Inc. (`http://www.weblogic.com`). This company offers a variety of Java-database connectivity solutions, including the popular jdbcKona family of JDBC drivers.

Windows Hardware Quality Labs (WHQL) (`http://www.microsoft.com/hwtest`). This is a definite bookmark for hardware developers who must make sure their device will work under the Windows operating system.

WYSE (`http://www.wyse.com`). For years, WYSE was known as a leading vendor of computer terminals. It now has a solid share of the thin client and network computer market with its Winterm product line. Its products use a variety of technologies to accommodate almost any enterprise environment. It was one of the first companies to build a network computer that could access Windows applications using the Citrix ICA protocol.

XDB Systems, Inc. (`http://www.xdb.com/`). This company offers a number of products geared toward Java development environments, Java-database connectivity, and data access in general.

Index

Message from the
Publisher

WELCOME TO OUR NERVOUS SYSTEM

Some people say that the World Wide Web is a graphical extension of the information superhighway, just a network of humans and machines sending each other long lists of the equivalent of digital junk mail.

I think it is much more than that. To me, the Web is nothing less than the nervous system of the entire planet—not just a collection of computer brains connected together, but more like a billion silicon neurons entangled and recirculating electro-chemical signals of information and data, each contributing to the birth of another CPU and another Web site.

Think of each person's hard disk connected at once to every other hard disk on earth, driven by human navigators searching like Columbus for the New World. Seen this way the Web is more of a super entity, a growing, living thing, controlled by the universal human will to expand, to be more. Yet, unlike a purposeful business plan with rigid rules, the Web expands in a nonlinear, unpredictable, creative way that echoes natural evolution.

We created our Web site not just to extend the reach of our computer book products but to be part of this synaptic neural network, to experience, like a nerve in the body, the flow of ideas and then to pass those ideas up the food chain of the mind. Your mind. Even more, we wanted to pump some of our own creative juices into this rich wine of technology.

TASTE OUR DIGITAL WINE

And so we ask you to taste our wine by visiting the body of our business. Begin by understanding the metaphor we have created for our Web site—a universal learning center, situated in outer space in the form of a space station. A place where you can journey to study any topic from the convenience of your own screen. Right now we are focusing on computer topics, but the stars are the limit on the Web.

If you are interested in discussing this Web site or finding out more about the Waite Group, please send me email with your comments, and I will be happy to respond. Being a programmer myself, I love to talk about technology and find out what our readers are looking for.

Sincerely,

Mitchell Waite

Mitchell Waite, C.E.O. and Publisher

200 Tamal Plaza
Corte Madera, CA 94925
415-924-2575
415-924-2576 fax

Website:
http://www.waite.com/waite

CREATING THE HIGHEST QUALITY COMPUTER BOOKS IN THE INDUSTRY

Waite Group Press

Come Visit

WAITE.COM

Waite Group Press
World Wide Web Site

Now find all the latest information on Waite Group books at our new Web site, **http://www.waite.com/waite.** You'll find an online catalog where you can examine and order any title, review upcoming books, and send email to our authors and editors. Our FTP site has all you need to update your book: the latest program listings, errata sheets, most recent versions of Fractint, POV Ray, Polyray, DMorph, and all the programs featured in our books. So download, talk to us, ask questions, on **http://www.waite.com/waite.**

The New Arrivals Room has all our new books listed by month. Just click for a description, Index, Table of Contents, and links to authors.

The Backlist Room has all our books listed alphabetically.

The People Room is where you'll interact with Waite Group employees.

Links to Cyberspace get you in touch with other computer book publishers and other interesting Web sites.

The FTP site contains all program listings, errata sheets, etc.

The Order Room is where you can order any of our books online.

The Subject Room contains typical book pages that show description, Index, Table of Contents, and links to authors.

World Wide Web:

COME SURF OUR TURF—THE WAITE GROUP WEB

http://www.waite.com/waite
Gopher: gopher.waite.com
FTP: ftp.waite.com

SATISFACTION REPORT CARD

Please fill out this card if you wish to know of future updates to
TWG's NC Guide, **or to receive our catalog.**

First Name: _____ Last Name: _____

Street Address: _____

City: _____ State: _____ Zip: _____

Email Address _____

Daytime Telephone: ( ) _____

Date product was acquired: Month _____ Day _____ Year _____ Your Occupation: _____

Overall, how would you rate *TWG's NC Guide?*

☐ Excellent ☐ Very Good ☐ Good
☐ Fair ☐ Below Average ☐ Poor

What did you like MOST about this book? _____
_____
_____

What did you like LEAST about this book? _____
_____
_____

How did you use this book (problem-solver, tutorial, reference...)?
_____

What is your level of computer expertise?
New ☐ Dabbler ☐ Hacker
Power User ☐ Programmer ☐ Experienced Professional

What computer languages are you familiar with? _____

Please describe your computer hardware:
Computer _____ Hard disk _____
5" disk drives _____ 3.5" disk drives _____
Video card _____ Monitor _____
Printer _____ Peripherals _____
Sound Board _____ CD-ROM _____

Where did you buy this book?
☐ Bookstore (name): _____
☐ Discount store (name): _____
☐ Computer store (name): _____
☐ Catalog (name): _____
☐ Direct from WGP ☐ Other _____

What price did you pay for this book? _____

What influenced your purchase of this book?
☐ Recommendation ☐ Advertisement
☐ Magazine review ☐ Store display
☐ Mailing ☐ Book's format
☐ Reputation of Waite Group Press ☐ Other

How many computer books do you buy each year? _____

How many other Waite Group books do you own? _____

What is your favorite Waite Group book? _____
_____

Is there any program or subject you would like to see Waite Group Press cover in a similar approach? _____
_____
_____

Additional comments? _____
_____
_____

Please send to: **Waite Group Press**
200 Tamal Plaza
Corte Madera, CA 94925

☐ **Check here for a free Waite Group catalog**

SATISFACION CARD

MACMILLAN COMPUTER PUBLISHING USA

A V I A C O M C O M P A N Y

Technical

Support:

If you cannot get the CD/Disk to install properly, or you need assistance with a particular situation in the book, please feel free to check out the Knowledge Base on our Web site at **http://www.superlibrary.com/general/support**. We have answers to our most Frequently Asked Questions listed there. If you do not find your specific question answered, please contact Macmillan Technical Support at **(317) 581-3833**. We can also be reached by email at **support@mcp.com**.